CONTENTS

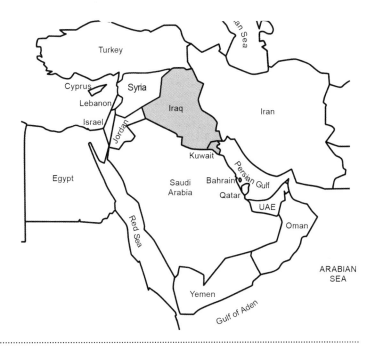

In order to simplify the use of this book, all names, locations and geographic designations are as provided in *The Times World Atlas*, or other traditionally accepted major sources of reference, as of the time of described events. Similarly, Arabic names are romanised and transcripted rather than transliterated. For example: the definite article al- before words starting with 'sun letters' is given as pronounced instead of simply as al- (which is the usual practice for non-Arabic speakers in most English-language literature and media). Because ranges are measured in feet and nautical miles in international aeronautics, all the ranges and measurements cited in this book are provided in metric and imperial measurements.

Helion & Company Limited
Unit 8 Amherst Business Centre, Budbrooke Road, Warwick CV34 5WE, England
Tel. 01926 499 619   Fax 0121 711 4075
Email: info@helion.co.uk   Website: www.helion.co.uk   Twitter: @helionbooks   Visit our blog http://blog.helion.co.uk/

Published by Helion & Company 2019
Designed and typeset by Farr out Publications, Wokingham, Berkshire
Cover designed by Paul Hewitt, Battlefield Design (www.battlefield-design.co.uk)
Printed by Henry Ling Ltd, Dorchester, Dorset

Text © E R Hooton and Tom Cooper 2019
Photographs © as individually credited
Colour profiles © Tom Cooper and David Bocquelet 2019

ISBN 978-1-911628-22-4

British Library Cataloguing-in-Publication Data.
A catalogue record for this book is available from the British Library.

For details of other military history titles published by Helion & Company Limited contact the above address, or visit our website: http://www.helion.co.uk. We always welcome receiving book proposals from prospective authors.

ABBREVIATIONS

AAA	anti-aircraft artillery
AAM	air-to-air missile
AB	air base
ADCC	Air Defence Command and Control Centre (RSAF)
ADOC	air defence operations centre (IrAF)
AEW	airborne early warning
AMC	Army Material Command (US Army)
An	Antonov (the design bureau led by Oleg Antonov)
AOI	(The) Arab Organisation for Industrialisation
ARM	anti-radar missile
ASCC	Air Standardisation Coordinating Committee
ATACMS	Army Tactical Missile System (US Army)
ATGM	anti-tank guided missile
ATMS	automated tactical management system
AWACS	airborne early warning and control system
AWACW	Airborne Warning and Control Wing (USAF)
BAC	British Aircraft Corporation
BAe	British Aerospace (nowadays BAE)
BAI	battlefield air interdiction
BOC	Base Operations Centre (RSAF)
bpd	barrel per day
CALCM	conventional air-launched cruise missile
CENTCOM	Central Command (US Military)
CIA	Central Intelligence Agency (USA)
CO	commanding officer
COIN	counter-insurgency
COMINT	communications intelligence
DIA	Defence Intelligence Agency (USA)
DMI	Directorate of Military Industries (Iraq)
ECM	electronic countermeasures
ECCM	electronic counter-countermeasures
EAF	Egyptian Air Force (official designation since 1972)
ELINT	electronic intelligence
EMED	Electrical-Mechanical Engineering Directorate (Iraqi Army)
FSS	Fast Sealift Ships
GCC	Gulf Co-operation Council (formal designation is actually 'The Co-operation Council for the Arab States of the Gulf')
GMID	General Military Intelligence Directorate (Iraq)
GP	general-purpose (bomb)
HE	high-explosive
HET	heavy equipment transporter
IADS	integrated air defence system
IAP	international airport
IDF	Israeli Defence Force
IDF/AF	Israeli Defence Force/Air Force
IrAAC	Iraqi Army Aviation Corps (official designation 1980-2003)
IrAF	Iraqi Air Force (official designation 1958-2003)
Il	Ilyushin (the design bureau led by Sergey Vladimirovich Ilyushin, also known as OKB-39)
IRI	Islamic Republic of Iran
IRIAF	Islamic Republic of Iran Air Force
JCS	Joint Chiefs of Staff (USA)
JIC	Joint Intelligence Committee (of Great Britain)
KLF	Kuwait Land Forces (Kuwaiti Army)

KOC	Kuwait Oil Company
LANTIRN	Low Altitude Navigation Targeting Infrared for Night
MAC	Military Airlift Command (USAF)
MANPAD	man-portable air defence
MEC	Middle East Command (British)
MiG	Mikoyan i Gurevich (the design bureau led by Artyom Ivanovich Mikoyan and Mikhail Iosifovich Gurevich, also known as OKB-155 or MMZ 'Zenit')
MODA	Ministry of Defence and Aviation (Saudi Arabia)
MPA	maritime patrol aircraft
MRAAM	medium range air-to-air missile
NAS	naval air squadron
NATO	North Atlantic Treaty Organisation
nav/attack	navigational and attack (avionics suite)
OCU	Operational Conversion Unit
OTU	Operational Training Unit
PDRY	People's Democratic Republic of Yemen (or 'Southern Yemen')
POW	prisoner of war
PVO	Protivovozdushnaya Oborona Strany (Soviet Air Defence Force)
OKB	Opytno-Konstrooktorskoye Byuro (design bureau)
RAF	Royal Air Force (of the United Kingdom)
RCC	Revolutionary Command Council (Iraq)
RGFC	Republican Guards Forces Command (Iraq)
RHAW	radar homing and warning (system)
RJAF	Royal Jordanian Air Force
RSAF	Royal Saudi Air Force
RSLF	Royal Saudi Land Force
RRF	Ready Reserve Fleet
RWR	radar warning receiver
SAD	Defence Companies (Syria, predecessors to the Republican Guards Division)
SAM	surface-to-air missile
SANG	Saudi Arabian National Guard
SAR	search and rescue
SEAD	suppression of enemy air defences
SHF	super high frequency
SIGINT	signals intelligence
SIS	Secret Intelligence Service (of Great Britain)
SOC	sector operations centre (IrAF & RSAF)
SSMD	Surface-to-Surface Missile Directorate (Iraq)
STOL	short takeoff and landing
Sqn	squadron
Su	Sukhoi (the design bureau led by Pavel Ossipovich Sukhoi, also known as OKB-51)
SyAAF	Syrian Arab Air Force
SyAADF	Syrian Arab Air Defence Force
Tacfire	Tactical Fire Direction System (US Army)
TEL	transporter/erector launcher (essentially: self-propelled launcher)
TLAM	Tomahawk Land Attack Missile (US Navy)
TRADOC	Training and Doctrine Command (US Army)
UAE	United Arab Emirates
UHF	ultra-high frequencies
USAF	United States Air Force
USN	US Navy
USSR	Union of Soviet Socialist Republics (also 'Soviet Union')

VG	variable geometry (wing)
VHF	very high frequencies
VTOL	vertical takeoff and landing
VVS	Voyenno-Vozdushnye Sily (Soviet Air Force)

FOREWORD AND ACKNOWLEDGEMENTS

On the morning of 2 August 1990, the citizens of the State of Kuwait (Dawlat al-Kuwait) awoke to find long columns of Iraqi armoured vehicles driving down their boulevards and dozens of Iraqi helicopters flying overhead. Sounds of fighting were rumbling from the distance and then military aircraft appeared in the sky: first those of the Kuwait Air Force (KAF), then those of the Iraqi Air Force (IrAF). Thus began an Iraqi invasion of Kuwait: an enterprise planned and organized only days before it was launched, but then one that was to trigger the last major conflict of the 20th Century – and help create the frighteningly uncertain World of the 21st Century.

While most histories of the following war – colloquially known as the 'Gulf War' or 'Desert Storm' in the USA in particular – start with the Iraqi invasion of Kuwait, they usually pay little attention to the history of the two nations and their mutual relations, and even less so to their relations with their neighbours. Similarly, while much has been published about US, British and French air warfare during Operation *Desert Storm*, little has been published about Iraqi operations (notable exceptions include books by James Woods and Pesach Malovany). Sadly, and much to the annoyance of Iraqi and Kuwaiti officers, even most serious accounts describe their operations either in derogatory terms or focussing upon 'Russian influence'. With the notable exceptions of Mr Woods and Colonel Malovany, ignorance drives most English language accounts of the events and Iraqi intentions in 1990-1991. In fact most accounts about Operations *Desert Shield/Desert Storm* focus upon the undeniably dominating role of US forces, with the Iraqi role reduced to what in theatrical terms is described as 'noises off'.

This purpose of this book is not only to present the 'other' – Iraqi – perspective of related affairs, but also to put numerous important background items within their context. Many people have assisted us but the authors would especially like to express their appreciation to Ms Annette Amerman, Branch Head & Historian, Historical Reference Branch, US Marine Corps History Division for her valuable assistance. Furthermore, our gratitude is due to Major-General Makki (Iraqi Army, retired) and to Brigadier-General Ahmad Sadik (Iraqi Air Force Intelligence Department, retired) for patiently providing information and advices. Ali Tobchi has helped not only with information and photographs, but with translation of diverse publications and documents, too, while Milos Sipos supplied plentiful minute details on the Iraqi Air Force.

1

UNEASY NEIGHBOURS

Kuwait is the northernmost of a string of kingdoms running down the coast of the Persian Gulf and the periphery of the Arabian Peninsula. Occupying just 17,818 square kilometres (6,880 square miles), it is one of the World's smallest countries: extending from Abdaly on the historically contested 240-kilometre-long frontier with Iraq to the 255-kilometre-long border with Saudi Arabia just north of the latter's town of al-Khafji. Indeed, the greatest distance

from north to south is about 200km (120 miles) and from east to west 170km (110 miles).

The terrain consists of flat, sandy and stony desert, with few low rolling hills: there are no lakes, no permanent rivers, and very few sources of fresh water. The climate is harsh with the average temperature in the 'coldest' month of January being 13.5°C (56°F). Temperatures begin to warm around March, when thunderstorms bring most of the average annual rainfall of less than 127mm (5in), briefly filling several *wadis* – an Arabic word for 'valley', though usually referring to a dry riverbed that contains water only during times of heavy rain. The largest of them in Kuwait is Wadi Hafr al-Batin, which forms the border to Iraq. The north-western *shamal* wind of June and July provides Kuwait with some of the hottest temperatures ever measured: these routinely exceed 45°C (113°F), while the highest ever recorded was 54.4°C. They in turn are offset by the moisture-rich south-easterly winds between July and October.

The coast includes nine islands, most of them uninhabited. The largest is Bubiyan, connected to the mainland by a 2.4-kilometre-long bridge. To the south of Bubiyan lies the great sweep of Kuwait Bay (Un al-Kuwayt), with Faylaka Island at its entrance: the bay is a natural, deep-water harbour which indents the shoreline for about 40 kilometres, providing natural protection. Most of the population of about 2.5 million people – only about 1 million of whom are native Kuwaitis – live in a string of conurbations along the southern shore of Kuwait Bay: al-Jahra in the west, Kuwait City and as-Salimiyah in the centre, and – 15-20 kilometres further east – a trio of towns, as-Funaytis, al-Ahmadi, and al-Fuhayhil, together with the country's biggest port and oil terminal, Mina al-Ahmadi.

KUWAIT'S HISTORY

The earliest population of Kuwait consisted of Semitic-speaking peoples of Arabian origin who migrated form southern and central Arabia into the valley of the Tigris and Euphrates rivers into Mesopotamia, around 3,500 BCE, where they supplanted the Sumerians and became the Assyro-Babylonians. Islam conquered Mesopotamia and then Persia, in 633-651 CE and until the early 10th Century, the coastal area was nominally controlled by the Abbasid caliphs of Baghdad. In 1258, the Mongols destroyed Baghdad and from that time the rulers of this city lost all influence of the area that is nowadays Kuwait, which together with the territories further south were controlled by diverse tribes. The situation remained the same when the Ottomans took control of Hejaz (nowadays western Saudi Arabia) in 1517.

The future Kuwait City came into being around 1613, as a fishing village under several clans from the Bani Utbah, a tribal confederation originally from Najd (present day central Saudi Arabia), who later occupied both Kuwait and Bahrain. From around 1750, Kuwait's future was influenced by the Wahhabis, a militant, anti-establishment Muslim sect founded by the stern reformer Muhammad Ibn Abd al-Wahhab, whose conquests in cooperation with the Saud clan drove refugees northwards from the interior of the Arabian Peninsula. These included the Sabahs who established themselves as rulers of Kuwait in 1752. Another wave of refugees arrived from Basra during a Persian siege of 1775-1779: they brought trade contacts and boat-building-skills.[1]

Together with their skilled sailors, the dhows built in Kuwait meant that the town had established itself as the region's principal commercial centre to both India and East Africa by the end of the 18th Century.[2] Regional conflicts led to a continuous flow of refugees who became the biggest catalyst for the port's prosperity.

At least nominally, the Ottomans returned to the area in 1875, when Kuwait became a part of the Ottoman Empire's Basra Vilayet (district), although no Ottoman official was permanently based in the town.[3]

BRITISH INVOLVEMENT

In 1792, the British made contact with Kuwait through the East India Company which was in the process of securing the sea lanes to India. During the following decade, they established close links to local rulers as a part of their efforts to curtail the influence and potential trade threat of the Ottoman Empire. The wily Sabahs were determined to maintain their autonomy and played off the two empires until January 1899, when the British government of India – or Raj – in New Delhi, persuaded Sheikh Mubarak as-Sabah ('Mubarak I') to declare Kuwait a British protectorate, and make London responsible for foreign- and defence affairs, while leaving him in control over internal affairs.[4]

During the next decade, the Raj sought to strengthen its position in Kuwait, which the Germans planned to become the southern terminal of their Constantinople-Baghdad Railway – a strategically important link between the Ottoman capital and the empire's southern fringes. London opened negotiations with Constantinople seeking Ottoman acceptance of Kuwait's autonomous status, including Bubiyan and Warbah islands. Negotiations led to the Anglo-Ottoman Convention of 1913: an agreement in which Kuwait was defined as an autonomous administrative division of the Ottoman Empire, with the local rulers acting as provincial sub-governors. Correspondingly, Sheikh Mubarak I was granted authority over an area 80 kilometres from the town of Kuwait and including the islands of Auhah, Bubiyan, Faylakah, Kubbar, Mashian, and Warbah.

In turn, the Ottomans limited their jurisdiction in the Persian Gulf, particularly with respect to Bahrain, Qatar and the Shatt al-Arab waterway (which separated Mesopotamia from Persia). Although never ratified, and rendered obsolete by the outbreak of the First World War, this treaty was to prove of crucial importance for the status of Kuwait and several countries further south in the coming years.[5]

During the First World War, Sheikh Mubarak I initially supported the Ottoman Empire, prompting Great Britain into declaring an economic blockade that heavily damaged the local economy. The British then invaded Kuwait and forced the Sheikh to remove the Ottoman symbol from his flag and replace it with the word 'Kuwait' written in Arabic. From 1915, he contributed to the British war effort against the Ottomans by supplying troops for the Mesopotamian Campaign. In exchange, London recognized the Emirate of Kuwait as an 'independent government under British protection'. The war saw the end of the Ottoman Empire and the creation of the modern-day Middle East through the Franco-British Sykes-Picot Treaty of 1916 – including Iraq, whose border with Kuwait was only vaguely defined. Sheikh Mubarak I did not live to see this because he died in 1917, and was succeeded by Sheikh Salim al-Mubarak as-Sabah.[6]

KUWAIT-NAJD WAR

The greatest post-war threat to Kuwait came from Saudi Arabia. Even before the war, the Ottoman grip on the Arabian Peninsula was slipping, while that of Emir (later King) Abdul Aziz Ibn Abdul Rahman Ibn Saud of Riyadh was growing. In 1913, Saud's forces occupied the Sanjak (province) of Hasa to become Kuwait's new southern neighbour, and then claimed the Emirate in 1919. When Sheik Salim of Kuwait ('Salim I') then announced his intention to

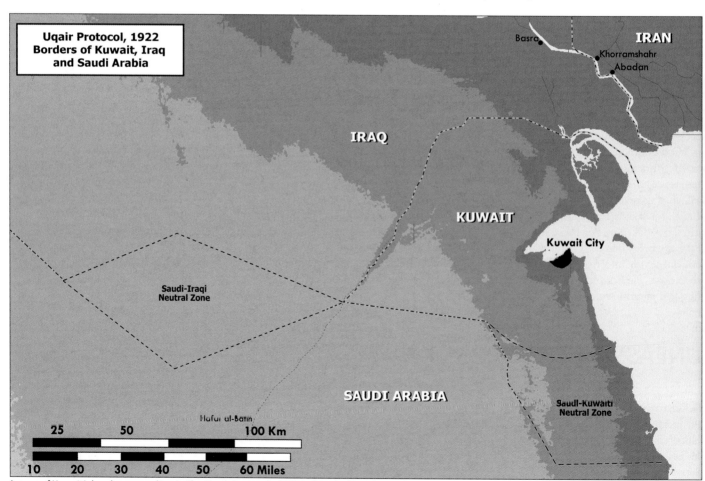

A map of Kuwait's borders according to the Uqair Protocol of 1922. (Map by Tom Cooper)

construct a commercial city in the south of his country, in 1919, this caused a major crisis. Saud sent troops, mounted nomadic tribesmen of the so-called Ikhwan ([the] 'Brethren') into southern Kuwait, defeating the Kuwaitis at the Battle of Hamdh and then advancing north where they were held at the Red Fort of al-Jahra, buying time for the Sheikh to seek British help. A combination of local resistance, British troops and aircraft of the Royal Air Force (RAF) proved decisive, although Saudi raids ended only after the Battle of ar-Regai in 1928. Saud was eventually forced to abandon his design and negotiate, but he maintained an economic blockade of Kuwait until 1937.

Meanwhile, in 1922, the British High Commissioner to Iraq, Percy Cox, forced Salim and Saud to sign the Uqair Protocol. In exchange for losing nearly two thirds of its territory, Kuwait received clearly defined borders, including the diamond-shaped 'Neutral Zone' of 5,700 square kilometres along the border between Iraq and Saudi Arabia in the west, and another 'Neutral Zone' in the south, towards Saudi Arabia. All the borders were drawn by Cox with a red pencil on the map without consulting Sheikh Salim. Iraq officially recognized this border in 1932, in its application to the League of Nations, and these remain generally recognised today.[7]

Modern Kuwaiti society is thus based upon a mix of refugees of very diverse backgrounds. The majority of its citizens were, and remain Muslim: about 60% are Sunni, and 40% Shi'a and predominantly of Persian ancestry. Nevertheless, the country has a very small, native Christian community and a similarly sized Baha'i community. During the second half of the 20th Century, large communities of expatriate Christians, Hindus, Buddhists, and Sikhs have also established themselves. Combined with their influence, trade activities and links to numerous other cultures resulted in what for many of the following decades was considered one of the most tolerant and liberal Arab societies.

GOLDEN TIMES

The British blockade during the First World War, followed by the Saudi trade blockade, then the switch of Indian and East African trading to Britain, and the World-wide economic depression of 1929 all contributed to wreck the pearling industry and ruin the Kuwaiti economy: during the 1930s, gold smuggling to India became the primary source of income, while poverty was widespread. What saved the country was the discovery of extensive underground reserves of crude oil in 1930: four years later, Sheikh Ahmad al-Jaber as-Sabah (Kuwait's 10th ruler, from March 1921 until 29 January 1950), granted the first oil concession to the Kuwait Oil Co. (KOC), jointly owned by the Anglo-Persian Oil Company (later British Petroleum), and the Gulf Oil Corporation. Further discoveries of crude and steadily rising exports boosted and revolutionised the sheikhdom's economy, making it vital to British strategic interests. For similar reasons, London occupied Iraq after an anti-British rebellion in 1941, and then participated – together with the Union of Soviet Socialist Republics (USSR or 'Soviet Union') – in the occupation of Persia, later the same year. Through such actions, British control of Kuwait was secured, apparently without necessity for a significant military presence in the country.

The post-war years saw oil exports fuel a further economic boom, or 'Golden Era', which was to last until 1982. During this period, Kuwait became the largest oil exporter in the Persian Gulf region. Ultimately, proven crude oil reserves grew to about 104 billion barrels – once making up nearly 15% of the known World's reserves (the Burgan Field is still the second largest oil field ever discovered). Although the benefits of the oil industry were never distributed on a per capita basis, successive governments of the 1950s had converted their desert patrimony into a 'welfare sheikhdom' – through intensively constructing local oil industry, roads, power plants and seawater evaporators and water purification plants. During the 1950s, a major public-work programme enabled Kuwaitis – of which there were barely 200,000 at the time – to enjoy the most modern standards of living.

2
KUWAIT CRISIS OF 1961

During the late 1950s, a wave of so-called 'pan-Arabism' swept over the Middle East. This began when Egyptian President Gamal Abdel Nasser emerged as a political victor over two former colonial powers – Great Britain and France – during the Suez War of 1956. Much of the Arab media then created a public image of Nasser as a person with all the personal attributes required for an Arab leader: indeed, with qualities that all the other Arab leaders 'lacked'. On 1 February 1958, Syria joined Egypt to form the United Arab Republic. Iraq and Jordan – both of which were ruled by two branches of the British-installed Hashemite dynasty – were the next countries to experience the full power of a wave of Arab nationalism: facing growing opposition and concerned about the safety of his throne, King Hussein II of Jordan requested support from his relative, King Faysal II of Iraq. Ordered to re-deploy to Jordan, commanders of the 19th and 20th Brigades of the Iraqi Army exploited the opportunity to stage a coup against Faysal: on 14 July 1958, they arrested the entire royal family and the prime minister, and executed them. Brigadier General Abd al-Karim Qassem then established himself in power in Baghdad. The coup in Iraq prompted public unrest which spread through Jordan and then into Lebanon. Monitoring these developments solely through the prism of the Cold War, and fearing a 'communist take-over', Washington and London launched military interventions in Lebanon and Jordan respectively. Unsurprisingly, these events had an impact upon Kuwait, too: Sheikh Abdullah was first forced to deny rumours about an impending union with Iraq and then, after consultations with Nasser, reached an agreement with Great Britain to be granted full independence on 25 July 1961 – although retaining the right to request British military assistance as, and when, he considered this necessary.

IRAQI THREAT

With no obvious external threats to Kuwaiti security, London was happy to support the nation's independence and had loosened its control already at an earlier date. In 1949, the British launched the development of a national army by converting the para-military Directorate of Public Security Force into an autonomous force, a status reached in 1953. Subsequently, they slowly but methodically forged an army that by 1961 included the 25th Commando Brigade with three commando battalions – but very few heavy weapons and no indigenous air support. Indeed, there were very few Kuwaitis within its ranks: most of the officers were Palestinians or Jordanians, while many of the soldiers were Iraqi.[1]

The British military presence in the Gulf in 1960 consisted of a small Royal Air Force (RAF) detachment of two Shackleton MR.Mk 2 maritime patrol aircraft (MPA) deployed at Muharraq Air Base (AB) in Bahrain, about 360 kilometres from Kuwait. The ground forces consisted of a battalion-sized battle group with elements deployed in Bahrain and Oman, and an afloat tank force of a half-squadron (eight Centurions). The main concentrations of British

military power in the Middle East at this time was in Aden (present day Yemen) and on Cyprus, 2,500 and 2,850 kilometres away from Kuwait, respectively.[2]

The primary potential external threat to Kuwait appeared to be Iraq, but was more sound than substance. For example, in 1961 British intelligence assessed the 60,000-strong Iraqi Army as being organised into five under-strength divisions (1st Infantry, 2nd Mountain, 3rd Armoured, 4th and 5th Infantry), but reported all of these as stationed in northern and central Iraq. Only the Basra-based 15th Independent Infantry Brigade was anywhere near Kuwait.[3]

This army was under the control of the government of Brigadier-General Abd al-Karim Qassem who ruled from Baghdad with an iron fist. Under the shadow of Nasser, Qassem followed the Egyptian-, and then Syrian example of turning to the Soviet Union as a major supplier of military equipment. In 1958-1960, Baghdad placed huge orders for Soviet arms: indeed, by 1961, about 75% of the equipment of the Iraqi Army was of Soviet origin having been delivered over the previous two years. Unsurprisingly, the majority of its troops were still undergoing conversion training on such items as 260 T-34 and T-54 main battle tanks (MBTs), 300-400 armoured personnel carriers (APCs), 120 SU-100 self-propelled guns, and 400 field- and anti-aircraft guns. Similarly, the IrAF was in no condition to fight a war having only a squadron of Ilyushin Il-28 bombers, two squadrons of Mikoyan i Gurevich MiG-17Fs, and a squadron of British-made Hawker Hunter F.Mk 6 fighter-bombers acquired before the coup of 1958 – all of which were deployed in central and northern Iraq. Moreover, the IrAF was preoccupied with introducing into service recently acquired MiG-19 interceptors. Indeed, by 26 June 1961, only the Hunter-equipped and Habbaniyah-based No. 6 Squadron was reported as ready for combat operations. Worse still, the only air base anywhere in southern Iraq was Wahda (former RAF Shoibiyah), 45km southwest of Basra: this was half-way through the process of reconstruction following a decision to relocate the IrAF Flying College from Rashid AB (in Baghdad) to there.[4]

Brigadier-General Abd al-Karim Qassem, who ruled Iraq with an iron fist from 1958 until 1963. (Albert Grandolini Collection)

British-made equipment used to dominate the Iraqi military of 1950s. This photograph shows a Churchill infantry tank (foreground) and several Centurions (background), during a parade in 1956. During the years of Qassem's rule, most of these tanks were donated to Jordan and replaced by Soviet-made vehicles. (Albert Grandolini Collection)

PREPARING FOR THE UNTHINKABLE

While never renouncing Iraq's claims on Kuwait, which had been made regularly since the 1930s, Qassem initially seemed willing to establish close cooperation with 'Iraq's sister Kuwait' and helped the Emirate join numerous Arab organisations. Unsurprisingly, ever since the coup in Iraq of 1958, the British Joint Intelligence Committee (JIC) believed that the primary Iraqi threat to Kuwait was through subversion – although 'even this was unlikely'. Contingency planning of the Aden-headquartered British Forces in the Arabian Peninsula, from March 1959, concluded that an Iraqi invasion would involve only two brigades with limited air support. Moreover, the JIC assessed that the assembly of such a force in the Basra area would be detected within days, although there would be little warning of an actual invasion.[5]

In November 1960, the British produced a two-option plan: 'Vantage'. 'Vantage-A' aimed to pre-empt an Iraqi invasion of Kuwait, and 'Vantage-B' would react to an invasion. Both were based on the assumption that the British could detect a threat at least a week in advance and that the Kuwaiti government would fully cooperate – both politically and, through the KOC, logistically. On 1 March, months before Kuwait's independence, the headquarters (HQ) of the British Forces in the Arabian Peninsula was re-organised into the Middle East Command (MEC), but remained based in Aden. Now under the command of Air Chief Marshal Sir Charles Elworthy, one of its priorities was to assess the potential threat to Kuwait. Correspondingly, in mid-April 1961, MEC sent the commander of its Kenya-based 24th Infantry Brigade, Brigadier Derek Horsford, to study local defence requirements. Horsford promptly recommended a revised plan, 'Bellringer': scheduled to replace 'Vantage' during the summer. However, there was no time to implement the same before the storm broke.[6]

QASSEM'S REACTION

Kuwait's road into independence seemed wide open until April 1961, when an unsubstantiated rumour about the country planning to become a member of the British Commonwealth provoked fury in the Arab world. Qassem, who like Nasser believed he had a mission to liberate the Arab World from imperialism, publicly observed that there were no frontiers between Iraq and Kuwait, and, after examining the historic background to Kuwait's independence from the Iraqi point of view, concluded his country had a claim to the territory – because, just like most of southern Iraq, this had been a part of the Ottoman Empire's Basra Vilayet. Furthermore, he claimed that Britain had obtained illegitimate rights in the former sheikdom through a forged treaty and a bribe. Such statements aside, the strongman in Baghdad decided to keep his related intentions a closely guarded secret. Unsurprisingly on 12 June 1961, the British Secret Intelligence Service (SIS) – which had an embassy-based presence in Baghdad since 1958 – concluded it was unlikely that Iraq would actually attack Kuwait.

Only seven days later, on 19 June, the Anglo-Kuwaiti Agreement of 1899 was formally ended but the Emir of Kuwait then signed a new defence treaty with Great Britain. The next day a furious Qassem sent the Emir a telegram that strongly hinted of Iraq's historic rights and his intention of protecting these. The strongman in Baghdad then went a step further and publicly announced that any agreements between Kuwait City and London were unlawful on the grounds that Kuwait was Iraq's 19th province. In the course of a

A column of brand-new T-54 MBTs of the Iraqi Army on the streets of Basra in 1961. Around 200 such tanks were acquired from the Soviet Union in 1959 and 1960, and most of the units to which they were distributed were still fresh from converting to them. (Albert Grandolini Collection)

press conference on 25 June 1961, he formally repeated such claims, pledging to defend Kuwait against the imperialists, and – to that end, and while talking about 'taking peaceful steps' – he announced his intention to deploy troops to 'liberate the local population'. To say that London, which acquired 40% of its oil from Kuwait, was 'alarmed' would be an understatement.[7]

Even then, and despite the steadily growing barrage of radio propaganda from Baghdad during the following days, there still remained hopes that the crisis could be solved in peaceful fashion – through mediation of the Arab League and in cooperation with the USA. At that point in time, the British Military Attaché in Baghdad reported a planned re-deployment of an Iraqi Army tank battalion and the assembly of railway flat-beds. Putting such rumours together with the perceived 'unpredictability' of Qassem, on 25 June 1961 London concluded that this was the first move in a potential invasion of Kuwait. The SIS was sceptical: concluding the Iraqis were either preparing for the National Day Parade on 14 July, or making their first moves in a long-planned offensive against Kurdish insurgents in the north of the country, planned to start in September. However, the governments in London and Kuwait City took counsel of their fears – even more so when additional alarming reports were received on 28 June. Even the JIC that – until that point in time considered an invasion 'unlikely' – then warned that, 'an invasion is imminent and would occur without warning'.

Given the uncertain situation, on the morning of 30 June 1961, the Emir of Kuwait – who had already requested support from the Arab League and referred the issue to the United Nations Security Council (UNSC), two days earlier – officially requested British

military assistance. From his point of view, the Arab League was too slow: although officially admitting Kuwait as a member and demanding a British withdrawal, its leaders were still pondering their next step. This was enough to prompt the government in Whitehall to put the MFG on alert and then order a military intervention. Any further doubts of the British and Kuwaiti governments disappeared the same evening, when the Egyptian Minister of State, Abd al-Qadir Hatim, publicly announced that he was informed of the Iraqi preparations for a military intervention. Apparently, nobody paid attention about the fact that at the time Egypt and Iraq were at odds and not only considered each other as rivals, but the former was plotting no less than three military coups against the latter.[8]

OPERATION VANTAGE

It might sound surprising that for Great Britain of 1961 approving a military intervention was much easier than actually executing one. However, the fact was that the British had only light forces deployed within the Persian Gulf. The only heavy armament consisted of the prepositioned half-squadron of eight Centurion MBTs in a tank landing ship: with this being relieved by a similar force, it provided a theoretical total of 16 tanks.[9]

On 26 June the Centaur-class commando carrier HMS *Bulwark* – carrying 13 Westland Whirlwind HAS.Mk 7 helicopters of Naval Air Squadron (NAS) 848, and 600 troops of 42 Royal Marine Commando, and escorted by three frigates – departed Singapore towards the Persian Gulf, supposedly to conduct hot weather trials following a minor refit. The ship arrived off Karachi in Pakistan two days later, to refuel, while the commander of 42 Commando

HMS *Bulwark* as seen in Singapore, in the early 1960s, while loaded with Whirlwind helicopters and vehicles of the embarked Royal Marines. (Tom Cooper Collection)

Advance party of No. 29 Squadron RAF, disembarking in Kuwait from an amphibious ship of the Royal Navy, escorted by a Ferret armoured car. (Tom Cooper Collection)

flew from there to Bahrain for a briefing. Subsequently, HMS *Bulwark* was ordered into the Persian Gulf at a speed of 24 knots. As soon as the ship was within range, at 1130hrs on 1 July 1961, the helicopters were used to deploy a company of the Royal Marines at Kuwait International Airport (IAP, then still under construction and known to the British as 'Kuwait New'), near Farwania. There they commandeered various vehicles and used these to establish a command post and defensive positions on the al-Mutlaa Ridge – a 306-metre high rocky outcrop which is the only defensive terrain in north-western Kuwait. With the IAP secured, Bristol Britannia transports of Nos. 99 and 511 Squadrons, RAF then flew in two companies of 2nd Battlion Coldstream Guards – an element from the 24th Brigade – from Bahrain, during the afternoon. For the next 48 hours, they were the entire British presence on the ground; Kuwait's airport had no radar and facilities described as 'very austere' made it difficult to despatch reinforcements, while the sole available port lacked docking facilities for large warships or troop transports.[10]

British engineers immediately started the work on Kuwait IAP but until this was completed, Bahrain acted as the airhead. Brigadier-General Horsford and the HQ of 24th Brigade arrived there on board de Havilland Comets of No. 216 Squadron, RAF, and Canadair North Star/Argonaut C.Mk 4s from No. 3 Squadron Royal Rhodesian Air Force: the brigade headquarters would remain in Kuwait until the crisis ended. Both the MEC's Hunter fighter-bomber squadrons – Nos. 8 and 208 – were re-deployed to Muharraq Air Base (AB), in Bahrain, where they were joined by a dozen English Electric Canberra B.(I).Mk 6 bombers from the Germany-based Nos. 88 and 213 Squadrons. It was only once the Kuwait IAP had been improved that British aircraft brought in further reinforcements, including 45 Royal Marine Commando. Meanwhile, Ferret scout cars of A Squadron of the 11th Hussars reconnaissance regiment were brought in by landing craft, between 4 and 6 July, followed by three infantry battalions

Troops of 42 Royal Marine Commando chatting with the pilot of a Whirlwind from NAS 848, after their landing in Kuwait on 1 July 1961. (Albert Grandolini Collection)

Royal Marines starting their march towards the al-Mutlaa Pass. (Albert Grandolini Collection)

(including 2nd Battalion the Parachute Regiment, 1st Battalion the Royal Inniskilling Fusiliers from Kenya, 1st Battalion the King's Regiment, and C Squadron of the 3rd Carabineers (Prince of Wales' Dragoon Guards), a tank squadron, a field artillery battery (from the 33rd Parachute Field Artillery Regiment), and an engineer company (from the 34th Field Engineer Squadron). Overall, by 6 July 1961, about 7,000 officers and other troops supported by tanks had turned Kuwait into an armed camp.[11]

As Kuwait IAP became operational, the RAF deployed a Type SC787 radar there: this lacked a height-finding capability but was adequate for detection and air traffic control – in turn enabling operations of combat aircraft. Furthermore, from 3 July 1961, two photo-reconnaissance Canberra PR.Mk 7 aircraft from No. 13 Squadron flew photo-reconnaissance sorties from Muharraq AB along the border with Iraq: however, their oblique cameras could not penetrate the severe haze which the British believed was concealing the assembly of Iraqi tanks. Permission was granted for flights 'inside' Iraqi airspace, all aimed to find the 'troop concentrations' – which did not exist. IrAF's ground observation posts detected and reported the intruders, but the air force failed to intercept them because neither the early warning radar system nor surface-to-air missiles ordered from Moscow had been delivered, while many of the best pilots were still undergoing conversion training on brand-new MiG-21F-13 interceptors in the USSR.[12]

Once in Kuwait, the troops settled down to a situation that was far from pleasant: after taking positions along the Mutlaa Ridge, they had to cope with temperatures over 50°C and sandstorms that reduced visibility to less than 100 metres (109 yards). It was under such adverse conditions that a Hunter F.Mk 6 from No. 208 Squadron – coded XG134 – crashed on the Mutlaa Ridge, killing the pilot. Eventually, most of the deployed forces became accustomed to such conditions and there were fewer problems than might have been expected. Even so, the British took great care that the deployed troops were constantly rotated between Kuwait and HMS *Bulwark*, to enable the men to get some rest. The carrier was also acting as a forward-deployed radar station and a communications centre,

because it carried Type 982 radar with a 150km (93-mile) detection range as well as a comprehensive communications suite. Indeed, its radios proved vital since the headquarters of the operation remained in Bahrain, more than 550km (342 miles) away from Kuwait.[13]

In mid-July 1961, the arrival of the much larger, Illustrious-class fleet carrier HMS *Victorious* provided not only her Type 984 3D radar with 270km (168 mile) range, but also Fairy Gannet AEW. Mk. 3 airborne early warning aircraft of B Flight NAS 849, and de Havilland Sea Vixen all-weather interceptors. This ship greatly improved the situational awareness of British commanders. In late July, HMS *Victorious* was relieved by the light carrier HMS *Centaur* with 17 Supermarine Scimitar F.Mk 1 and Sea Vixen FAW.Mk 2 interceptors from NAS 807 and 891, and 11 other aircraft including four Skyraider AEW.Mk 1s from D Flight of NAS 849. Nevertheless, coordinating their operations with those of the RAF proved difficult, not only because the Royal Navy used ultra-high frequency (UHF) communications and the air force the very high frequency (VHF), but also due to vast distances. The latter had forced the British to improvise: when no other solution was found for handling theatre-wide communication signals, these were relayed by Canberra bombers between Aden and Bahrain, while RAF Hunting Percival Pembrokes from A Flight No. 152 Squadron were used for liaison duties between Bahrain, Sharjah and Aden.

A CRISIS IN A CRISIS

The arrival of the British troops divided Kuwaiti society, with many regarding it as an imperialist gesture, reminiscent of the Anglo-French conspiracy with Israel against Egypt, in 1956: this time, it would have been the forces deployed in Kuwait that were 'conveniently available'. Many Arab countries initiated not only intense diplomatic activity but also propaganda campaigns, demanding a British withdrawal – even more so because when Kuwait was granted access to the Arab League, this was on the understanding that the British would depart and be replaced by Arab troops. Matters were not helped when three sappers from the British Army accidentally drove a scout car across the border into

British troops with Saladin armoured cars in Kuwait in 1961. (Albert Grandolini Collection)

Once 'Kuwait New' – the future Kuwait IAP – was made operational by British engineers, the RAF began deploying Hunter fighter-bombers there. The trio barely visible in the background were partially armed with unguided rockets. (Albert Grandolini Collection)

Iraq, where they were arrested and remained imprisoned for several weeks. Still, with the Iraqi military action limited to patrol boats firing upon boats bringing food from Iran to Kuwait in defiance of a luke-warm attempt by Baghdad to impose a blockade, once the Iraqi national holiday of 14 July 1961 passed without any military action, the British felt more secure. Indeed, their withdrawal began

almost as soon as Elworthy announced – on 7 July – a policy of 'minimum defensive forces': having never observed any Iraqi troop movements south of Basra, and ultimately finding not a single Iraqi army unit deployed along the border to Kuwait, on 20 July 1961, London ordered the withdrawal of 42 Commando and 2 Para to Bahrain, while 45 Commando was shipped back to Aden. They

Centurion MBTs of the British Army in hull-down positions along the Mutlaa Ridge, in north-western Kuwait. (Albert Grandolini Collection)

HMS *Victorious* in around 1958. Notable on the top of the bridge is the large mounting for the Type 984 3D radar – one of the most modern systems of that type at the time. As of 1961, Skyraider AEW aircraft (two can be seen to the left, next to three Supermarine Scimitar fighter-bombers), and de Havilland Sea Venom interceptors (nine of which can be seen to the right), had been replaced by more modern Gannets and Sea Vixens, respectively. (US Navy National Museum of Naval Aviation, photo No. 1996.488.037.041)

were followed by the Hunters of No 208 Squadron. By 23 July, the British thus had only 2,300 troops still in Kuwait.[14]

Nevertheless, the danger was not over even once Qassem denied any military intentions: on the contrary, it seems that he had indeed planned an invasion, and it seems that the SIS had learned of this and then used the British Military Attaché's reporting as a cover story in events that were eerily echoed three decades later. On 25 June 1961, the Iraqi strongman ordered the 3rd Armoured Division's commander, Major-General Khalil Said, to prepare an invasion plan, 'as soon as possible'. Said did so with help of his operations officer, Brigadier-General Abd al-Jabbar Khalil Shanshall (who would later serve as the Chief-of-the-General-Staff and then

Iraq's Defence Minister). Their plan envisaged the re-deployment of the entire Diwaniya-based 1st Infantry Division to southern Iraq, from where its 1st (Musayeb), 14th (Nassiriyah), and 15th (Basra) Brigades would – with support form the IrAF – advance to secure Kuwait's towns, while a battalion would land on the coast to prevent units of the Kuwaiti army escaping into Saudi Arabia. Finally, the 3rd Division was to secure the rear areas of this advance. Said then presented this plan to Qassem, who approved it and appointed him the commanding officer (CO) of the 1st Infantry Division – without informing his General Staff of either the change of command or his intentions. Preparations for the invasion then continued with officers conducting reconnaissance of both land and sea approaches – and that even after the remaining British forces were withdrawn from Kuwait, in late September, and were replaced by the first contingent of an Arab League force (primarily 1,200 Saudi Arabian troops, which had crossed the border on 1 September 1961). Indeed, as late as of November 1961, units of the 1st Infantry Division of the Iraqi Army ran a related exercise, although the troops were never told about its purpose. Nevertheless, the prompt British intervention – followed by deployment of the Arab League's troops, and then the need to deal with the Kurdish insurgency in the north of his country led Qassem quietly to drop the plan which remained a state secret until 1992.[15]

On 8 February 1963, Qassem was overthrown and shot in a military coup supported by the IrAF and the Ba'ath Party. He was succeeded by Major-General Abdul Salam Arif, who – in October 1963 – not only recognised the international border, but officially 'granted' the (uninhabited) islands of Bubiyan and Warbah to Kuwait. Nevertheless, subsequent governments in Baghdad for the next two decades continued to demand their return to Iraq, always with an explanation of the necessity to protect the major Iraqi naval base in Umm Qasr. For these reasons the RAF continued flying regular reconnaissance sorties along the border until May 1968, while maintaining forces in the region ready to intervene – and that until the complete British withdrawal from all bases 'east of Suez' in 1971.[16]

3

KUWAIT, IRAQ AND IRAN

Despite its peaceful conclusion, the 'Kuwait Emergency' of 1961 had far-reaching consequences. On one side, the government subsequently began developing a welfare state, and spending more on social services than either Great Britain or Sweden. Internationally, it took care to reach an agreement with Saudi Arabia regarding the Neutral Zone separating the two countries, to demarcate the territorial waters with Iran, and to bolster it ties and establish diplomatic relation to a wide range of nations abroad. On the domestic plan, Emir Abdullah insisted on keeping the riches of the country within the hands of the indigenous population, and significantly bolstered spending for defence purposes. [1]

Subsequently, financial involvement became a trademark of Kuwaiti foreign politics. As the country established itself as a major international creditor, in the mid-1960s, it began granting ever larger loans to foreign governments and private businesses, as well as becoming a significant founder of the Fund for Arabic Economic Development. Kuwait did not formally join the other Arab states in fighting Israel in June 1967, but did deploy to Egypt a small force that took part in the War of Attrition, in 1969-1970, and then in the October 1973 Arab-Israeli War. Moreover, during a conference of Arab leaders in Khartoum, in September 1967, Kuwait agreed to join Saudi Arabia and Libya in financing Egypt and Jordan to help defray the immense costs of the continuous armed conflict with Israel. Quickly learning to exploit their position to exercise influence well outside their borders, the Kuwaitis invested heavily abroad: between late 1960s and mid-1980s, their interests grew from about US$200 million to over US$100 billion. Amongst others, they purchased nearly 10% of the Volkswagen corporation, a 21.6% share in British Petroleum, and then the majority of Gulf Oil. In 1968, Kuwait helped Saudi Arabia by placing an order for British Aircraft Corporation's (BAC) Lightning interceptors, and thus London, to finance an order for 50 General Dynamics F-111K strike aircraft in

the USA (as replacements for the still-born BAC TSR.2).[2]

While Kuwait and Saudi Arabia eventually received Lightnings, London cancelled its order for F-111Ks due to growing economic problems which influenced the July 1967 decision to abandon all the bases east of the Suez Canal. Six months later, this was followed by the decision to withdraw entirely from the Persian Gulf.[3]

The British withdrawal from the Gulf was completed in November 1971 and with the USA heavily committed in South-East Asia, Iran sought to exploit the resulting power vacuum and strengthen its regional position by seizing the Tunb Islands: two rocks strategically positioned near the Straits of Hormuz. Kuwait's response to the British withdrawal was to play a leading role helping the sheikhdoms in the Gulf to unite into the Federation of Persian Gulf States – later the United Arab Emirates (UAE) while improving relations with Tehran, cancelling its defence treaty with London, and establishing diplomatic relations with China and the Soviet Union.

THE SAMETA INCIDENT

Kuwait's relations with Iraq remained on something of a roller coaster. The failure in 1948-1949 to strangle the infant Israel at birth had discredited the traditional conservative regimes based upon monarchies and societies deeply influenced by religious leaders. Countries like Iraq, Egypt, and Syria had become secular societies with more representative leaderships pursuing a vaguely socialist path. Unsurprisingly, most Iraqis regarded with contempt the ancient governments where rulers had harems and even slaves, but which were funded by vast oil wealth. The government of Kuwait was regarded as one of them. Seeking to resolve the situation, in December 1972, Kuwait City opened a new round of talks with the government led by President Ahmed Hassan al-Bakr and his Deputy, Saddam Hussein at-Tikriti – who acted as 'soft man' and 'hard man', respectively. Unimpressed, in March 1973 Baghdad claimed Warbah and Bubiyan, which the Kuwaitis refused to cede. Indeed, although the Iraqi government proposed a major trade agreement on 3 March 1973, it withdrew this offer when the Kuwaitis expressed their interest only on condition that there would be no territorial concessions.

A fortnight later, on 20 March, Iraqi troops approached the border crossing point of Sameta (or 'Sanita'), and demanded the Kuwaiti border guards to leave it. When the latter refused, the Iraqis tried to force them out, provoking a firefight in which superior force prevailed. While appealing to the Arab League, Kuwait proclaimed a state of emergency and mobilised its armed forces. However, a counterattack by its commandos was thwarted by Iraqi resistance. Kuwait thus regained Sameta only in late April 1973, following mediation by the Arab League. Even then, Baghdad continued to press for the occupation of the two islands, or at least their lease. Nevertheless, when a similar crisis developed between Iraq and Iran over the Shatt Al-Arab, in 1974-1975, Kuwait permitted a temporary deployment of a sizeable Iraqi garrison on the islands south of Umm Qasr to help shield the port: these remained in position until 1977. Meanwhile, reportedly, Egyptian president Anwar el-Sadat mediated between Baghdad – which was making an offer to lease Bubiyan and Warbah for 99 years – and Kuwait City, and there were rumours that an agreement had been reached, but no details were ever published.[4]

Ultimately, the Sameta incident not only made Kuwaitis more aware of their northern border, but also reinforced their determination not to cede any territory. Instead, the Kuwaiti government continued its cautious manoeuvring on the international level: it supported Baghdad's protests against the Iranian occupation of the Tunb Islands, which were also claimed by the UAE, but it rejected Iraqi proposals for a defensive alliance of the Arab states in the Persian Gulf.[5]

INTERNAL PROBLEMS

Upon independence, Kuwait was – at least officially – a parliamentary monarchy. Feeling it necessary to promote national unity, the Sheikh allowed elections for a constituent assembly: this produced the Constitution which was signed into a law on 11 November 1962.[6] Based upon democratic principles, this combined the presidential and parliamentary systems: it guaranteed the Sabah's dominance as the head of state and armed forces commander; with the cabinet acting as the executive branch, but retaining a role for the people in government. It set up the National Assembly (Majlis of Kuwait) with 50 seats and the right to censure the government and dismiss the prime minister. While ceding the right of the royal family to rule, the Majlis had a say in the choice of the crown prince. Furthermore, the Constitution introduced the civil law system based on a mix of English common law, French civil law, Egyptian civil law, and Islamic law. As such, it was largely secular, with Sharia law regulating the family law for Sunni Moslems, and separate courts for the Sunni, Shi'a, and non-Muslim population. While functioning reasonably well during the 1960s, by the early 1970s the political system experienced growing instability due to expatriate workers' unrest. Although Kuwait was the primary sponsor of the Palestinian Liberation Organisation (PLO), continuous political agitation within the growing Palestinian community of some 250,000 (about a quarter of the contemporary population) led to a crisis which caused Emir Sabah as-Salim as-Sabah ('Sabah III') in August 1976 to suspend the constitution, dissolve the Majlis, and drastically curtail press freedoms. He died of a heart attack on New Year's Eve 1977, and was succeed by the Crown Prince Jaber al-Ahmad al-Jaber as-Sabah ('Jaber III'), who within two months appointed Sheikh Sa'ad al-Abdullah as-Salim as-Sabah as his prime minister to leverage the take-over by his clan. Political tensions remained high over the following two years, especially following the overthrow of the Shah of Iran and then the Camp David peace-treaty between Egypt and Israel – which led the Kuwaitis to join the Arab League's economic and political boycott of Egypt, while continuing to support the PLO and Syria.

IRAN-IRAQ WAR

The outbreak of the Iran-Iraq War, in September 1980, added to Kuwait's woes. Considering at least a third of the Kuwaiti native population were Shi'a, it is unsurprising that the government became seriously concerned about the theocracy established in Iran by the Shi'a clergy led by Ayatollah Ruhollah Musavi Khomeini, its close links to the PLO, and announcements it would export its 'Islamic Revolution'. Such concerns drove Kuwait closer to Iraq, prompting the government to allow its territory to act as a conduit of a growing amount of military supplies and fuel.

When an offensive by the Islamic Republic of Iran Air Force (IRIAF) crippled the Iraqi oil industry and continual overspending by Saddam Hussein's government nearly bankrupted the northern neighbour in late 1981, Kuwait City kept Iraq afloat by granting ever-increasing loans. Already by the end of that year, Baghdad owed up to US$6 billion.[7] Aware of such developments, Tehran repeatedly warned that it would 'take appropriate action' against any neighbouring country which backed Baghdad. When these warnings were ignored, IRIAF McDonnell-Douglas F-4E Phantom II fighter-bombers struck the petrochemical complex in Umm Aayah, on 1 October 1980, causing a large fire. The failure of Kuwaiti air defences to react, and the continuous flow of contraband to Iraq, encouraged Tehran, whose Phantoms returned on 12 and 16 November 1980 to hit two posts on the Iraq-Kuwait border with US-made Hughes AGM-65A Maverick air-to-surface missiles, first flying low-level passes to force the occupants to flee. A few days later, Kuwait City remained silent when Iraqi warships used Kuwaiti territorial waters during clashes with the Islamic Republic's Navy.

In February 1981, a new Majlis of Kuwait was elected by only 90,000 eligible voters. Once constituted, the parliament showed no opposition to continued support for Iraq even after the IRIAF hit another border crossing in April of the same year. On 21 October 1981, a pair of IRIAF F-4Es struck Umm Aayash oil refinery again, in turn provoking an air battle that all three involved parties quickly hushed up: the Iranians announced that they had shot down up to four 'Iraqi Mirages', the Iraqis claimed no involvement at all, the Kuwaitis claimed to have shot down one of the Phantoms but their TV aired a video showing a wreck with the IrAF's insignia, while – years later – a member

Sheikh Jaber al-Ahmad al-Jaber as-Sabah ('Jaber III'), who ruled Kuwait during the turbulent 1980s and 1990s. (official release)

of the US Marine Corps team present in Kuwait at the time reported several Mirages and Skyhawks as written off during this period. Apparently in reaction to these 'incidents', in early 1982 Kuwait granted Baghdad another loan of US$6 billion. Little wonder then that around the same time Tehran rejected efforts by Saudi Arabia (which was also actively involved in supporting Iraq) to mediate in the conflict with Baghdad, and pay for damage caused by the Iraqi invasion of Iran.[8]

On 12 December 1983, Tehran opened a 'new front' with a terrorist bombing campaign staged by its Islamic Revolutionary Guards Corps (IRGC) and its proxy, Hezbollah of Lebanon: this was to go on for the better part of that decade. Emir Jaber narrowly escaped one car bomb that killed his driver in May 1984. Moreover, the IRIAF then began targeting Kuwaiti ships underway in the Persian Gulf: when Washington turned down a request for FIM-92A Stinger man-portable air defence missiles (MANPADS) the Kuwaitis quickly placed an order for heavier 9K33 (ASCC/NATO-code 'SA-8 Gaskin') self-propelled surface-to-air (SAM) systems in Moscow, worth US$327 million, on 15 August 1984.[9]

However, the Iran-Iraq War remained a relatively distant affair until February 1986, when the Iranians captured the Faw Peninsula in southern Iraq, during their Operation *Valfajr-8*, in what was very much a military operation which also aimed to increase political pressure upon Kuwait City. Perhaps unexpectedly, Kuwait – together with Saudi Arabia, Bahrain, Qatar and the United Arab Emirates – responded by granting the Iraqis permission to use its airspace; permanently to garrison Bubiyan and Warbah; and to increase the flow of Soviet arms shipments through its ports, thus shortening the usual route via the Jordanian port of Aqaba. Several times over the following years, Iraqi aircraft that were either damaged in combat with IRIAF interceptors, or running short of fuel, made use of these agreements. In hundreds of other cases, the IrAF flew air strikes against targets in Iran from within Kuwait airspace.[10]

If Kuwait hoped such support for Baghdad would guarantee its borders with Iraq, this was in vain: IrAF pilots not only carried maps showing Bubiyan as Iraqi territory, but Iraqi helicopter crews carrying foreign reporters frequently declared the island as 'theirs' (i.e. Iraqi), and that, 'one day it would be their (Kuwaiti) turn'.[11] Indeed, Saddam Hussein never abandoned Iraqi pretensions upon Kuwait: early during the Iran-Iraq War, he renewed his proposal of 1975 for a 99-year lease of Bubiyan and Warbah, but Kuwait City refused that, and also a proposal from 1984 for a 20-year lease in exchange for a definitive agreement on the border.[12] Although Kuwait continued providing extensive financial aid to Baghdad, this fuelled a profound sense of Iraqi entitlement, because most of that country regarded its war against Iran as an action of 'shielding fellow Arabs from the Persian-Shi'a threat': indeed, many of the Iraqis became convinced that the Kuwaiti loans were 'gifts' from their 'brothers in the south'.[13]

OPERATION EARNEST WILL
Meanwhile, during 1986 the Iranian-run terrorist bombing campaign began targeting Kuwaiti oil installations and in January 1987, the Kuwaiti authorities charged 16 citizens with being involved: six were sentenced to death. So concerned was the government that it removed Shi'a from all sensitive jobs in the oil industry and defence. When the Iranians intensified their attacks on shipping bound for, or returning from, Kuwait, the government began seeking foreign support and Washington granted permission to transfer 11 of its super-tankers to the US Flag in July 1987, followed by another three in October. The US Navy began escorting tankers under Operation

Earnest Will and when the SS *Bridgetown,* one of the re-flagged super-tankers, struck an Iranian-laid mine the US Navy and US special forces launched a determined hunt for Iranian minelayers, and attacked several offshore oil platforms known to have been used by the IRGC as observation posts. On 15 and 16 October 1987, the Iranians retaliated by launching anti-ship missiles from the Faw Peninsula against tankers in Kuwaiti waters: two – including the re-flagged SS *Sea Isle City* – were severely damaged.[14]

In March 1988, the Iranians intensified their pressure with IRGC deploying three gunboats to fire upon a Kuwaiti military outpost on Bubiyan, while an Iranian missile exploded harmlessly about 100km south of Kuwait City, a month later. Tehran subsequently stated these attacks were in retaliation for Kuwait's support of Iraq and the use of the Bubiyan as a staging area for Iraq's successful counter-offensive, Operation *Ramadan Mubarak*, that recaptured the Faw Peninsula in April 1988.[15]

During the next three months, a combination of Iraqi air strikes on Iranian oil refineries, strategic mistakes by the IRGC's top commanders, and a series of massive Iraqi offensives destroyed Iranian military power and forced Khomeini into 'drinking the cup of poison': Tehran announced its acceptation of the UN-mediated cease-fire, and the Iran-Iraq War came to an end on 20 August 1988. Breathing a sigh of relief, the Kuwaitis were unaware that their troubles had not ended. Attempting to return to 'normality', they focused upon a gathering pro-democracy campaign which in late 1989 called for the restoration of the Majlis. The Emir responded by granting permission for elections but only 62% of the exclusively male electorate cast their ballots on 10 June 1990, and government-supporters won all 50 seats for elected members. They joined 25 appointed members to form a new parliament.[16]

OIL ON TROUBLED WATERS
By the time the election campaign in Kuwait was underway, events sparked by Iraq's parlous post-war economic condition were afoot that would soon end the country's independence. The pointless, massive and bloody Iran-Iraq War, and extensive spending for advanced weapons systems that eventually proved ineffective had wrecked the flourishing pre-war economy, leaving Baghdad with virtually no foreign reserves and a massive debt. Indeed, while the Iraqi population grew by a third between 1980 and 1988, the country had lost US$160 billion in oil revenues, suffered US$90 billion of damage to its infrastructure, and also spent US$92 billion for military equipment, pensions, and repairs of its oil industry. Worse yet: financing of the war forced Iraq to indebt itself by as much as US$150 billion. Although the oil-rich Gulf monarchies provided more than US$125 billion in loans – including US$60 billion from Saudi Arabia and US$65 from Kuwait – Iraq was in such a bad position for most of the 1980s that its negotiators could offer almost nothing as security. By 1990, Baghdad had to serve US$10 billion a year. Unable to demilitarise without facing mass unemployment, still determined to earn himself a place in history as a great Arab and victorious military leader, and in the best traditions of the policy of 'guns, butter, and bankruptcy', Saddam showed no interest in changing his overall strategy. On the contrary, he continued spending lavishly on the Iraqi armed forces: in 1989 and 1990 Baghdad placed orders for arms worth an additional US$5.5 billion.[17]

If there was any hope of recovery, it was based upon Iraq's control over oil reserves worth more than US$100 billion. However, the IRIAF offensive upon the country's oil industry early during the Iran-Iraq War caused so much damage that even as of 1988-1989

Saddam Hussein. (Wikipedia Commons)

the production was still down at a mere 2,100 barrels per day (bpd), compared to 3,000,000bpd before the war. Combined with the 'Oil Shock' of 1986 – when the oil price dropped to US$18 per barrel – this meant that the whole of 1987 production brought in only US$11.3 billion. In attempt to help, in 1988 Saudi Arabia and Kuwait began providing some 300,000bpd, mostly pumped out of the former Neutral Zone. However, the Iraqi port facilities were so badly damaged that this oil could not be exported by sea, but had to go through pipelines. In turn, the two main Iraqi conduits to the markets in the West – the H-pipeline to Haifa in Israel, and the T-pipeline to Tartous in Syria – were cut in 1967 and 1981, respectively, leaving Baghdad with only the northern pipeline through Turkey, which had a capacity of a mere 500,000bpd. Moreover, neither Saudi Arabia nor Kuwait were willing to reduce their own shares of the depressed market, or to reduce their oil production to push up the price: indeed, while announcing to the UN that Kuwait would drop the interest of all the loans it had handed out to impoverished nations, in September 1988, Kuwait actually increased production by 40%, although the state of the oil market meant that despite this – and substantial foreign investments – it was also suffering from a declining income.[18]

CLEARING THE DECKS

These grievances with his 'little southern neighbour' shaped Saddam's foreign policy in the late 1980s – including his decision to move against Kuwait in 1990. Emboldened by his 'success' against Iran, he regarded himself as not only a natural-born-leader, but also

the future 'Liberator of Palestine' and, therefore, Israel's prime foe – a standpoint further reinforced by the Israeli air strike in 1981 upon the site of the French-built nuclear reactors under construction outside Baghdad.[19]

From April 1989, Saddam frequently spoke of a coming military confrontation with Israel and the staff from all the brigades of the Iraqi Army – and all the way up to the corps-level – were ordered to conduct personal reconnaissance of the armistice line between Israel and Jordan. Simultaneously, Dassault Mirage F.1EQ fighter-bombers of the Iraqi air force flew photo-reconnaissance sorties inside Jordanian airspace to take photographs of the Israeli nuclear complex in Dimona – prompting Israeli complaints to Amman, which in turn reined in the Iraqis.[20]

Saddam also took steps to strengthen his strategic position. Denied membership in the Gulf Cooperation Council (GCC) – a defence alliance between Saudi Arabia, Kuwait, Bahrain, Qatar and the United Arab Emirates, established in 1981 – he formed the Arab Co-operation Council (ACC) including Iraq, Jordan, Egypt and North Yemen. Egypt – which had closely cooperated with Iraq during the war with Iran – was especially delighted to join, because the country was still keen to rejoin the Arab mainstream after being ostracised following its peace treaty with Israel. A month later, Iraq signed a non-aggression and military assistance pact with Saudi Arabia, and King Fahd agreed to convert much of Iraq's wartime debt into a 'gift'.[21]

The Iraqi-Saudi pact put the Emir of Kuwait under pressure and he opened talks to end the long-running border dispute with Baghdad

– only to receive renewed claims to Bubiyan and Warbah islands. Unsurprisingly, despite visiting the Iraqi capital in November 1989, the Emir failed to resolve either issue. In an effort to achieve at least some sort of progress, he began to push for a repayment of the Iraqi debt. Saddam concluded this a 'disrespectful move' and an element of a conspiracy between Kuwait, United States and Israel.[22]

In March 1990, the leader of the PLO, Yasser Arafat, correctly informed Saddam that the Israeli cabinet was considering an attack upon strategic targets and missile bases of Iraq. This was publicly confirmed by the Deputy Chief-of-Staff Israeli Defence Force (IDF), General Ehud Barak, at the end of the month. An appeal by the Egyptian President Hosni Mubarak for Israel and the USA to abandon the plan appears to have worked, but left Saddam seriously concerned about another Israeli 'pre-emptive strike'. He responded on 1 April 1990 by placing his air force on alert and intensified preparations for launching an attack on Israel.[23]

Before launching a war against Israel, Saddam decided to 'clear the decks'. Later in April he sent a message to the President of the Islamic Republic of Iran (IRI), Hashemi Rafsanjani, proposing to set aside their differences so Iraq would be able to stand against their common enemy. Furthermore, in a volte-face, he re-accepted the 1975 Algiers Treaty with Iran and made concessions with regard to Iraqi claims for the Shatt al-Arab, and ordered a complete withdrawal of the Iraqi military from those parts of Iran it still held occupied. Finally, the strongman in Baghdad ordered an acceleration of prisoner-of-war exchanges with Iran.[24]

NEGOTIATIONS OF 1990

The pace of events now accelerated. In May 1990, when Baghdad hosted a summit of the Arab League, Saddam publicly called for the liberation of Jerusalem, and attacks on Israel and the USA – while demanding a payment of US$27 billion from Kuwait, whose 'greed for oil' he equated with an 'act of war' against Iraq. Kuwait,

Saudi Arabia, and the UAE reacted by offering to lower their oil output, but the Organisation of Petroleum-Exporting Countries (OPEC) ignored the fact that most of its members were exceeding their oil quotas further lowering the price and thus increasing Iraq's problems. An Iraqi delegation again visited Kuwait City in June 1990, to find a solution to their differences, but without success. Although OPEC subsequently agreed to cut production and the new oil minister of Kuwait, Rashid Salem al-Amiri, pledged to observe the 1.5 million bpd quota in attempt to drive the price up to US$21, nothing happened: most of that organisation's members continued ignoring their quotas as usual.

Already convinced that a part of Kuwait's overproduction came from so-called 'slant drilling' – exploitation from across the border under Iraq's soil from oilfields around Rumailah – on 16 July Saddam had his foreign minister, Tariq Aziz complain about this 'theft' to the Arab League, also about Kuwait exceeding its OPEC quota, and claimed that his southern neighbour's refusal to resolve border disputes and to cancel Iraq's massive debt 'amounted to military aggression'. Ominously, Aziz announced that this would force Iraq to retrieve, 'stolen funds and recover territories'. Nobody listened. The next day – celebrated in Iraq as the 'Revolutionary Day' – Baghdad formally complained to OPEC about the 'theft' of Rumaila's oil, threatened military action and demanded US$2.4 billion compensation. Saddam did propose negotiations with the Emir, but upped his demands to include another US$12 billion compensation for Kuwait's role in depressing oil prices, writing off Iraq's war debts, and a long-term lease on Bubiyan island. While such claims did create considerable unease, no Arab seriously expected that Iraq would invade: everybody was convinced that Saddam was 'merely sabre-rattling'. Unsurprisingly, Emir Jaber refused.[25]

Saudi Arabia's King Fahd and Egypt's President Mubarak

Sheikh Sa'ad al-Abdullah as-Salim as-Sabah was the chief Kuwaiti negotiator with Baghdad of 1990. (official release)

Egyptian President Hosni Mubarak vainly tried to mediate between Baghdad and Kuwait City. (official release)

now became involved in trying to defuse the situation. Mubarak hastily arranged a meeting between the Vice-Chairman of Iraq's Revolutionary Command Council (RCC; the de-facto government of Iraq since 1968), Izzat Ibrahim ad-Duri and Kuwait's Premier and Crown Prince, Sheikh Sa'ad al-Abdullah as-Salim as-Sabah. Saddam seemed to agree and even summoned the US Ambassador, April C Glaspie to a hastily arranged meeting on 25 July, where he claimed his intentions would be peaceful and he sought no confrontation – but also that everything would depend on the meeting arranged by the Egyptians.[26]

Although Glaspie was appointed to Baghdad on 5 September 1988, this was her first meeting with Saddam, and it was arranged so quickly, she had no time to receive instructions from the State Department. Unsurprisingly, she was later castigated for seeming to suggest that Washington would not oppose any Iraqi action by stating that the United States took no position on the issue but sought a peaceful resolution. Actually, this was Saddam's interpretation of her reply when he asked her about the US position on the border issue, and it was a standard diplomatic reply.[27]

In its final attempt to conciliate Iraq, OPEC set up a meeting in Geneva on 26 and 27 July, during which the decision was taken to increase the price to US$21 a barrel. King Hussein in Jordan then visited Kuwait on 30 July, to brief Crown Prince Sa'ad, and observed that Saddam was very angry – but that there would be no military threat. In return, the Prince asked him why Iraqi troops were deployed along his border? Hussein refused to believe the reports.

THE US STANDPOINT

Another important fact at the time was that not only the US Ambassador to Riyadh, but also the British, French, Soviet and Japanese ambassadors to Baghdad had all departed for summer vacations. This was because most, but especially the Americans, were convinced that Saddam, through self-interest, could be reined-in by US economic aid – including wheat sales – whose influence grew following the collapse of the USSR, which still remained one of Iraq's most important allies. Indeed, the National Security Directive No. 26, which US President George W Bush (Senior) signed in October 1989, stated;

> Normal relations between the United States and Iraq would serve our longer-term interests and promote stability both in the Gulf and the Middle East. The United State should propose economic and political incentives for Iraq to moderate its behaviour and to increase our influence with Iraq.[28]

Such directives were not unexpected: the US intelligence services had been monitoring the growing Iraqi military might for some years, and began perceiving it as a threat. As early as of 1979, the CIA's study 'Capabilities for Limited Contingencies in the Persian Gulf' concluded, 'It seems likely that we and Iraq will be increasingly at odds' – and recommended that Washington should be willing to demonstrate its capabilities and, if necessary, make commitments early in any crisis, so that an escalation of hostilities could be avoided. Of course, for the next ten years, the US leadership was preoccupied with Iran and for this reason Washington began providing Iraq with low-level, covert support. However, with the end of the Iran-Iraq War, President Bush's administration re-evaluated its policy towards Iraq – and chose to ignore the 1979-study. Instead the 1989 National Intelligence Estimate for Iraq concluded that while the country was too exhausted to contemplate the use of conventional military force for another big war, it was likely to continue modernising its

US President George H W Bush. (US DoD)

capability for power-projections against Israel. As if attempting to confirm this, on 2 April 1990 – shortly after the US intelligence learned that the SSMD was constructing permanent missile sites in the west of Iraq – Saddam then announced that Iraq possessed binary chemical weapons, and added, 'By God, we will make the fire eat up half of Israel, if it tries to do anything against Iraq'.[29]

GENIE OUT OF THE BOTTLE

Increasingly sceptical about the might of the US, Saddam noted that in 1983 Washington had, 'quit Lebanon after some Marines were killed' and had began to convince himself that the USA was a 'paper tiger'. In February 1990, he demanded US Navy warships to withdraw from the Persian Gulf, and complained about the US Air Force (USAF) operating Boeing E-3A Sentry airborne early warning and control (AWACS) aircraft over eastern Turkey. When the strongman in Baghdad then called for attacks on Israel and the USA, in May 1990, Washington flexed its economic muscles by suspending a US$500 million commodity credit programme for provision of grain (amid allegations of corruption), and senior officials of the State Department travelled to Baghdad to warn Saddam that the future of his relations to the USA was in his hands. Yet by the early summer 1990, the sole concern of the Central Intelligence Agency (CIA) with regard to Iraq, was the country's growing arsenal of weapons of mass destruction (WMD).[30]

The situation began to change only after Tariq Aziz's complaint to the Arab League, on 16 July 1990: this rang alarm bells in the chancelleries throughout the region and beyond. Seriously concerned, Washington sought clarification of Iraqi intentions via its ambassador in Iraq, but could deduce nothing because even the Iraqi foreign ministry ignored Glaspie. On 23 July, the British Military Attaché reported to his American contacts in Baghdad that while driving down to Kuwait he counted some 3,000 vehicles moving war material in a southerly direction. Two days later, the CIA warned that there was a 60% chance that the Iraqi armed forces would attack Kuwait. The following day, satellite imagery revealed much of the scale of the Iraqi build-up along the border, while the Defence Intelligence Agency (DIA) issued a report that revealed the scale of the Iraqi military concentration – although also concluding that this was a part of policy of intimidation. It was only on 24 July, that the DIA expanded its related reports with the remark: 'These forces could initiate military operations against Kuwait at any time and with no warning'.[31]

By chance, on July 23 there was a meeting of Saudi Arabia's Higher Officers Committee (including commanders of all military branches) chaired by the Chief-of-Staff, General Muhammad al-Hammad at the Ministry of Defence and Aviation (MODA) in Ryiadh, and this came to a similar conclusion, that: the Iraqi armour was moving towards the border of Kuwait. Still, it considered this deployment 'sabre rattling' and showed more concerned about threats – real or imagined – from Israel, Iran, and the People's Democratic Republic of Yemen (PDRY, or 'Southern Yemen'), while expressing concern that Iran and Iraq might unite against Saudi interests in regards of oil prices. Indeed, the Saudis were further reassured when Mubarak returned to Kuwait with Saddam's assurances that the military activity was simply 'routine manoeuvres' and he had no intention of using force.[32]

Finally, the situation appeared to have been 'defused' when ad-Duri and Kuwait's Crown Prince Sa'ad al-Abdullah as-Salim as-Sabah met in Jeddah, in Saudi Arabia, on 31 July. Convinced that Iraq's demands were 'reasonable', and surprised that they were rejected once again, ad-Duri shouted: 'How do you confront me without a solution? This means you are driving me to kill you!'[33]

The Iraqis walked out the next day, but still: the Kuwaitis remained unconcerned – indeed, they were convinced that the threats were the usual verbal fire and brimstone, common in Arab diplomatic exchanges. Back in Kuwait City, as-Salim described the meeting in Jeddah as a 'summer cloud which would soon be blown away'. Similarly, the Saudis denied that there had been a row and noted the meeting ended with all three parties sitting down for a dinner and then agreeing that there would be another round of talks in Baghdad.[34]

In fact that day the RCC in Iraq (including Izzat Ibrahim, Taha Yasin Ramadan, Deputy Premier Sa'adun Hammadi, Foreign Minister Tariq Aziz and Information Minister Latif Nusaif Jasem) met in secrecy to agree an invasion of Kuwait. A few hours later, the Iraqis closed their border with Kuwait and the Republican Guards Forces Command (RGFC) opened a forward operations centre in Basra.[35]

4
WAR CLOUDS LOOMING

The fact that Tehran formally accepted the UN-negotiated cease-fire and thus ended the Iran-Iraq War is widely considered in Iraq as a 'victory' in the Iran-Iraq War. If so, it was a pyrrhic victory, one in which Iraq not only failed to achieve the territorial gains for which Saddam Hussein invaded the neighbour but also suffered up to a million casualties (including the injured and the civilians), and left up to 70,000 prisoners of war in Iran. Moreover, it was a war that left the Iraqi military ill-positioned for another major conflict.

IRAQI ARMY: CAPABILITIES AND INTENTIONS
Despite plenty of flawed and patronising analyses by Western observers, during the Iran-Iraq War the Iraqi military grew in

strength and developed in capability beyond the wildest expectations of its commanders. By 1988, it was the most powerful, capable, and professional Arab military force. It had won its spurs, especially during the last year of that conflict, through conducting a series of set-piece battles, usually run at a slow pace, but with good fixed- and rotary-wing support. It learned to make extensive use of electronic warfare to discover enemy intentions, to constantly run careful reconnaissance of the battlefield, to prevent the Iranian armour from providing support to the infantry, and then learned to conduct combined arms operations not only at the tactical level, but also at the operational level; indeed to stage multi-axis, multi-corps offensives deep into the enemy territory. Its operations were backed by excellent staff work – especially in the fields of transport and logistics – and massive artillery support (supplemented by chemical weapons), and its engineering branch was one of the best in the Middle East.[1]

Certainly enough, the poor economic situation of Iraq in 1988 forced Baghdad to reduce its armed forces: indeed, the crisis reached such proportions that the Iraqi Army would have had to be reduced even if the economic situation had been rosier. The Army alone totalled about 775,000 officers and other ranks, organised into 8 corps, 55 divisions, and 196 manoeuvre brigades. Furthermore, the RGFC had its own corps headquarters, 6 divisions and 26 manoeuvre brigades. Combined, the two forces had about 4,300 MBTs, 3,500 artillery pieces, and 410 helicopters.[2]

The US intelligence services recognised that Iraq was exhausted by the war with Iran. Consequently the Army – which in 1989 the Americans estimated at 45 divisions and 125 brigades – was expected to be reduced to 25 divisions and 75 brigades by 1995, although Iraq was expected to continue expanding its strategic capabilities, especially against Israel. In fact, by the end of 1988, Baghdad disbanded a total of 15 divisions of the Army and reduced troop numbers to 425,000, organized into seven corps and 25 divisions. Indeed, many of the latter were reduced in strength, while many troops were deployed to help repair wartime damage in diverse cities. However, at the same time Baghdad expanded the RGFC by activating two divisions and two independent brigades, bringing its total strength to 110,000. Moreover, in 1990, Saddam ominously proclaimed he needed an army of 50 divisions (an increase of 66%).[3]

On 4 May 1989, the popular Minister of Defence, Adnan Khairallah Talfah – highly regarded not only by Saddam as his chief advisor on military affairs, but also for his will to oppose Saddam on professional matters – was killed in a helicopter crash during a sand storm. His tragic death, Saddam's wish to restore his personal control of the armed forces (which he had loosened in response to the loss of the Faw Peninsula in 1986), and his interest in thwarting any attempts at coup d'état, were reflected in a series of reshuffles in the chain of command. In Khairallah's place, Saddam appointed Lieutenant-General Abd al-Jabbar Shanshall, an officer who played a minor role in the liberation of the Faw Peninsula. Further down the chain of command, Lieutenant-General Nizar Abd al-Karim Faysal al-Khazraji remained the Chief-of-Staff, but now with Lieutenant-Generals Muhammad Abd al-Qadir and Sultan Hashim Ahmed as his new Deputies for Training and Logistics, respectively. Finally, four of the army's seven corps received new commanders – three of whom were from the RGFC.[4]

LEARNING LESSONS
After the end of the war with Iran, the Iraqi armed forces studied their experiences carefully. Early in 1989, a conference on the 1988 Faw Campaign was held at the al-Bakr University for Senior

Khairallah (centre, in green uniform and black beret) with the commander of the IrAF in the period 1984-1988, Lietuenant-General Hamid Sha'ban at-Tikriti (centre right, in khaki uniform and blue beret), were two out of three of the architects of the final series of Iraq's military victories against Iran in 1988. Two years later, only Khazraji remained. (via Ali Tobchi)

Officers; one conference discussing the strategic importance of the city of Basra was held in May 1990; and another – a month later – discussed the importance of regular training. Furthermore, all the corps commands held conferences to assess the roles of diverse services under their commands.[5]

Ironically, most of these conferences recognised that the Iraqi military had grown in size and developed in capability beyond its wildest expectations, but they also underlined the earlier errors of selecting senior commanders for their political, rather than military, credentials. The army also recognised the importance of Khairallah and Khazraji as architects of victory through persuading a reluctant Saddam to allow the military to exploit its professional talents to a greater degree. The result was the conclusion that the 'stunning' victories of 1988 were achieved precisely because the professionalism was married with traditional military principles of covert concentration and the application of overwhelming force. That aside, the Iraqis had learned numerous lessons at both the tactical and operational levels during the war with Iran. They proved capable of containing most threats by developing a strongpoint system, backed with fire-bases and fortified assembly points for counter-attacks, the most extensive of which – about 40km deep – was constructed along the Fish Lake (shielding Basra). Here, the Iraqi gunners had learned, rapidly and effectively, to allocate fire; even when their defences were penetrated; to meet new threats and then interdict enemy communications. Moreover, the Iraqi gunners had acquired excellent equipment, mostly of Soviet design but including 45 of the latest Austrian-made GHN-45 and South

African G-5 long-range guns and Brazilian-made SS-40 Astros II multiple rocket launchers (MRLS).[6]

While the Iraqi tank force was made up mostly of obsolete, Soviet-designed T-54/55 (or their Chinese-manufactured variants), and T-62 MBTs, its core consisted of the formidable T-72, whose armour proved capable of brushing off hits by the 105mm gun installed in the majority of Western-made tanks, and whose own 125mm gun proved capable of penetrating most of its Western contemporaries. Mechanised formations were well-supported by helicopters of the Iraqi Army Aviation Corps (IrAAC), especially types equipped for anti-armour operations, like the Aerospatiale SE.316B/C Alouette III, Aerospatiale SA.342 Gazelle, and Mil Mi-25. Although lacking armour and proving vulnerable even to small-arms fire, especially the Gazelles equipped with French-made HOT third generation anti-tank guided missiles (ATGMs), remained a serious threat. Unsurprisingly, delegations from many Third World armed forces made pilgrimages to Iraq to garner insights into the knowledge and experiences from eight years of combat and – in some cases – to explore the potential for offering new weapons systems. Still, the Iraqi military had its limitations – especially when compared to the Israel Defence Force (IDF) and the armies of the North Atlantic Treaty Organisation (NATO): although confident as never before or after, its professional officer corps was aware of such issues and thus threw itself into the task of improving the conduct of combined arms operations, starting in 1989.[7]

At least initially, the question was: whom would Iraq fight next? Saddam's answer was Israel. Indeed, in early 1989, he met

Lieutenant-General Iyad Futaykh ar-Rawi, commander of the Republican Guards Forces Command of Iraq as of 1988-1990. (via Ali Tobchi)

the commander of the RGFC, Lieutenant-General Iyad Futaykh ar-Rawi to discuss offensive and defensive options against the 'Zionist Entity'. As a result of that meeting, the Guards divisions subsequently ran a series of exercises aimed at not only keeping them sharp, but also improving their effectiveness.[8]

SADDAM'S FALCONS: A FORCE-IN-BEING

The Iraqi Air Force of 1988-1990 was a seasoned, combat-proven service at the peak of its power and capabilities. Not only the long war with Iran, but especially the immense investment into new equipment during the 1970s and 1980s converted it into a force capable of dominating the airspace well outside that of Iraq. However, at this crucially important moment in time, nobody less than Saddam Hussein – the very man that authorised the massive investment into the Iraqi air power of 1980s in particular – effectively castrated the IrAF.

Ever since the 1960s, the commander of the air force was supported by four deputies, all with the rank of major-general. The most important amongst these was the Deputy Operations: a major-general in charge of the Directorate of Operations, essentially the 'operational brain' of the air force, that controlled all the units equipped with ground-attack, fighter- and transport aircraft, as well as all the personnel-related affairs. This position was usually occupied by an officer with a background of serving on fighter-bombers. The second most important was the Deputy Air Defence: the officer in charge of the Directorate of Air Defences was usually a former interceptor pilot, who supervised all air defence activities, including interceptors, SAMs, and anti-aircraft artillery.

In 1988, the long-serving commander of the Air Force, Lieutenant-General Hamid Sha'ban at-Tikriti retired from active service. A former Hunter-pilot trained in Great Britain, Sha'ban was an energetic, aggressive officer who commanded the air force not only in the period 1984-1988, when he organized and ran the crucial campaign of strategic bombardment of the Iranian economy, but also in the period 1976-1980, when he played the critical role in purchasing most of the aircraft, armament and weaponry operated by the IrAF as of 1990. Instead of following the tradition based on decades of experience and enabling Sha'ban's logical replacement through appointment of his Deputy Operations, Major-General Salim Sultan al-Basu – the mastermind of the aerial offensive that broke the back of the Iranian capability to continue the war against Iraq – Saddam picked one of his cronies and relatives as the new commander. In early 1989, he appointed his cousin and a former MiG-21-pilot, Colonel Muzahim Sa'ab al-Hassan at-Tikriti as the

T-72s of an RGFC division on parade in Baghdad in 1990. (via Ali Tobchi)

new commander IrAF.[9]

With hindsight, it is on hand that this – politically-motivated – decision resulted in a major weakening of the Iraqi air force at a crucial point in time. While certainly a versed MiG-21-pilot, former base-commander, and staff officer fresh from completing higher military education at Egypt's prestigious Gamal Abdel Nasser Academy for Higher Military Studies, Hassan was simply not up to the task. He had flown only point-defence interceptors at earlier times and thus not only lacked experience in commanding complex operations of advanced multi-role aircraft, but also those including multiple formations of mutually-supporting combat-support-aircraft, interceptors, bombers, and fighter-bombers. Moreover, unlike those of Sha'ban, Hussein's principal aides were also of low calibre: together with Hassan, and contrary to Sha'ban and Basu at earlier times, they all lacked the connections within the High Command in Baghdad necessary to influence the planning of the General Headquarters (GHQ) at strategic and operational levels. This was even more important considering that the position of the commander of the IrAF was subordinated to the Chief-of-Staff of the Armed Forces, who was always and exclusively an Army officer, and that the Iraqi Army generals had no clear understanding of the capabilities of modern air power. Finally, there are strong indications that, just like Hassan, his new deputies also had no clear knowledge of the actual capabilities of all the aircraft, equipment, and personnel of the IrAF as of 1988-1990.[10]

Unsurprisingly, the situation resulted in a weak leadership that was ill-prepared for what it was about to face – and that at the time Saddam led the country towards a direct confrontation with nobody less than Israel, as noted in a post-1991 Iraqi study:

> Our air force and air defence were assigned the task of confronting the potential Zionist aggression by responding in the form of air attacks with limited numbers of aircraft targeting the strategic and vital targets in the Israeli depth.[11]

All of this mattered very little to Saddam: while justifiably proud of the IrAF, he was a strong believer in the 'fleet in being' philosophy. From his point of view, it didn't matter if the air force could not operate effectively, as long as it was well-equipped and existent, and its personnel were under his control.

FORCE-MULTIPLIERS AND INTERCEPTORS[12]
The flying component of the IrAF consisted of about 50 operational squadrons with around 620 combat aircraft, most of which were staffed by combat-seasoned personnel.[13] As of 1988-1990, the air force was working on several so-called 'multiplier' platforms: foremost amongst these were three Ilyushin Il-76 transports modified to carry French-made Thomson-CSF Tigre-G radars. The first prototype, designated Baghdad, had just one such radar installed in a big plastic radome instead of the rear loading ramp and proved a disappointment. The later two prototypes – designated Adnan-2 (in memory of Khairallah) – received two Tigre-G antennas inside a conventional rotor dome mounted atop a pedestal in front of the fin. However, while their French radars proved highly effective in detecting low-flying aircraft from the ground, when installed on Adnan-2s they lacked both range and look-down capability and despite work to improve their performance none was officially operational. More effective proved the conversion of a Boeing 727 airliner into a platform for COMINT- and SIGINT gathering, and data-links enabling it to fuse the collected information directly into the Kari's ADOC (see below for details) in real time. Nick-named

Faw-727, this aircraft became operational in early 1988. Nevertheless, the IrAF's principal reconnaissance platform was the MiG-25RB (ASCC/NATO-codename 'Foxbat'), a Soviet-made jet capable of reaching operational speeds of Mach 2.3 while flying at an altitude of 21,000 metres (68,890ft), equipped with reconnaissance cameras and a reasonably advanced ELINT-gathering system. Iraqi MiG-25RBs were supported by Mirage F.1EQ-2/4/5/6 fighter-bombers capable of carrying French-made Thomson-CSF TMV-018 Syrel pods for electronic support measures (ESM) and Raphael-TH pods including a side looking radar (SLAR). Just like the Faw-727, these used a data-link system to download the collected intelligence to a network of ground stations: connected with the Kari's ADOC with help of electro-optical cables made by the Finnish company Ericsson, they thus enabled the IrAF commanders to manage the air battle in real time. Finally, Iraqi Mirages had a significant reconnaissance capability in the form of the ability to carry the COR-2 and Harold pods, equipped with conventional reconnaissance cameras.[14]

For air defence purposes, the IrAF operated a total of 102 modern interceptors. While the US intelligence subsequently obtained a reasonably good picture of this force, it was far from perfect: for example, the Office of Naval Intelligence assessed IrAF fighter strength at 29 advanced MiG-29 (ASCC/NATO-codename 'Fulcrum'), 22 MiG-25PD/PDS (ASCC/NATO-codename 'Foxbat'), 22 MiG-23MF/ML (ASCC/NATO-codename 'Flogger'), 29 Mirage F.1EQ-2/EQ-4 and five Mirage F.1EQ-5/6s, and noted that the MiG-23s and MiG-25s lacked the look-down/shoot-down capability, and that their equipment had 'poor' reliability. Actually, the Iraqis were confident their MiGs could match the American fighters. In their opinion, their most potent interceptors were 19 MiG-25s armed with R-40RD and R-40TD (ASCC/NATO-codename 'AA-6 Acrid') medium range air-to-air missiles. The IrAF had a total of 30 pilots for these, of which 20 were qualified for daylight operations only. The high operational costs of this complex type and related maintenance problems meant that only 10 MiG-25PD/PDS were usually operational, and that each of the two units flying them could usually deploy only a pair of aircraft simultaneously.[15]

On the contrary, the MiG-29 proved a disappointment for the Iraqis and they thus accepted only 33 out of 137 ordered. The first of two units to operate these became operational in early 1988, while the second was still working-up as of 1990. Iraqi MiG-29s were armed with R-27R (ASCC/NATO-codename 'AA-10 Alamo') and R-60M/MK (ASCC/NATO-codename 'AA-8 Aphid') missiles, and thus lacked the most advanced Soviet short-range air-to-air missile, the R-73E (ASCC/NATO-codename 'AA-11 Archer'). However, and unknown outside Iraq for years longer, the IrAF modified them to carry the highly effective, French-made Thomson-CSF TMV-002 Remora ECM self-protection pods. Together with their combat-experienced pilots – roughly half of whom were qualified for night operations – Remora-equipped MiG-29s were to cause quite some difficulties later on.[16]

Operated by a total of four squadrons, the 35 remaining Iraqi MiG-23MLs – armed with R-24R and R-24T medium-range air-to-air missiles (ASCC/NATO-code 'AA-7 Apex') and R-60s – were flown by combat-proven pilots, but their radar and fire-control system proved unreliable. However, several of them were also adapted to carry Remora pods. Iraq did operate about 30 older MiG-23MS, MiG-23MFs and about a dozen MiG-23UB two-seat conversion trainers, but these were considered as obsolete by the IrAF and used for training purposes only.[17]

A source of particular pride for the IrAF were four squadrons

The Iraqi fleet of Mirage F.1EQ fighter-bombers and pilots of four squadrons operating this type were a matter of great pride in Baghdad – with good reason: advanced equipment like Syrel ESM-pods, visible under the centreline hardpoint of this example, was the core of IrAF's war-fighting capability. (Ahmed Sadik Collection)

In the period 1988-1987, the IrAF applied and flight-tested numerous modifications to a wide range of its aircraft, including the adaptation of Soviet-made Kh-29 PGMs to one Mirage, or French-made AM.39 Exocet missiles on one MiG-23ML. Another test included the installation of French-made in-flight refuelling probes on a handful of MiG-23BNs and (visible on this photograph) one Su-22M-4K. (via Ali Tobchi)

equipped with Dassault Mirage F.1EQ multi-role fighters, frequently assessed as 'operated by its best pilots and ground crews' – in Iraq and abroad. Between 1977 and late 1987, Iraq placed orders for a total of 105 Mirage F.1EQ-2/EQ-4/EQ-5 and EQ-6 multi-role fighters and 15 Mirage F.1BQ two-seat conversion trainers. According to official Iraqi documentation, 64 single-seaters and 12 two-seaters were still intact as of 1990: they were operated by four squadrons staffed by about 150 qualified pilots. While all single-seaters were equipped with advanced variants of Cyrano-IVM radar and fire-control system with limited look-down/shoot-down capability, only about 30 were assigned the air defence role. On the contrary, the majority of F.1EQ-5/6s – the only variants that could carry such advanced weapons as laser-guided Aerospatiale AS.30L and radar-guided AM.39 Exocet missiles, but also the few remaining Matra Baz-AR ARMs, custom-built to Iraqi requirements and capable of effectively countering US- and Israeli-made air defences – were retained for ground attack and anti-ship operations. Moreover, the Mirages played a crucial role in the IrAF because of their electronic warfare capabilities using French-made Thomson-CSF TMV-004 Caiman broad-band offensive stand-off jammers, Remora self-protection jammers, and Matra Sycomor chaff and flare dispensers.

French-made in-flight refuelling pods and extensive training made their pilots experts in in-flight refuelling operations at critically low altitudes.[18]

The balance of the IrAF's interceptor fleet consisted of about a dozen squadrons equipped with about 150 MiG-21 (ASCC/NATO-codename 'Fishbed') point defence interceptors. While armed with reasonably advanced R-60 and R-13M (ASCC/NATO-codename 'AA-2 Atoll') air-to-air missiles, their avionics were hopelessly obsolete. Indeed, after flying nearly 50% of all the sorties flown by IrAF's fixed-wing fleet during the war with Iran, the majority of Iraqi MiG-21s were badly worn out and in urgent need of overhauls – if not an outright replacement.[19]

BOMBERS AND FIGHTER-BOMBERS

The IrAF of 1990 also possessed a potent offensive capability. Over the previous two years it replaced old and worn out Tupolev Tu-16 (ASCC/NATO-codename 'Badger') and Tu-22 (ASCC/NATO-codename 'Blinder') bombers with 25 advanced Sukhoi Su-24MK (ASCC/NATO-codename 'Fencer') strike aircraft, capable of penetrating enemy airspace at very high speed and very low altitude along a pre-programmed route, almost like a cruise missile. The

The major new intake for the IrAF in the period 1988-1990 included the delivery of 25 powerful Su-24MK fighter-bombers. However, the type proved complex to fly and maintain, and both units equipped with it – No. 8 and No. 18 Squadrons – were still working up as of August 1990. (via Ali Tobchi)

Fencer was a big brute of an aircraft, complex to maintain and troublesome to fly, but capable of carrying more than 3,000kg (6,613lbs) of bombs or guided weapons over a range of 1,000km (621 miles) at a speed of more than 1,111km/h (600 knots). By virtue of its complex fire-control system, it was compatible with a wide range of precision guided ammunition (PGM), including Kh-25 (ASCC/NATO-codename AS-10 'Karen' or AS-12 'Kegler', depending on variant), Kh-28 (ASCC/NATO-codename 'AS-9 Kyle') anti-radar missiles (ARM), and Kh-29 (ASCC/NATO-codename 'AS-14 Kedge') laser- and electro-optically guided missiles. It also featured a comprehensive electronic countermeasures (ECM) suite, including radar warning- and missile-launch warning-systems, and large wing fences with integrated chaff and flare dispensers. As of 1990, two squadrons of the IrAF were in the process of working-up on this type.

The rest of the IrAF's strike fleet was based upon two types. Six squadrons were equipped with Sukhoi Su-22 (ASCC/NATO-codename 'Fitter') – an old but sturdy 'warhorse' of the war with Iran, available in several variants. The last three of these – Su-22M-2K, Su-22M-3 and Su-22M-4K – were all compatible with PGMs like Kh-25, Kh-28 and Kh-29. Indeed, the Su-22M-4Ks could deploy their Kh-29s in combination with Thomson PDL.1EQ Patrick laser-designator pods carried by Mirage F.1EQ-5s and F.1EQ-6s. Moreover, the IrAF's Su-22s could be equipped with the Soviet-made SPS-141 ECM-pod, which proved effective against US-made MIM-23B I-HAWK SAMs in Iranian service. The internal variant of the SPS-141 was installed into about half of the MiG-23BN fighter-bombers (ASCC/NATO-codename 'Flogger'). While proving shorter-ranged and less-popular than the Su-22, this type was still operated by two squadrons of the IrAF.[20]

There is no doubt that the IrAF's commanders, ground crews and pilots were far better qualified and more experienced in 1988-1990 than ever before, or after, and in all aspects of aerial warfare, including counter-air, suppression of enemy air defences (SEAD), interdiction and strategic strikes, reconnaissance, and close-air support. They were not only well-trained in electronic warfare, but considered the availability of operational ECM-systems on their aircraft a matter of life or death. Indeed, the war with Iran taught the Iraqis how to combine Syrel-carrying Mirages or the Faw-727, Kh-28-toting Su-22s and combat air patrols of MiG-23s, MiG-25s and MiG-29s, and multiple formations of Tu-16s, Tu-22s, Su-22s and MiG-23BNs into big strike packages, and then deploy their ECM-systems in highly effective fashion. On the contrary, IrAF's capability to fight for air superiority remained rather limited: all intercept operations during the war with Iran were run under strict ground control, according to a carefully rehearsed plan and usually resulted in the deployment of medium-range air-to-air missiles only. Iraqi interceptor pilots next to never engaged the Iranians in air combat at short range, and frequently jettisoned all their stores and flew back to base when encountering just one of the vaunted Grumman F-14A Tomcat interceptors of the IRIAF.[21]

KARI IADS

The nerve centre of both the Directorate of Operations and Directorate of Air Defence, IrAF was the Kari integrated air defence system (IADS) and automated tactical management system (ATMS). The 'brain' of the same was the Air Defence Operations Centre (ADOC) constructed inside a massive fortified facility at the former al-Muthana AB, in the Baghdad suburb of Mansour. The ADOC was responsible for compiling the national strategic and tactical picture, for determining strategic directions and tactical air defence priorities, and could also coordinate operations of radars, communications, electronic counter-measure systems, manned interceptors, surface-to-air missiles, and anti-aircraft artillery. The Kari was sub-divided into four geographically-distributed air defence sectors (ADSs): at the heart of each was a sector operations centre (SOC) for air battle management and up to five intercept operations centres (IOCs). These command posts controlled 28 primary and some 275 secondary surveillance radars deployed in approximately 100 sites. Between 15 and 20 were static and equipped with long-range E/F-band (2.6-3GHz) radars such as P-35M and P-37 (ASCC/NATO-codename 'Bar Lock'), supported by PRV-11 (ASCC/NATO-codename 'Side Net') E-band height-finders, augmented by Thomson-CSF TRS.2205 Volex III, Thomson-CSF TRS.2215 and 2230 Tigre-S medium-range 'gap-fillers'.[22]

The ADOC was linked to a well-developed network of electronic warfare sites, including such as Unit 128 – which was a dedicated communications-intelligence (COMINT) and signals-intelligence-gathering asset. Well-integrated, and highly-automated, the Kari enabled the commanders at ADOC in Baghdad to control the air battle over any piece of Iraqi airspace at any time of the day.

The ADOC was connected to the SOCs and all 14 major air bases (the HQs of which acted as wing-commands, each controlling up to three or four squadrons of combat or combat-support aircraft), by a multiple and hardened network of fibre-optic cables that provided redundancy. The cables connecting the ADOC and the SOCs linked

Table 1: Kari IADS Organisation

ADS	HQ	Areas of Responsibility	Missile Brigades	Number of Missile Batteries	Warning and Control Regiments
1	Camp Taji	Central/Eastern	145, 146	16	50, 51, 52
2	Wallid AB	Western	147	11	12
3	Ali Ibn Abu Talib AB	Southern	148, 149	17	71, 72, 73
4	al-Hurrya AB	Northern	195	6	81, 82

Table 2: Distribution of Iraq's Air Defence Assets[25]

Type	Mosul/Kirkuk	Baghdad	H-2/H-3	Talil/Jalibah	Basra	Total
Missiles	122	552	90	10	118	892
AA sites	39	380	138	73	167	797
Guns	110	1,267	281	180	442	2,280
SA-2	1	10	1	1	2	15
SA-3	12	16	-	-	-	28
SA-6	-	8	6	-	8	22
SA-8	1	15	-	-	-	16
Roland	2	9	6	2	5	24
ZSU-23-4	-	8	-	-	5	13
S-60	8	10	3	2	14	37

One of the rare photographs taken inside the ADOC of the Kari IADS, at Muthenna AB, in northern central Baghdad. (Albert Grandolini Collection)

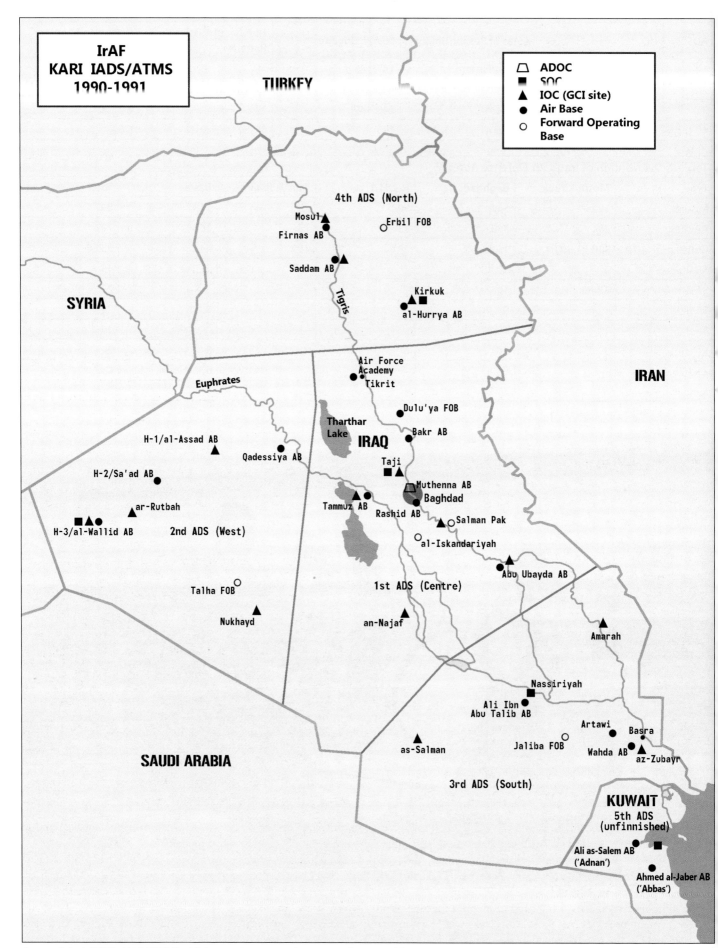

IrAF
KARI IADS/ATMS
1990-1991

⬠	ADOC
■	SOC
▲	IOC (GCI site)
●	Air Base
○	Forward Operating Base

TURKEY

4th ADS (North)

Mosul ▲
Firnas AB ●
Erbil FOB ○

Saddam AB ● ▲

Kirkuk ▲ ■
● al-Hurrya AB

SYRIA

IRAN

Euphrates

Air Force Academy
● Tikrit

Dulu'ya FOB ●

Tharthar Lake

IRAQ

Bakr AB ●

H-1/al-Assad AB ▲

Qadessiya AB ●

Taji ■ ▲

Muthenna AB ⬠
Baghdad

H-2/Sa'ad AB ●

▲ ●
Tammuz AB

Rashid AB ●

▲ ○ Salman Pak

ar-Rutbah ▲

■ ▲ ●
H-3/al-Wallid AB

2nd ADS (West)

○ al-Iskandariyah

● ▲
Abu Ubayda AB

Talha FOB ○

1st ADS (Centre)

Nukhayd ▲

an-Najaf ▲

▲ Amarah

SAUDI ARABIA

as-Salman ▲

Nassiriyah ■

Ali Ibn Abu Talib AB ●

Jaliba FOB ○

Artawi ●
Basra
● ▲
Wahda AB
az-Zubayr

3rd ADS (South)

KUWAIT
5th ADS (unfinnished)

Ali as-Salem AB ●
('Adnan')
■

Ahmed al-Jaber AB ●
('Abbas')

A map of the IrAF's Kari IADS/ATMS with its most important elements, air bases, and forward operating bases, as of 1990-1991. (Map by Tom Cooper)

DESIGNATIONS OF IRAQI AIR BASES

With next to nothing known about the rich military history of Iraq, outside the country most official designations of the IrAF's air bases were entirely unknown for decades prior to 2003. Correspondingly a number of designations based on local geography, though also on misunderstanding or misspelling of some of names, were in widespread use in the West. For the reader's easier orientation, Table 3 lists both 'Western' and official, native designations of major Iraqi ABs and FOBs in service as of August 1990.

Table 3: IrAF Bases, Native and Western Designations[26]		
Western Designation	**Official IrAF Designation**	**Background**
Mosul	Firnas AB	named after a legendary Andalusian Arab who attempted to fly using feathered wings
Kirkuk	al-Hurrya AB	'Liberty' in Arabic
Qarayyah West	Saddam AB	named after Saddam Hussein
Balad (also Balad Southwest)	al-Bakr AB	named after former Iraqi President Ahmad Hassan al-Bakr
Taqqaddum	Tammuz AB	named after the Babylonian month of Tammuz (July)
H-1 New (also al-Assad)	al-Qaddessiya AB	former water-place Ain al-Assad
H-2	Sa'ad AB	named after an Islamic warrior
H-3	Al-Wallid AB	named after an Islamic warrior
Mudaysis	Talha FOB	
Kut (also al-Kut)	Abu Ubaida Ibn al-Jarrah AB	named after an Islamic warrior, also 'Imam Ali Base'
Tallil	Ali Ibn Abu Talib AB	named after an Islamic warrior
ex-RAF Shoibiyah	Wahda AB	'Unity' in Arabic

All of the major air bases of the IrAF were either newly-constructed or vastly expanded and heavily fortified during the 1980s. This is a view of al-Bakr AB: home-base of three MiG-23ML squadrons and two Su-24MK squadrons as of August 1990. (Photo by Martin Rosenkranz)

modems capable of switching between direct land lines, microwave and troposcatter communication links, while the SOCs were linked to the IOCs by similar cables for voice and data. Finally, the IOCs were linked to more than 600 observation posts where operators had hand-held pads in which the observer entered heading, altitude, and formation size data, and then transmitted by pushing the button. Like contemporary Soviet IADS and ATMS, the whole system was designed and laid out to be operated by men with limited secondary education: most of the responsibility lay on the shoulders of the better-educated officers. Unsurprisingly, the Kari was an extremely

hierarchical system and damage to key sites (see Table 1) and its communication system could render it ineffective.

Supported by surveillance- and fire-control radars, and a network of visual observation posts, the SOCs were responsible for battle management using interceptors, SAMs, and anti-aircraft artillery. They could track up to 120 targets and compiled the regional tactical picture which was relayed to the ADOC. Commanders of every SOC had the right to decide how to engage the target, even the type of intercept and the number of missiles to be fired. The IOCs – usually consisting of two vehicles carrying a container with necessary command, control and communication equipment and parked inside a concrete shelter – could track only a limited number of targets. While capable of quickly dispersing if necessary, their task was to follow the orders issued by the SOCs and execute the task.[23]

Integrated within the Kari were a total of about 67 SAM-sites operated by the IrAF and some of 30 operated by the Army. The centrepiece were older Soviet-made SAM-systems such as Volga and Volkhov (ASCC/NATO-codename 'SA-2 Guideline'), and Neva and Pechora (ASCC/NATO-codename 'SA-3 Goa'). Between 1974 and 1989, Iraq imported enough equipment for 39 SA-2 and 52 SA-3 SAM-sites, of which 43 were identified as still operational as of late 1990 and 1991 (see Table 2 for details): their primary task was

the protection of military production facilities and three air bases in western Iraq. The Air Force's SAM-sites were augmented by four French-made Roland SAM-battalions deployed for protection of military and civilian sites, and six battalions equipped with Soviet-made 2K12 Kub (ASCC/NATO-codename 'SA-6 Gainful'), which were assigned to shield the SSMD's missile sites and al-Wallid AB near the border with Jordan. In addition to SAMs, the Iraqis deployed 7,600 anti-aircraft artillery pieces, including up to 1,800 in Baghdad alone. These ranged from heavy 130mm KS-30 flak to 14.5mm machine guns – the latter often positioned on rooftops or 10-13ft (3-5m) tall earth berms.[24]

Table 4: Iraq Air Force and Air Defence, Order of Battle, 1 August 1990[27]			
Unit	Base	Aircraft Type	Notes
Chief of Staff IrAF: Lieutenant-General Muzahim Sa'ab al-Hassan			
Deputy Operations: Major-General Hamid Raja-Shalah Hassan at-Tikriti			
or Major-General Safa Tawfiq Rashidin at-Tai			
Deputy Air Defence: Major-General Shahin Yassin Muhammad			
Direct-Reporting Units			
No 3 VIP Transport Sqn	Baghdad IAP	JetStar, Falcon 20	est. 1935
No 4 VIP Transport Sqn	Baghdad IAP	SE.316B, Mi-8, Bo.105, MBB.105, Commando Mk 2	est. 1935
No 53 Squadron	Baghdad IAP	Falcon 50	
Air Force Academy	Tikrit AB	Zlin 142, EMB.312, L-29, L-39, MiG-15UTI	est. 1973
Flight Leaders School	al-Wallid AB	Jet Provost, F-7B	est. 1966; fighter weapons school
No 7 OCU	al-Wallid AB	F-7B	est. 1960
No. 17 OCU	al-Wallid AB	MiG-21FL/UM	est. 1966
No. 20 OCU	unknown	Su-22UM	est. 1980; status unclear
No. 21 OCU	unknown	SA.342	est. 1980
No. 27 OCU	Sa'ad AB	MiG-21FL/PFM/UM	est. 1980
No. 30 Squadron	unknown	SE.316B	est. 1975
No. 31 Squadron	unknown	SA.342	est. 1978
No. 55 Squadron	unknown	Mi-8	est. 1974
No. 57 OCU	al-Wallid AB	F-7B	est. 1982
No. 59 OCU	Tammuz AB	MiG-23UB	est. 1983
No. 69 OCU	Bakr AB	Su-22M-3K/UM-3K	est. 1981
No. 84 OCU	unknown	Bo.105	est. 1985-1986; liaison & VIP-transport unit
No. 88 Squadron	unknown	SA.342	est. 1969
No. 106 Squadron	unknown	Bo.105	Est. 1985-1986; liaison & VIP-transport unit
1st ADS (Centre), HQ Taji			est. 1980
No. 11 Squadron	Rashid AB	MiG-21MF	est. 1961
No. 23 Squadron	Baghdad IAP	An-24/26	est. 1975
No. 33 Squadron	Baghdad IAP	Il-76MD	est. 1978
No. 70 Squadron	Rashid AB	MiG-21MF/R	est. 1973; detachment at Ali Ibn Abu Talib AB
SAR Flight	Rashid AB	2x Mi-8	
145 Missile Brigade	Baghdad IAP	6x SA-2, 6x SA-3	
No. 6 Squadron	Tammuz AB	MiG-29	est.1954

No. 10 Squadron	Tammuz AB	7 Tu-16, 4 B-6D	est. 1960
No. 36 Squadron	Tammuz AB	6 Tu-22	
No. 87 Squadron	Tammuz AB	MiG-25PU/RB	est. 1981
No. 96 Squadron	Tammuz AB	MiG-25PD	est. 1985; detachment at Jaliba FOB
No 114 Squadron	Tammuz AB	Su-25K	est. 1988; also reported as No. 109 or No. 121 Squadron
No. 115 Squadron	Tammuz AB	Su-25K	est. 1985
No. 116 Squadron	Tammuz AB	Su-25K	est. 1986
SAR Flight	Tammuz AB	2x Mi-8	
146 Missile Brigade	Tammuz AB	2x SA-2, 4x SA-3 battalions	
No. 8 Squadron	Bakr AB	Su-24MK	est. 1958
No. 18 Squadron	Bakr AB	Su-24MK	est. 1973
No. 63 Squadron	Bakr AB	MiG-23ML	est. 1984
No. 93 Squadron	Bakr AB	MiG-23ML	est. 1987; detachment at Firnas AB
2nd ADS (West), HQ Wallid AB			est. 1982
No. 47 Squadron	al-Wallid AB	MiG-21bis	est. 1979; from al-Hurrya AB
No. 39 Squadron	Qaddessiya AB	MiG-29	est. 1974; detachment at Talha FOB
No. 97 Squadron	Qaddessiya AB	MiG-25PDS	est. 1983
No. 73 Squadron	Sa'ad AB	MiG-23ML	est. 1984;
3rd ADS (South), HQ Nassiriyah			est. 1982
No. 14 Squadron	Ali Ibn Abu Talib AB	MiG-21bis	est. 1966
No. 49 Squadron	Ali Ibn Abu Talib AB	MiG-23BN	
SAR Flight	Ali Ibn Abu Talib AB	2x Mi-8	
No. 29 Squadron	Abu Ubaida Ibn al-Jarrah AB	MiG-23BN	est. 1966
SAR Flight	Abu Ubaida Ibn al-Jarrah AB	2x Mi-8	
No. 5 Squadron	Wahda AB	Su-22M-4	est. 1953; from Firnas AB
No. 11 Squadron	Wahda AB	MiG-21MF	est. 1961
No. 109 Squadron	Wahda AB	Su-22M-4	est. 1978
SAR Flight	Wahda AB	2x Mi-8	
148 Missile Brigade	Wahda AB	3x SA-2, 5x SA-3 battalions	
No. 101 Squadron	Umm Qassr AB	SA.321	est. 1977
149 Missile Brigade	Umm Qassr	3x SA-3 battalions	
4th ADS (North); HQ Kirkuk			est .1982
No. 1 Squadron	al-Hurrya AB	Su-20	est. 1931
No. 37 Squadron	al-Hurrya AB	MiG-21bis	est. 1979
No. 44 Squadron	al-Hurrya AB	Su-22	est. 1977
SAR Flight	al-Hurrya AB	2x Mi-8	
195 Missile Brigade	al-Hurrya AB	3x SA-2, 3x SA-3 battalions	
No. 9 Squadron	Firnas AB	MiG-21MF	est. 1959; detachment at Abu Ubaida Ibn al-Jarrah AB
SAR Flight	Firnas AB	2x Mi-8	
No. 79 Squadron	Saddam AB	Mirage F.1EQ	est. 1981;
No. 81 Squadron	Saddam AB	Mirage F.1EQ-5/6	est. 1985
No. 89 Squadron	Saddam AB	Mirage F.1EQ-4	est. 1985
No. 91 Squadron	Saddam AB	Mirage F.1EQ-2	est. 1982-1983
5th ADS (Kuwait);			
HQ Kuwait City (est. 1990; no flying units assigned, and build-up never completed; included SAM-units only)			

ARTILLERY AND BALLISTIC MISSILES

One aspect which deeply influenced the Iraqi leadership was that of the surface-to-surface missiles (SSMs). These were controlled by the Surface-to-Surface Missiles Directorate (SSMD), which was spun off from the Army's Artillery Directorate shortly before the end of the war with Iran (for organisation of the SSMD, see Table 5).

In Baghdad, the experiences from the IrAF's offensive against the Iranian economy, and the large-scale deployment of SSMs during the so-called 'War of the Cities' against Iran, were reflected in the fear that Israel might repeat the 1981 Osirak air raid on a much larger scale, primarily targeting facilities for the production of chemical weapons, but also the dams that fed irrigation systems. Together

An al-Hussayn missile as put on display during the Baghdad Arms Show in May 1989. (US DoD)

with Saddam's predilection to conserve the IrAF, this combination of factors resulted in the SSMD becoming the primary means of striking Israel. Correspondingly, reconnaissance operations conducted in 1989 along the armistice line between Israel and Jordan resulted in Iraq's General Military Intelligence Directorate (GMID) preparing a list of 32 targets with target folders, and dividing them between the SSMD and the IrAF. To aid the former the Electrical-Mechanical Engineering Directorate (EMED) prepared three major missile bases in western Iraq.[28]

Early in 1990, SSMD operations against Israel were discussed in at a meeting attended by Saddam, Defence Minister Shanshal, Chief of the Directorate of Military Industries (DMI) Hussein Kamel, Chief-of-the-General-Staff al-Khazraji, IrAF Commander Lieutenant-General Hassan (see next sub-chapter for details), GMID-Director Saber Abd al-Aziz and SSMD's commander Lieutenant-General Hazem Abd al-Razzaq al-Ayyubi. Many aspects were discussed, including the advantages of static and mobile

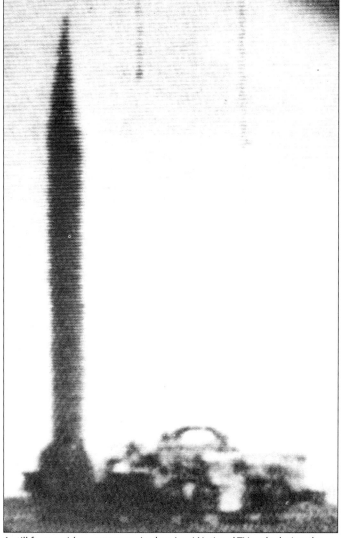

A still from a video sequence aired on Iraqi National TV early during the war with Iran, and showing an R-17E (or 'Scud') missile in firing position. The 224th Missile Brigade and its Scuds played an important role in that conflict. (Tom Cooper Collection)

Table 5: SSMD, Order of Battle, 1988-1991		
Unit	Equipment	Notes
223rd Missile Brigade	al-Hussein	est. mid-1990; al-Hussein was a stretched-range derivative of the Soviet-made R-17E (ASCC-designation 'SS-1c Scud-B'; grew to two battalions with 10 TELs as of 1990
224th Missile Brigade	al-Hussein	est. 1974; originally equipped with R-17E; re-equipped with al-Hussein in 1987
225th Missile Brigade	Luna-M	
226th Missile Brigade	SS-30, SS-40, SS-60 Astros	

By 1988-1990, Brazilian-made artillery rocket systems like SS-30 and SS-40 (visible in this photograph) were the principal MRLS of the Iraqi Army. Ironically, the same were acquired in even larger numbers by the armed forces of Saudi Arabia because they had financed the Iraqi order for Astros. (US DoD)

launchers, with Saddam demanding both. In September 1990 the EMED began construction work on both active and dummy sites, and then created a communications network, improved road access, and provided protection in the shape of both conventional air defences and ground-based commandos (some of them from the RGFC). To facilitate Saddam's demands, not only was the 224th Missile Brigade re-deployed to western Iraq, but in mid-1990 the new, 223rd Missile Brigade was established and equipped to operate al-Husseins from both static and mobile launchers. By February 1990, US intelligence had detected five clusters of static missile sites in western Iraq, including 28 launchers. Meanwhile, SSMD's crews and attached civilian engineers worked hard on improving the missile's performance and payload, and developed chemical warfare warheads. On 31 January 1990, the Iraqis carried out their first test from the east towards the west (rather than the west-east operations during the war), including four al-Husseins. The chemical warhead was tested on 18 April of the same year and further tests followed later on to improve their propulsion and guidance.[29]

THE KUWAITI ARMED FORCES[30]

With its origins in the Directorate of Public Safety, the Kuwaiti Army was established in 1953 and slowly expanded: the 6th Mechanised Brigade was created in 1959, and followed in 1962 by two armoured brigades; the 15th Mubarak and the 35th Shaheed Brigades, which absorbed the troops of the former 25th Commando Brigade. Supporting even this modest force proved difficult due to the small population, and there were no major developments until 1980 when the government felt forced to introduce conscription.

As often in the case of oil-rich countries of the 1970s and 1980s,

Kuwait went on a spending spree acquiring large quantities of advanced armament. Between 1965 and 1978 it acquired 70 Vickers MBT Mk.1 tanks and then 267 Chieftain Mk.5s from the United Kingdom. However, just as the Iranians had quickly discovered, the Chieftain was underpowered and suffered from overheating problems, although having formidable armour and a good gun.[31]

Spreading the largesse around, during the same period, France and the United States each supplied 18 self-propelled 155mm howitzers (including M109A1Bs), while the USSR sold five launchers for Luna-M 'FROG-7' artillery missiles (ASCC-codename 'FROG-7'). Another wave of modernisation was initiated in the 1980s, when orders were placed for 231 vehicles from the US-made M113 family (mostly APCs, but including 56 M901s equipped with TOW ATGMs), and 245 Soviet-made BMP-2 IFVs. Finally, in the late 1980s, an order was placed for 150 Yugoslav-made M-84M MBTs and BM-21 MRLS. The Emirate also acquired American, Belgian and Soviet infantry weapons together with French, Soviet and US anti-armour missiles, which only added to the logistical burden.

The Kuwaitis held most of this equipment, together with many of the troops, in just one facility, constructed some 30 km south of Kuwait City at a cost of US$100 million: the resulting 'military city' was vulnerable to air and missile strikes, but well-suited to thwart the possibility of a military coup. The military city was constructed with US support: the Americans assisted the Kuwaiti military build-up through their small United States Liaison Office Kuwait (USLOK; assigned to the US Embassy in Kuwait City), as the two countries grew closer during the Iran-Iraq War. Eventually, by 1988 the army, which was officially designated the Kuwaiti Land Forces (KLF) that year, had reached a nominal strength of

Nearly all of the equipment of the Kuwait Army in the 1960s was of British origin. This column of vehicles mounting Vickers Vigilant anti-tank guided missiles belonged to the 2nd Infantry Battalion, and was photographed during a contemporary military parade. (Albert Grandolini Collection)

By the time of the Iraqi invasion of Kuwait, only a handful of Yugoslav-made M-84 (an indigenous variant of the T-72) had reached Kuwait. Most of the remaining MBTs were subsequently delivered to Saudi Arabia and had to be stored until the Kuwaiti military was re-formed in late 1990. (US DoD)

10,000 men. However, most of its troops were poorly-paid and poorly-treated Bedouin mercenaries with a strong predilection for deserting, while the majority of the officers and NCOs were recruited from the ruling families and loyal tribes and promoted on basis of favouritism. Training was basic, with very few exercises at brigade-level and even here there was little coordination and no effective higher command. Agreements had been signed with Egypt and Turkey for the provision of advanced training, but neither took effect before the Iraqi invasion. Maintenance and logistics were stifled by bureaucracy that had priority over military effectiveness,

Table 6: KLF, 1 August 1990			
Unit	Base	Primary Equipment	Notes
Amiri Guard Battalion			
Commando Battalion			
6th Mechanized Brigade	Mutlaa Ridge	BMP-2s, M113s, Vickers Mk.1	northern Kuwait
15th Mechanized Brigade	Kuwait City	Chieftain, M113	central Kuwait
35th Armoured Brigade	Salmi Road	Chieftain, M113, BMP-2s	western Kuwait, incl. 7th and 8th Tank Battalions, 57th Mechanized Infantry Battalion, 51st Artillery Battalion

A Mirage F.1CK-2 (recognizable by its light grey camouflage pattern), an SA.330 Puma, a Gazelle, a Super Puma, and three other helicopters of the KAF, seen shortly before the Iraqi invasion. (Albert Grandolini Collection)

and the KLF was still heavily dependent on foreign technicians, mostly civilians from Bangladesh, Egypt, France, India, Jordan, Pakistan and the United Kingdom, the advice of whom was usually ignored. Unsurprisingly the conclusion was that: 'The order of battle was a little more than a hollow shell'.[32]

Overall, the strong feeling of national pride, race, and religion reflected an unrealistic assessment of the country's security situation. Therefore, Kuwait and its friends and neighbours never anticipated an invasion by a fellow Arab nation and the existence of the GCC together with limited US military support appeared to act as a counterbalance to the Iraqi threat, although Kuwait (like Saudi Arabia) stopped short of accepting an American military presence. The KLF was never regarded as anything more than a 'trip-wire' or a 'speed bump' to a serious incursion and its presence was intended to buy time for an international response.[33]

KUWAIT AIR FORCE

Like the KLF, the Kuwait Air Force (KAF) – commanded by Brigadier-General Dawood S al-Ghanim since 1986 – also existed to serve as a trip-wire. Its backbone consisted of survivors of 30 McDonnell-Douglas A-4KU Skyhawk strikers and 10 TA-4KU conversion trainers ordered in November 1974 and delivered by 1983: while they provided an effective interdiction- and CAS-platform, they lacked advanced self-protection equipment, yet were also still used to fly combat air patrols (CAPs) as Mirage F.1s ordered

from France in April 1974 (following the Sameta Incident), were inadequately equipped to meet contemporary threats. The 18 F.1CK interceptors and two two-seat Mirage F.1BK conversion trainers were delivered between 1977 and 1983, together with 24 SA.342L/K Gazelle attack helicopters and 12 Aerospatiale SA.330H transport helicopters. However, not only did at least one Mirage crash soon after delivery: all were equipped only with the basic Cyrano IV radar and fire-control system, very limited self-protection equipment and lacked even Matra Super 530F medium range air-to-air missiles.[34]

The Sameta Crisis also prompted Kuwait into bolstering its ground-based air defences. In 1974, the KAF placed an order for two AN/TPS-32 3D long-range surveillance radars and four batteries (each with six launchers) of MIM-23B I-HAWK SAMs. Eight French-made TRS-2100 Tigre low-altitude radars and five batteries with 20 transporter/erector-launchers (TELs) of Soviet-made 9K33 Osa-AK (ASCC/NATO-codename 'SA-8 Gecko') SAM-systems. The latter were operated by the KLF and not integrated into the KAF's IADS – which was otherwise a miniature version of the Kari: supported by French-made Mitra computers with 12 consoles, this was installed in an underground site in Kuwait City. Rather unsurprisingly, the Kuwaiti air defences put up a mediocre performance when put to the test during the Iranian attacks, that included surface-to-surface and anti-ship missiles, in 1987. Nevertheless, the experience gained during this period led to the Kuwaitis deploying their I-HAWKs as listed in Table 7. Another

A pair of Mirage F.1CKs (front aircraft wearing the serial number 704) as seen following overhauls in France, in March 1989. (Photo by Jean-Francois Lipka)

A pre-delivery photograph of the TA-4KU (serial number 881). This light striker was the backbone of the KAF until 1990. (George van der Schor Collection)

long-term effect of the Sameta Crisis was the contract for Yugoslav companies to construct two heavily fortified air bases: Ahmed al-Jaber AB, south-west of Kuwait City, was opened in 1979; while Ali as-Salem Sabah, west of Kuwait City, was declared operational a year later. The command of each also acted as a wing-command of the KAF, that as of August 1990 was organised as listed in Table 8.

In another attempt to bolster the KAF, in 1983 Kuwait City placed an order for 13 additional F.1CK-2s and 4 additional F.1BK-2s, and six Aerospatiale AS.532SC Cougar helicopters armed with AM.39 Exocet anti-ship missiles. Even then, several of the Mirages were quickly lost in accidents, while their radars reportedly proved unreliable, and they still had to be augmented by Skyhawks in the air defence role. The resulting 'chronic problem in air defence' finally had to be solved through an order placed in Washington, in July 1988, for 40 McDonnell-Douglas F/A-18C/D Hornet multirole fighters (including 8 F/A-18D two-seaters), together with AIM-7M Sparrow and AIM-9L Sidewinder air-to-air, AGM-65G Maverick air-to-surface, and AGM-84D Harpoon anti-ship missiles. None had been delivered by the summer of 1990, by which time the KAF

was in the process of receiving 12 BAe Hawk T.Mk 64 trainers and four Lockheed L-100-30 Hercules transports, and still heavily dependent upon foreign technicians, foremost the Pakistanis.

Table 7: Kuwait Air Force & Air Defence, MIM-23B I-HAWK SAM-sites, August 1990		
Unit	Equipment	Base
1st Hawk Battalion	MIM-23B	Mutlaa Ridge
2nd Hawk Battalion	MIM-23B	Bubiyan Island[35]
3rd Hawk Battalion	MIM-23B	Ahmadi
4th Hawk Battalion	MIM-23B	al-Adourmi
Unknown	MIM-23B	Ras al-Jalayh

One of about 20 SA.342L Gazelle attack helicopters as in service with Nos. 33 and 34 Squadrons, KAF, in July-August 1990. (KAF)

The 9K33 Osa-AK (SA-8 Gecko), was a Soviet air defence system operated by both the Iraqi Army and the Kuwaiti Land Force. This ex-Iraqi example was captured in 1991 and ever since has been on display at the RAF Museum in Duxford, in Great Britain. (Photo by Tom Cooper)

Table 8: KAF Order of Battle, 1 August 1990	
Unit	Aircraft Type
Commander of KAF: Brigadier Dawood S al-Ghanim	
Ahmed al-Jaber AB	
Air Defence Brigade	SA-7
No. 9 Squadron	14 A-4KU/TA-4KU
No. 12 Squadron	12 Hawk T.Mk 64
No. 25 Squadron	15 A-4KU/TA-4KU
Ali as-Salem Sabah AB	(CO Col Saber as-Swaidan)
No. 18 Squadron	11 Mirage F.1CK/F.1BK
No. 31 Squadron	SA.330F/H Puma
No. 32 Squadron	SA.330F/H Puma
No. 33 Squadron	10 SA.342K Gazelle
No. 34 Squadron	10 SA.342L Gazelle
No. 61 Squadron	10 Mirage F.1CK-2/F.1BK-2
No. 64 Squadron	4 AS.532C Cougar
Kuwait International	
No. 41 Squadron	4 L-100-30
No. 42 Squadron	2 DC-9-32

UNKNOWN AND UNCERTAIN: SAUDI ARABIA[36]

For Iraq's southern neighbours the end of the war with Iran could not come too soon: for almost a decade they were haemorrhaging money to support Iraq which in turn led to Iranian military harassment. For Saudi Arabia in particular, the task of defending a quarter of the world's oil reserves was challenge enough because the indigenous population consisted of between 8 and 12 million people, of whom about a million were young men aged 18–22. Conscription was officially adopted in 1970, but differences between different tribes, passive opposition from the youngsters who were often supported by their families, and growing corruption made it impossible to execute this universally. Moreover, obsession with the security of the royal family and retention of the acquired equipment resulted in very conservative training, while general lack of know-how and conservative instruction by foreigners made the kingdom over-reliant upon foreign mercenaries for technical support.

Originally established in 1902, but converted into the Royal Saudi Land Forces (RSLF) only in 1976, the Saudi Army had been expanded into six motorised infantry brigades by the time of the Arab-Israeli War of 1948, and several of these were committed to the unsuccessful struggle against the emerging Jewish state. A much more serious threat for the integrity of Saudi Arabia emerged during the 1950s in the form of a severe financial crisis caused by overspending, and then from Nasser's Egypt of the 1960s. Growing political differences with Cairo culminated in Nasser's support for the overthrow of the conservative Yemeni kingdom in 1962: this resulted in pan-Arabism spreading into Saudi Arabia and causing a wave of defections not only from the Saudi military, but even from units of the Royal Jordanian Air Force deployed in the country in order to bolster its defences. On advice from London, the Saudi government subsequently began financing a covert war against the Republican government in Yemen supported by Egypt.[37]

Following the period of austerity in the late 1950s and early 1960s, the war in Yemen prompted Riyadh into re-starting substantial improvement of its defences from 1965. Over the following decades, ever-larger acquisitions were funded by a surge in oil prices in the

An AMX-30 of the RSLF: together with 350 M60A1/A3s, 290 of these lightly armoured but well-armed and fast MBTs formed the backbone of Saudi mechanised units. (Albert Grandolini Collection)

Installed on the chassis of the AMX-30 tank, mobile Shahine SAMs provided air defence for the RSLF's mechanised units. (Albert Grandolini Collection)

wake of the October 1973 Arab-Israeli War, as the Saudi-dominated OPEC flexed its economic muscles by controlling the output and distribution of 'black gold'. A bi-product of the tensions with Yemen and geographic circumstances (including the latent lack of water and other supplies in the desert kingdom) was the decision taken in 1964 to concentrate the entire army – then only some 25,000 strong – in three major bases, originally dubbed 'cantonments', and later 'military cities', strategically positioned close to borders: each of these was to become home for two brigades, support troops, and several squadrons of the Royal Saudi Air Force (RSAF). This elegant solution provided a symbolic gesture of defence, while keeping the armed forces away from urban conurbations and thus presenting no direct political threat to the rulers. The design and project management of these military cities was assigned by the Ministry of Defence and Aviation (MODA) to the US Army Engineer Corps in 1965. Aided by US construction companies, the work on the first, the King Faysal Military City near Tabuk, began in 1969 and was completed in 1971 at a cost of nearly US$82.5 million.[38] The next two bases were constructed to cover the coastal plain along the Persian Gulf. The first of them was the King Khalid Military City, constructed 60 kilometres south of Hafr al-Batin (contract signed in January 1974), to protect the Trans-Arabian Pipeline (TAP) that links as-Sammam and Jordan. Its octagonal design was completed only in 1987 – because the US Army first had to build the port of Ras al-Mishab to handle the necessary materials and suppliers.

During the same period, the RSLF was provided with a cornucopia of modern equipment, including 290 French-made AMX-30 and 150 US-made M60A1 MBTs (later reinforced by 200 additional M60A3s), 1,638 tracked armoured fighting vehicles (AFVs) on the chassis of the US-made M113 armoured personnel

carrier (APC), 517 French-made AMX-10 infantry fighting vehicles (IFVs), and 90 M109A2 and 51 AuF-1 155mm self-propelled howitzers. Anti-armour units were equipped with US-made BGM-71 TOW and M47 Dragon and French-made HOT ATGMs. By 1981, these helped convert two brigades into armoured units, and three into mechanised units. The profusion of equipment posed severe logistics problems foremost related to supply of water, fuel and adequate cooling systems: a traditional problem of the RSLF of the 1970s and 1980s were overheated crew compartments exposing the men to heat-stroke.

Nevertheless, the Iran-Iraq War, Western commercial interests, and growing corruption of top officials prompted further purchases, including 90 towed 155mm howitzers (72 FH70s and 18 M198s), in 1983; and also 15 Bell 406CS Combat Scout light helicopters and 16 Sikorsky S.70A-1 Desert Hawk transport helicopters for the Army Aviation Command, established in 1986 at King Khalid Military City.[39]

For the air defence of its formations, between 1974 and 1979, the RSLF acquired 32 AMX-30 tracked launchers and 61 sheltered-launchers for the Thomson-CSF R.460 Shahine SAMs (a development of the R.440 Crotale missile), together with necessary radars and support systems. In 1984, this was followed with an order for 36 mobile and 12 air-transportable shelter launchers, additional radars and data-link systems for a total of 17 SAM-batteries within the frame of the US$4 billion Project Al-Thakeb.

As of 1990 – and at least on paper – the RSLF thus totalled 38,000 troops equipped with 550 MBTs, organised into seven conventional brigades (two armoured, four mechanised, and one infantry), and one airborne brigade that included two battalions of paratroopers and three companies of special forces. The Royal Guard added

As of 1990, the Army Aviation Command of the RSLF was still a diminutive force, equipped – amongst others – with 15 Bell 406CS Combat Scout light helicopters. As visible in this photograph, these could be armed with BGM-71 TOW anti-tank guided missiles. (US DoD)

The second major helicopter type in service with the RSLF was the S.70A-1 Desert Hawk – essentially an export variant of the US Army's UH-60A Black Hawk. (US DoD)

another brigade. However, the force was a hollow shell, short by up to a third of its nominal strength, and suffering from a severe shortage of experienced non-commissioned officers and technical specialists. So many troops were regularly absent without leave that most of the brigades had only half their establishment. This was one of the reasons why the MODA contracted Pakistan in 1981 to provide 15,000 troops for two brigades: one at Tabuk in the north-west and one at Khamis Mushayt in the south. In 1987, one of the two Pakistani-staffed brigades was replaced by the Moroccans.

However, it was not just a shortage of manpower which undermined the RSLF. Although trained in some of the best Western military educational facilities, once they returned to Saudi Arabia officers were discouraged from independent thought or autonomous action until they rose in rank to that of a battalion commander, and at all levels they faced tremendous pressure to keep their superiors happy. Many lost all professional standards and competence. Unsurprisingly, their NCOs lacked authority and responsibility, while the majority of troops tended to have only very limited education. Training time was eroded by both religious and family obligations with the result that exercises were confined to battalion level and largely limited to arm-of-service with next to no combined arms training or preparation for a fluid battlefield. Even close air support training was focused upon static operations. Ultimately, the country was dependent upon the United States for its security but at the same time was refusing either to provide any kind of bases for Washington's forces, or to conduct any kind of joint exercises. Instead, Riyadh insisted that any kind of cooperation would be based upon Saudi forces with American arms and technical assistance.[40]

SAUDI ARABIAN NATIONAL GUARD

If the RSLF was a slender reed, Riyadh could always depend upon the Saudi Arabian National Guard (SANG) raised from Bedouin tribesmen and the Ikhwan as a bodyguard during the First World War, and gradually expanded until by 1990 it had about 10,000 enthusiastic volunteers who enlisted for three years. Until the late 1980s the SANG was organised into some 17 motorised infantry and 4 mechanised battalions, of which eight were combined into the 2nd King Abdul Aziz (Motorised) Brigade (KAAB), and the 10th Imam Mohammed Bin Saud (Motorised) Brigade (IMNSB). More than half of the remaining battalions were still in the process of being formed as of 1990, while others were either of ceremonial character or created in ad hoc fashion. The SANG had a screening role in the overall ground defence concept of the country, and to this end standardised upon 539 examples of the Cadillac-Gage LAV-150 Commando 4x4 wheeled AFV, supported by towed 105mm howitzers.[41]

ROYAL SAUDI AIR FORCE

Originally established as a US-supported attempt to create a native air force, the RSAF experienced a significant growth in the 1950s which ended with the financial crisis of 1958. In 1965 there was a new attempt at growth when Riyadh placed an order for English Electric (later BAC) Lighting F.Mk 53 supersonic interceptors and BAC Strikemaster jet trainers and light strike aircraft. Shortage of qualified pilots meant that most of the Lightnings had to be crewed by contracted British personnel. Clashes with South Yemen in the early 1970s led to a major shopping spree. In 1975, Saudi Arabia placed an order for 34 Lockheed C-130H Hercules transports and 11 KC-130H tanker aircraft. Two years later, the RSAF started receiving 79 Northrop F-5E Tiger II light fighter-bombers and 35 F-5B/F trainers under Project Peace Sun. In 1983, these were augmented by 12 RF-5E Tigereye reconnaissance fighters.

The outbreak of the Iran-Iraq War and the Israeli air strike on Iraq, in June 1981, convinced Riyadh that a further build-up of the air force was necessary. Correspondingly, an order was placed for 5 Boeing E-3A Sentry AWACS and 76 McDonnell-Douglas F-15C/D Eagle interceptors in the USA (Project Peace Sun II). Although the Eagles were supposed to have a strike capability, in reality this barely existed – which proved a major problem because while the Tiger IIs were extremely effective in this role, they were short-ranged and lacked advanced self-protection equipment. Furthermore, the US Congress turned down the request for Sentries, in turn prompting the Saudis and other Arab countries to turn to the European manufacturers. After financing Iraqi acquisitions of Mirage F.1EQ-4/5s and Mirage 2000s (together with Egyptian orders for Mirage 2000s and Dornier-Breguet Alpha Jets), in late 1981 and early 1982, in February 1986 Saudi Arabia signed a contract for Project Al-Yammamah. Originally valued at a 'mere' £500 million, this stipulated deliveries of 48 Panavia Tornado interdiction-strike (IDS), 24 Tornado air defence variant (ADVs), and 63 training aircraft (including 30 BAe Hawk T.Mk 65s, 30 Pilatus PC-9s and 2 BAe Jetstream T.Mk 31s). While the first Tornado IDS were taken from an order for the RAF and arrived in 1986, the first Tornado ADVs followed only four years later – and promptly proved a major disappointment due to problems with avionics integration. After receiving eight, the Saudis halted deliveries and then converted half of the order for ADVs into additional IDS, with which they were highly satisfied. The Al-Yamamah deal – ultimately valued at US$4.1 billion – also included air-to-air and air-to-ground guided weapons (amongst them brand-new Alarm ARMs and JP.233 anti-runway dispenser systems), and eventually prompted BAe to deploy 4,100 technical experts and advisors in Saudi Arabia.[42]

Meanwhile, the Pentagon convinced the US Congress to grant permission for Saudi Arabia to 'rent' 5 E-3A Sentries, 3 Boeing KC-135 Stratotankers and 2 McDonnell-Douglas KC-10A Extender tankers with USAF crews, forward deployed at Dhahran AB from late 1980 as the 'European Liaison Force-1' (ELF-1). Finally, after even more extensive negotiations, the Saudis were granted permission to buy 5 E-3As, together with 8 Boeing KE-3A tankers (an export variant of the KC-135, powered by CFM-56 engines) for US$3.2 billion, in 1985 and 1986. This acquisition was followed with a major buy of guided missiles, including 1,700 AIM-9Ls, 700 AIM-9P-4s, and 100 AGM-84 Harpoons.[43]

Overall, and while certainly the best-equipped and trained of all the branches of the Saudi military, by August 1990 the RSAF was still a force consisting of a mass of modern aircraft, commanded by officers with little operational experience, operated by pilots and ground crews with even less practical experience, and heavily dependent upon foreign technical assistance. It was only thanks to the latter that the service could demonstrate an operational availability rate of 80-85%.

The pillar of the RSAF since 1990 is the fleet of five E-3A Sentry AWACS operated by No. 18 Squadron. (George van der Schoor Collection)

Table 9: RSAF Order of Battle, August-September 1990[44]		
Unit	Aircraft Type	Notes
Commander of RSAF: Lieutenant-General Ahmad al-Buhairi		
Tabuk (King Faysal AB)		
No. 17 Squadron	RF-5E	ground attack & reconnaissance
Hafr al-Batin (King Khalid Military City)		
no permanently assigned units		
al-Jubail Airport		
Royal Saudi Navy	AS.332	ASW & SAR
Dammam, King Fahd IAP		
no permanently assigned units		
al-Ahsa AB		
no permanently assigned units		
Jeddah (Prince Abdul Aziz AB)		
No. 4 Squadron	C-130H	Transport
No. 16 Squadron	C-130H	Transport
No. 20 Squadron	C-130H	Training
Riyadh (King Khalid IAP/Military City)		
no permanently assigned units		
Riyadh (King Faysal Air Academy)		
No. 1 Squadron	B737, B747, BAe125	VIP-transport
No. 8 Squadron	Cessna 172	elementary training
No. 9 Squadron	Strikemaster	jet training
No. 11 Squadron	Ce.550, Gulfstream	training & liaison
No. 33 Squadron	B757, Gulfstream, Beech 300	Transport
al-Kharj (Prince Sultan AB)		
No. 18 Squadron	E-3A, KE-3A	AEW & tanker
No. 37 Squadron	Hawk T.Mk 65	weapons training & light attack
Dhahran AB		
No. 7 Squadron	Tornado IDS	strike/interdiction
No. 13 Squadron	F-15C/D	air defence
No. 14 Squadron	AB.212	SAR
No. 21 Squadron	Hawk T.Mk 65	weapons training & light attack
No. 22 Squadron	PC-9	Training
No. 29 Squadron	Tornado ADV	air defence; including nucleus of No. 34 Squadron
No. 42 Squadron	F-15C/D	est. in September 1990
No. 66 Squadron	Tornado IDS	strike/interdiction; working up
Taif (King Fahd AB)		
No. 3 Squadron	F-5E	ground attack
No. 5 Squadron	F-15C/D	air defence
No. 10 Squadron	F-5E	ground attack
No. 12 Squadron	AB.212	Training
Khamis Mushayt (King Khalid AB)		
No. 6 Squadron	F-15C/D	air defence
No. 15 Squadron	F-5E	ground attack

The F-15C Eagle was the primary interceptor of the RSLAF since the mid-1980s. This example from No. 6 Squadron was photographed in 1992, outside one of the underground hardened aircraft shelters at Khamis Mushayt. (Photo by Jean-Francois Lipka)

Often overlooked was the large RSAF fleet of F-5E and RF-5E Tiger II fighter-bombers, with which four squadrons were equipped. These two RF-5Es were photographed during a refuelling stop in Great Britain, in the course of their delivery flight. (Mlpix/Martin Hornliman Collection)

IADS PROBLEMS

Through the 1970s and 1980s, the RSAF also constructed seven huge air bases, all of which were to play a crucial role in the coming conflict. The most important of them was the King Khalid Military City, which served as the home both of the RSLF's Aviation Command and the GCC's Peninsula Shield Force. Commanded by Saudi Major-General Turki Hedaijan (supported by a 25-man staff) this consisted of a Qatari tank battalion with 24 AMX-30 MBTs, one Omani and one Emirati mechanised battalion each, and a motorised rifle company from Bahrain. The Peninsula Shield Force was supposed to act as a cadre for two brigades with 10,000 troops who were to act as a rapid intervention force. However, financial and manning problems meant that by 1990 it had only about 3,000 officers and other troops organized into the equivalent of one composite brigade. Indeed when the crisis over the Iraqi invasion of Kuwait erupted, the Peninsula Shield Force was quickly disbanded and Hedaijini assigned the command of a RSLF brigade deployed

in the north.[45]

At least initially, the construction of RSAF air bases went hand in hand with a carefully-phased acquisition of advanced air defence systems, which began with acquisition of the British-made Type 40 series radar systems (capable of supporting Lightings by calculating precise intercept vectors), a total of 16 batteries (96 launchers) for Hughes MIM-23A HAWK SAMs (later upgraded to the MIM-23B I-HAWK standard), and the first nation-wide communication network. The next step was initiated in 1984, when the Royal Saudi Air Defence (RSAD) was established as an independent branch of the armed forces under Lieutenant-General Prince Khaled Ibn Sultan – who was also assigned the responsibility for creating a national air defence system. Correspondingly, in February 1985, Riyadh placed a US$8.5 billion contract with Boeing Industrial Technology Group for a command, communications and control (C3) system within the framework of Project Peace Shield – in addition to an earlier order – and promptly followed by another US$1.7 billion contract

With No. 34 Squadron still working up, No. 29 Squadron was the only RSAF unit operational on the Tornado ADV as of August 1990. (Photo by Jean-Francois Lipka)

Due to protracted development of the Tornado ADV, the RSLF eventually increased its order for Tornado IDS. As of 1990, this was the backbone of the Saudi strike fleet. These two examples were photographed while launching from Dhahran AB for a training sortie, loaded with practice bomb dispensers. (US DoD)

with Litton Industries for related communications systems. These three contracts led to the delivery of 28 Westinghouse AN/TPS-43 short-range radars, AN/TPS-72 medium-range radars and 17 AN/FPS-117 long-range, 3D surveillance radars, and 34 AN/TPS-63 low-altitude, 2D surveillance radars. These were to be integrated into an IADS with the help of six AN/TQS-73 control systems, and tied to the RSAF's E-3A AWACS and the RSLF's Shahine 2 SAMs with help of data links and a network with tropospheric scattering and microwave communications systems.

On paper at least, the Saudis should thus have received one of the most advanced IADS world-wide: centred at the Air Defence Command and Control Centre (ADCC) in Riyadh, this was to control six zones (each with its own ADOC, and five own SOCs) together with two Base Operations Centres (BOCs) responsible for in-flight refuelling and search and rescue (SAR) operations. However, Project Peace Shield proved far too ambitious: many elements were still not delivered by the summer of 1990, while there were serious software and systems-integration problems, causing the programme to fall years behind schedule. Officially

activated on 26 September 1990, the Piece Shield continued to suffer serious weaknesses and caused numerous problems even when the Americans rushed additional equipment to Saudi Arabia. Unsurprisingly, the entire project was quietly terminated in January 1991. The RSAD thus went into its first war still operating MIM-23B I-HAWKs supported by various early warning radars for point defence purposes only.[46]

5

AMERICAN UMBRELLA

Following the end of the US involvement in the Vietnam War in 1973, there was little enthusiasm in Washington for adventures abroad. Nevertheless, there was also no return to the isolationism of the 1920s: instead Washington applied the so-called Nixon Doctrine, named after US President Richard B Nixon. This envisaged equipping regional allies – like Iran under the Shah Reza Pahlavi – with US-weapons, to act as ultimate guarantors of Western interests. The Pentagon maintained only a nominal presence in the Persian Gulf – in the form of a small base in Manama, in Bahrain, which served as headquarters for the US Navy's Middle East Task Force. In reaction to the Shah's demise and the Soviet invasion of Afghanistan, during the early 1980s the administration of President Ronald W Reagan developed a new strategy in which the USA would meet any threat to Saudi Arabia and the world's primary sources of oil and gas. The refusal of GCC states to accept the large-scale deployment of US troops – and related opposition from the US Congress – hindered this idea, but Reagan expanded support facilities elsewhere, such as in the Indian Ocean, and from April 1981, had rapid-deployment forces available at sea. The Reagan administration also provided the necessary command framework through converting the Rapid Deployment Joint Task Force established by President James L 'Jimmy' Carter in March 1980, into the multi-service United States Central Command (US-CENTCOM) in 1983: this became responsible for coordination of all reactions to threats in south-west Asia and north-east Africa.

CENTCOM

For political and diplomatic reasons, CENTCOM would not have its headquarters in its area of responsibility, but at MacDill Air Fore Base (AFB) in Florida. This made it difficult for its commanders to establish relations with the local forces but this was neither immediately necessary nor possible: until early 1990 its primary focus was on thwarting a Soviet invasion of Iran.[1]

Since 23 November 1988, the commander of CENTCOM was the burly and emotional General H Norman Schwarzkopf, an outspoken officer prone to 'volcanic' outbursts, which earned him

the nickname "Stormin' Norman". As the son of a former military advisor to the Shah (indeed, the man who helped create the Imperial Guard of Iran), Schwarzkopf had a great deal of personal experience in the region – to a degree where he felt that local tensions were far more likely to spring a regional conflict that the Soviets. His prime subordinate commands were the Central Commands of the US Army (USArCent) and the USAF (USAFCEnt), respectively. The former was based within the HQ of the 3rd Army, commanded by Lieutenant-General John J Yeosock since 1989, while the later was based within the 9th Air Force, commanded by Lieutenant-General Charles A 'Chuck' Horner since 1987.[2]

Schwarzkopf's first job upon assuming command of CENTCOM was to create a contingency plan to meet a Soviet invasion of Iran, Oplan 1002-90, but he felt that Iraq might be a greater threat to the regional stability, especially after the end of the Iran-Iraq War. Correspondingly, on 16 April 1990, he produced the outline of *Oplan 1002-90: Deterrence, Counterair, Interdiction and Defensive Operations, and Counteroffensive Campaign of Friendly Arab Peninsula States*. Soon after, Horner produced a supportive three-phase plan for aerial operations. On 25 April 1990, Schwarzkopf issued the paper 'Iraq, Regional Warning Problem' and increased the priority of related intelligence collection against Iraq. A month later, on 21 May, he reported that the heavily-armed Iraq had economic and territorial grievances with Kuwait, but also concluded, 'Iraq is not expected to use military force to attack Kuwait or Saudi Arabia to seize disputed territory or resolve a dispute over oil policy.'

Eventually, it was Washington's growing concern over Iraqi statements and actions that prompted the White House to, on 12 July 1990, request permission to deploy two KC-135 tankers to the

General Schwarzkopf (right) takes command of the US-CENTCOM in November 1988. (US DoD)

UAE. The Emiratis first turned this request down, but then granted permission, although their brand-new Mirage 2000 interceptors were incompatible with such aircraft, and their pilots (who were still mainly Pakistanis) had no training with the USAF's in-flight refuelling system. Despite these problems Operation Ivory Justice, began on 24 July.

Meanwhile, between 23 and 28 July, CENTCOM ran the war game *Internal Look* to test Oplan 1002-90 in a scenario including the invasion of Kuwait by six 'heavy' Iraqi divisions, but with sufficient time to deploy the primary tool of the US Army for response to any kind of a major diplomatic crisis, the XVIII Airborne Corps. The outcome was rather drastic: the 'blue' forces held the 'red' (Iraqi) troops beyond the Saudi oil fields, but lost half their troops in the process. As a result, Schwarzkopf began reworking Oplan 1002-90, aiming to publish the revised version on time for a conference scheduled in October and November 1990.[3]

A particularly worrying experience of *Internal Look* was that it highlighted a severe shortage of ships necessary to bring in reinforcements and supplies despite significant preparations to meet this eventuality. This was caused by the sharp reduction in US and European merchant fleets since the 1960s, which gradually compromised plans for the strategic sealift and rapid deployment of US forces even to Europe. Certainly enough, the USA did invest some US$7 billion into the Military Sealift Command (MSC) and its 96 Ready Reserve Force (RRF) ships, 25 Maritime Prepositioning Ships (MPS), and 8 Fast Sealift Ships (FSS), as well as 4 hospital and aviation logistics ships. However, this project was largely designed to support the US Marines: only the FSS were based in the United States and planned for the use by the Army, while the majority of RRF vessels proved to be not only obsolete, but poorly maintained.[4]

In 1990, the prospects of upgrading the strategic sealift force seemed ever more remote as the collapse of the USSR progressed with even President George H W Bush and his Defence Secretary, Richard B 'Dick' Chaney questioning the need not only to maintain the sealift capability, but also powerful military forces in Europe. Instead, they began seeking for ways to slash defence spending. Congress shared such opinions and was planning to cut the US Army to 535,000 by 1995, while in July 1990 an exercise was launched simulating the army's withdrawal from Europe.[5]

US ARMY

In August 1990, the US Army still had 740,471 active troops, and 1.5 million reservists and troops of the National Guard. The US Marine Corps (USMC) had 199,877 active troops and 102,200 reservists. Together, the US Army and the USMC had more than 15,000 MBTs and nearly 7,000 self-propelled and towed guns. Moreover, the USAF could call upon more than a million personnel and had 3,164 combat aircraft, while the USN and the USMC could provide another 1,000 combat aircraft.[6]

For the US Army, the end of the Vietnam War in 1973 saw it at the nadir of its fortunes, for while it had achieved much more than generally recognised it clearly failed to achieve Washington's goals, and reflected social ills such as drug abuse and racism. A 1973 Harris Poll of the public rating placed the Army only one level above garbage disposal workers in terms of respect.[7] At the end of the First World War, a British officer was heard to say, 'Now we can get down to proper soldiering' – a view many US Army officers must have felt in 1974, especially when returning their attention to potential operations against the Warsaw Pact. Yet in that year it would have proved a slender reed because limited funding for training meant only four out of 13 active divisions in the United

General William Eugene dePuy, the first commander of the US Army Training and Doctrine Command, one of the principal architects of the major reform of the US Army's doctrine after Vietnam, and initiator of the debate that resulted in the AirLand Battle doctrine.

States were assessed as 'combat ready'. The army was also short of 20,000 troops, and with combat arms 14% under strength. It would have to rebuild itself from the bottom up: a difficult task especially as defence spending – while steadily increasing in monetary terms – declined in terms of Gross National Product from 8.7% in 1964 to 5.0% in 1980.[8]

ROUND-OUTS

With all the army's leaders being Vietnam combat veterans, they began by restoring discipline and respect for the chain of command so that by 1990 there had been a massive drop in desertions and drug use, although the abolition of conscription led to problems with maintaining strength and capability. The all-volunteer force brought its own problems in terms of higher rates of pay and the need to divert defence budget resources into supporting soldiers' families – for a full third of the four lowest ranks were usually married and the troops found their pay, especially in Europe, insufficient to keep together body and soul: indeed, in 1979 the army commissaries accepted US$10 million of food stamps.

Only half of those recruited in 1980 had a high school education, while problems of discipline and suitability meant that 40% of troops were discharged before completing their first enlistment. Such problems were gradually solved and by 1990 almost all recruits were high-school graduates, 75% were in the highest mental categories, while there were still more than enough recruits to meet all requirements. The US Army thus opted to maintain an active force of 780,000 high quality troops, rather attempting to expand its strength. To do so operationally it opted to integrate brigades of the Army Reserve and the National Guard, which augmented – or 'rounded out' – selected divisions with a full brigade in the case of a crisis. This meant that by the end of 1980s, more than half of the combat forces belonged to the new, 'Total Army'. The round-out system was selected because reserve units were cheaper than active ones during peacetime, but also because many within the US Army believed the defeat in Vietnam was caused by the lack of Washington's will to mobilise reserves. Thus, the Total Army concept provided a political trip-wire forcing politicians to provide the forces as and when required.[9]

TRADOC

Meanwhile, the US Army returned to the basics through the recently established Training and Doctrine Command (TRADOC). This was initially commanded by General William E. DePuy, who reformed training with an emphasis upon leadership in the field based upon his own experience from Vietnam, where he found this was severely wanting, and had relieved many officers, including seven battalion commanders. Under DePuy's ideas, the US Army was to be trained at all levels to reach high combat capability standards with the aid of computer-based training and evaluation technology, including the Multiple Integrated Laser Engagement System (MILES), used for individual and unit training, and battle training centres based upon the idea behind the US Navy's Fighter Weapons School (famous as 'Top Gun'). Similarly, officers were subjected to simulator-based Battle Command Training Program, producing realistic command conditions in courses overseen by retried, but always battle-hardened generals.[10]

AIRLAND BATTLE

DePuy and his successors – Lieutenant-General Donn A Starry and General Glenn K Otis – also addressed the question of doctrine, the way the Army was expected to fight in the future. The prime threat of 1970s and 1980s was the Warsaw Pact, which had three tanks and guns for every one of NATO. The October 1973 Arab-Israeli war provided a grim indication that conventional operations resulted in a more lethal battlefield than anything previously known, with massive losses in men and material, and incredible expenditures of ammunition. The same conflict had also shown that warfare was no longer dominated by numerical superiority and fire-power volume, but by fire-power precision. In response to these conditions, by the time the USA celebrated its Bicentenary, in 1976, DePuy produced the *Field Manual 100-5 Operations*, which was based not only on discussions with the various branches within the Army, but also the USAF, and allies.[11]

FM 100-5 focused upon the European combat zone and advocated an active defence, jabbing with mechanised forces at enemy weak points and exploiting precision firepower with help of the Tactical Fire Direction System (Tacfire), as well as fire and movement – or 'shoot-and-scoot' tactics.[12] The manual made it clear the task was integrated with the USAF, and introduced the term 'AirLand Battle'.[13] In this, air power was used against enemy's second echelon. While the AirLand Battle had a Eurocentric focus, under DePuy's successors during the following decade this concept evolved into a very dynamic doctrine into which the USAF integrated its operations from 1984. Indeed, by 1990 it envisaged operations up to 150 kilometres deep within periods of up to 72 hours, exploiting initiative, mobility and synchronised responses with aerial interdiction, long-range fire, and electronic warfare, all aiming to stun even an advancing enemy with deep, lighting-fast manoeuvres of mechanised forces, supported by attack helicopters. Executing this doctrine as of 1979 seemed highly problematic as even optimistic assessments deemed only 6 out of 10 divisions in the

USA as combat ready, and only 3 out of 4 in Europe. The US Army remained in the doldrums with regard to equipment, with the only new heavy weapon introduced before 1980 being the M198 towed 155mm howitzer.[14]

A renaissance for the US armed forces, including the Army, began following a combination of events from 1979, including the occupation of the US Embassy in Tehran and the Soviet invasion of Afghanistan, followed by the induction of President Reagan in early 1981. He pushed for increased spending for defence, dedicating 5.9% of the gross national product (GNP) in 1982, and rising to 6.5% in 1986. Although the spending began to decline rapidly following the collapse of the Soviet Union – dubbed 'The Evil Empire' by Reagan – by that time the reform of the US armed forces was largely complete.[15]

Further development of the doctrine during the 1980s was heavily influenced by NATO, which first developed a coherent policy for the use of tactical, operational, and strategic air power and included a concept of indirect army-support known as 'battlefield air interdiction' (BAI). The research and theories of the so-called 'deep attack' were merged with the evolving FM 100-5 and the AirLand Battle concept in 1979, to produce the demand for the USAF and allied air forces to seek 'centres of gravity' of the enemy military power: objects, installations or units whose destruction would wreck the enemy ability to conduct operations. Such attacks were to be run against the background of theatre-wide aerial superiority, established not only by the US and allied air forces, but also through the involvement of the US Army and the US Navy.[16]

EQUIPMENT UPGRADES

The need for new equipment, especially for the mechanised and aerial forces, was demonstrated during the October 1973 Arab-Israeli War where the quality of Soviet armament was often superior to the 'latest generation' of US Army armament.[17] Research and development of replacements had already begun, but production became possible only during the Reagan era. The mechanised forces received the 63-tonne M1 Abrams MBT, powered by a gas turbine, and the M2/M3 Bradley IFV. The Abrams was initially equipped with a variant of the British-designed 105mm cannon, but from August 1985 was upgraded to the M1A1 standard through the introduction of the 120mm M256 smoothbore gun based on the German-designed Rheinmetall weapon. Moreover, from 1988 the US Army received up-armoured M1A1HAs (HA stood for 'heavy armor'), which offered greatly improved protection against the latest Soviet weapons through the incorporation of depleted uranium into their turret armour array. During the same period, the mechanised infantry received 1,371 M2 Bradleys (delivered from May 1981), while the M993 chassis of that vehicle was used to mount the M270 Multiple Launch Rocket System (MLRS).[18] In many ways, the latter was similar to the Brazilian SS-30/40/60 Astros MRLS used by the Iraqi Army, but carried a 2.3 tonne rocket pod launching unguided rockets equipped with sub-munition warheads out to a range of 31.5 kilometres. Moreover, these pods could also fire the MGM-140 Army Tactical Missile System (ATACMS) with a range of 160km.[19] The Army's aviation underwent a similar, wholesale upgrade, in the form of the introduction to service of the Bell OH-58D Kiowa scout helicopter, the Sikorsky UH-60 Blackhawk utility/transport helicopter, and the McDonnell-Douglas AH-64A Apache helicopter gunship armed with AGM-114 Hellfire ATGMs.

In similar fashion, the USAF received a new generation of aircraft of which the most important were the McDonnell-Douglas F-15A/B and – starting in the early 1980s – F-15C/D

Eagle interceptors that, in response to a growing requirement for deep interdiction, eventually evolved into the F-15E Strike Eagle. Equipped with the Low Altitude Navigation Targeting Infrared for Night (LANTIRN) pods – which actually completed operational test and evaluation during Operation *Desert Storm* – the F-15E was expected to replace the highly effective General Dynamics F-111, whose F-variant was compatible not only with tactical nuclear weapons, but also with a wide range of PGMs. The high cost of the Eagle meant that it had to be augmented by the new lightweight fighter in the form of the General Dynamics F-16A/B and then F-16C/D Fighting Falcon, which replaced the old McDonnell F-4 Phantom II. Furthermore, in 1977 the USAF introduced the unusual Fairchild A-10A Thunderbolt II, an extremely agile, yet well armoured purpose-built tank-buster. Finally, for long-range strike the air force continued to rely upon the venerable Boeing B-52 Stratofortress, but this was upgraded to deploy Boeing AGM-86C Conventional Air-Launched Cruise Missiles (CALCMs) – a variant of the nuclear-tipped AGM-86B – with the conventional blast/fragmentation warhead. The AGM-86C was the first weapon to have its inertial navigation system supported by an integrated GPS-system (instead of the AGM-86B's terrain contour-matching guidance system). The CALCM became operational just in time for Operation *Desert Storm*. Finally, shrouded in secrecy until 1988 was the revolutionary Lockheed F-117A Nighthawk. Developed in reaction to experiences from the October 1973 Arab-Israeli War, this was the first aircraft to be designed around so-called 'stealth' or 'low observable' technology, a sub-discipline of military tactics emphasising passive electronic countermeasures to make aircraft less detectable by radar, infrared, and other detection methods. The F-117 was constructed to reduce its radar cross-section through a combination of its internal construction, aerodynamic shape, and application of special (American and British) materials, with the aim of enabling the aircraft to operate undetected deep within enemy airspace.[20]

US NAVY AIRCRAFT

US naval air power also went through a post-Vietnam War renaissance with the most significant element being the introduction of the Grumman F-14A Tomcat interceptor. While equipped with advanced AWG-9 radar and fire-control system, and long-range AIM-54 Phoenix air-to-air missiles, this was the first US fighter designed to dog-fight small and nimble jets, like Soviet-made MiG-21s. Shackled by financial restrictions that left it under-powered, the F-14A was never upgraded to fully meet the US Navy's ambitious plans for a multi-role fighter: instead, the Pentagon opted to augment it with the simpler and lighter McDonnell-Douglas F/A-18A/B Hornet, and then the slightly more advanced F/A-18C/D. The primary all-weather and night strike platform remained the venerable Grumman A-6E bomber, a veteran type that proved its worth during the Vietnam War. Nevertheless, and just like the type in the process of being replaced by the Hornet – the Vought A-7E Corsair II – this was meanwhile equipped with a wide range of PGMs, including AGM-88 high-speed anti-radar missiles (HARMs), diverse variants of the AGM-65 Maverick air-to-ground missile, and laser-guided bombs from the Paveway I/II/III series. Finally, the US Navy adopted a unique approach to low-risk deep strike through the jet-powered RGM/UGM-109 Tomahawk Land Attack Missile (TLAM), which could be carried both by surface ships (RGM-variant) and attack submarines (UGM variant).

US Navy and USAF aircraft were equipped with weapons which demonstrated growing precision not just in the air-to-air role but also in the laser-guided air-to-surface role. The older missiles proved disappointing but the AGM-65D Maverick with its imaging infra-red seeker would prove an especially valuable battlefield tool. Similarly, further development of laser-guided bombs (LGBs) reached ground-breaking dimensions: kits were developed to adapt conventional free-falling or 'dumb' bombs into guided 'smart' bombs with seekers and fin-controlling guidance systems as GBU-16 Paveway II and the 'intelligent' semi-autonomous guidance as GBU-24 Paveway III. In similar fashion, kits were developed to convert dumb bombs into the electro-optically-guided GBU-15 which could operate when laser-guided ordnance could not.

6
UMM AN-NIDAA[1], IRAQI INVASION OF KUWAIT

Saddam's desire to strike Israel had in turn hardened his attitude towards Kuwait and his wish to 'clear the deck'. Exactly when he began thinking of the military option – Project 17 (Mashroo Sabatasher) – is uncertain, but in May 1990 General Sabari Ibrahim's GMID began detailed studies of Kuwait's terrain and armed forces, while on 19 June the SSMD was ordered to transfer a FROG battalion from the 225th Missile Brigade to the Basra area and, four days later, it was ordered to return to the Guards Corps those units which had been guarding missile bases in western Iraq. A few days later, Saddam met the Chief-of-Staff RGFC, Lieutenant-General Aayad Futayyih Khalifa ar-Rawi, ostensibly to discuss operations against Israel, and asked him, 'to take a look at the Iraq-Kuwaiti border', words that would light a fuse setting off numerous explosions with the chain reaction continuing to the present day. A day later, ar-Rawi was ordered to write up a detailed plan to accomplish the task of 'retrieving' Kuwait, with a small top secret planning staff, closely supervised by Saddam: all of the senior officers involved had to swear on the Qoran to maintain secrecy.[2]

IRAQ'S STRATEGIC PLANNING

The invasion of Kuwait was to be confined to the Republican Guards Corps Command and while Lieutenant-Generals Hussein Rashid (Operations Chief of the Army) and Saber Abd al-Aziz (Head of Military Intelligence) were informed of Saddam's intentions, they were forbidden from sharing the information even with the Defence Minister Shanshall (who, as described above, had had helped plan the 1961 operation), or with Army Chief-of-Staff Lieutenant-General Nizar al-Khazraji. Instead, Rawi and his staff exploited both updated contingency planning left over from the Qassem area and lessons from the war with Iran.

There was no shortage of information for the GMID had received verbal instructions from Saddam on 12 July to support this effort through a terrain analysis, and detailed reporting on the enemy order of battle. Correspondingly, between 25 and 31 July Iraqi intelligence not only provided intricate information on the status of the KAF and the ground-based air defences, but also on all vital targets in Kuwait, including major communication facilities, the locations of all the embassies, a detailed list of Kuwait's top civilian- and military officials, and KLF activity. Additional information was collected from numerous 'friendship delegations' sent to Kuwait from February 1990, to cement civilian and military ties, some of which received guided tours of major government offices, especially those related to the oil industry, and even military installations.[3]

IrAF MiG-25RBs provided photo-reconnaissance while flying

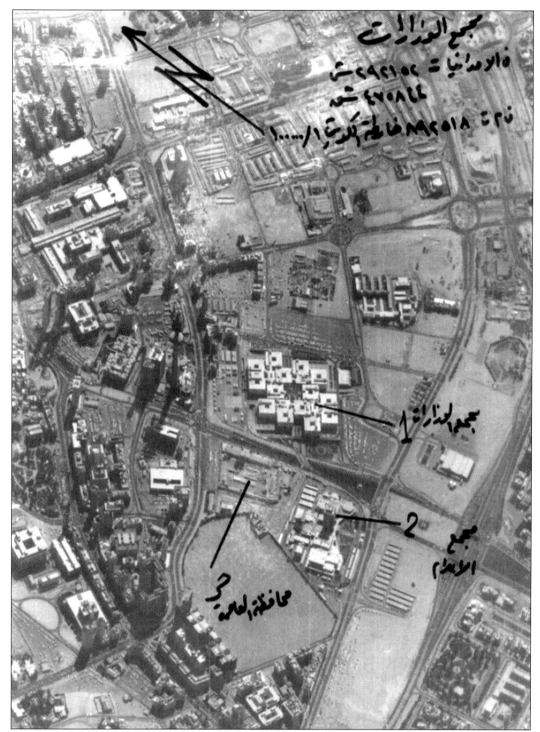

One of the reconnaissance photographs of important objects inside Kuwait City, taken by an Iraqi MiG-25RB in July 1990. (Ahmad Sadik Collection)

four sorties over Kuwait during the first fortnight of July, producing more than 800 images of 124 targets. The same aircraft also flew reconnaissance of northern Saudi Arabia and Bahrain, while the sole Boeing 727 electronic warfare aircraft ran several COMINT and SIGINT-sorties. The GMID also placed an order for satellite photographs of Kuwait and northern Saudi Arabia with the French-based commercial company SPOT (*Satellite Pour l'Observation de la Terre*), which operated two satellites equipped with high-resolution optical cameras. These images were handed over without questions from Paris, and if the French government suspected anything it did not inform anyone.[4]

Nevertheless, there remained a crippling shortage of detailed information, especially about the KLF and local terrain, while planners had to work with a handful of outdated 1:100,000 scale maps. For example, the HQ of the Hammurabi Armoured Division RGFC received only aerial photos and tourist maps of Kuwait City, and that during the evening of 31 July – while the GMID believed that the invading force would be facing not just three Kuwaiti brigades, but four, including the non-existent '80th Infantry Brigade' in the al-Jahra area.[5]

Eventually, Rawi's team produced two options for Project 17; the capture of Kuwait's islands, or the total occupation of the country. The former involved taking Bubiyan and Warbah as well as a 30-50 kilometre wide strip of the Kuwaiti coast to secure the approaches to the naval base of Umm Qasr. The latter was developed when the GMID concluded that no serious resistance was to be expected, and that the US forces in the region were too weak to offer serious resistance. Finally, the GMID assessed that the operation would

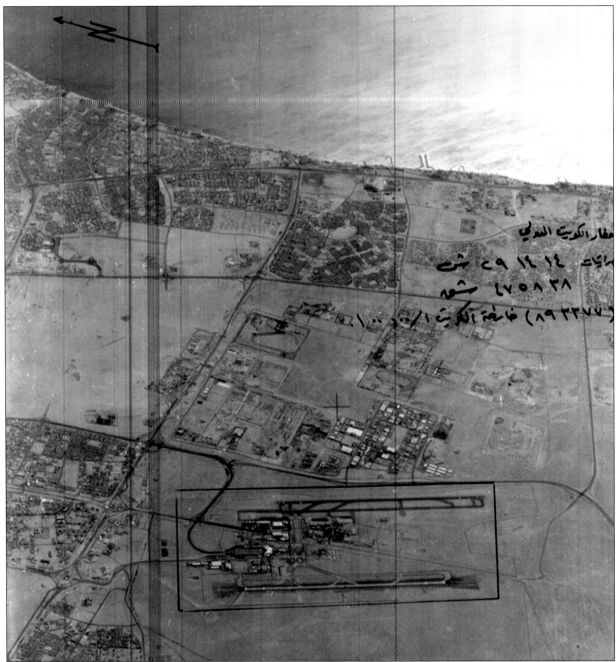

A view of Kuwait International Airport, as seen on another photograph taken by an IrAF MiG-25RB prior to invasion. (Ahmad Sadik Collection)

take four days at most, and – to prevent an 'internationalisation' of the conflict – priority was given to the decapitation of Kuwait's government, the seizure of the islands, air bases, and Kuwait International Airport (IAP).[6]

Major adaptations in Rawi's plan were the decisions not to use massed artillery or chemical weapons – ostensibly due to a lack of enmity towards the inhabitants of the '19th Province', but also because there were no Kuwaiti troop concentrations. On the contrary, all the commanders were advised to keep both civilian and military casualties to an absolute minimum, while the IrAF was ordered to simply to keep the KAF on the ground. In turn, the absence of the huge artillery train – which had characterized the 1988 offensives against Iran – was one reason why US Intelligence believed Saddam planned only a demonstration.[7]

What helped conceal Saddam's intentions was his high-profile propaganda campaign against Israel, although ominously he also spoke darkly about an international conspiracy. Indeed, this was the primary topic during his meeting with senior RGFC commanders,

on 2 July, when Saddam informed them that the country was facing an economic and propaganda plot with Kuwait acting as a major conspirator, and then discussed their capabilities and preparedness.[8]

Meanwhile, Saddam announced plans for large-scale manoeuvres in southern Iraq, supposedly to prepare his military for operations against Israel. Thus, when the Arab League met in Baghdad, on 15 July, and the RGFC began 'assembling for exercises' near the border with Kuwait, codenamed Operation *Arab Cooperation* (Amaliya Al Taawon Al Arabi) – and the CIA failed to detect this assembly for a week longer, by when the Guard's brigade commanders were being told their deployment was only a 'show of force to coerce Kuwait into the 'correct' response'. Indeed, the officers in question would learn the truth about the Project 17 only a week later: and even then many were convinced that the objective was merely to gain the Kuwaiti oilfields south of the Rumaila: not a few found it hard to believe the real objective was to 'regain the 19th Province'.[9]

For the reminder of July, the staff of RGFC's divisions concentrated on detailed planning of the invasion, testing solutions

The Vickers MBT Mk.1 was the result of a private venture aiming to make a simple, low-cost tank solely for export. Based on the design of the earlier Centurion, but having only 80mm of armour on the glacis and the turret front, the 39-tonne tank was armed with the new and more effective L7 105mm main gun. A total of 70 were sold to Kuwait in the mid-1960s. Originally delivered in green overall livery, and serving with the 6th Mechanised Infantry Brigade, Kuwaiti Mk.1s received a camouflage pattern in sand or tan colour sprayed in the form of irregular stripes, as shown here. (Artwork by David Bocquelet)

Starting in 1976, Kuwait acquired a total of 267 Chieftain Mk.5s, of which about 213 were operational with the 35th Armoured Brigade as of August 1990. They saw brief but heavy action during the morning of the Iraqi invasion, but were subsequently forced to withdraw into Saudi Arabia, thus leaving the Iraqis to capture no less than 136 intact Chieftains (between 50 and 75 subsequently entered service with the Iraqi Army). All Kuwaiti Chieftains were painted in light stone (BS381C/361) overall. Individual insignia consisted of a four-digit hull number, and 35th Armoured Brigade's tactical insignia (a black and yellow square), applied on the front section of fenders. (Artwork by David Bocquelet)

Kuwait originally acquired 18 M109A1Bs that served with the 51st Artillery Battalion, and saw quite intensive action on 2 August 1990. As usual, all were painted in light stone or tan colour overall, and wore the individual vehicle number on the front fender. Due to the lack of fuel but also their slow speed, most had to be left behind during the withdrawal of the 35th Armoured Brigade to Saudi Arabia. Only six survivors crossed the border, but they were subsequently reinforced by 31 M109A2s acquired from surplus stocks of the US Army. (Artwork by David Bocquelet)

Between 1980 and 1990, Iraq received about 1,000 T-72A and T-72M-1 tanks from the USSR and Poland, respectively, some 60 of which were lost during the war with Iran. In 1989, local assembly of T-72s from parts imported from Poland was launched at a factory built in Taji by a West German company. Based on the T-72A, the resulting vehicle was designated Saddam, and then Lion of Babylon (Assad Babil). Many of these received an additional 30mm plate of laminated armour welded on their glacis. By 1990, nearly all were painted in the same, carboard brown colour overall, slightly darker than the BS381C/361 light stone – which quickly faded in the sun to a very light sand colour. The majority of T-72s served with the Hammurabi and Medina Armoured Divisions, and the Tawakkalna ala Allah and Nebuchadenzzar Infantry Divisions, the rest with the 3rd 'Sallahaddin' Armoured Division of the Army. Insets show tactical insignia of the Medina, Tawakkalna and Nebuchadnezzar Divisions, RGFC. (Artwork by David Bocquelet)

Iraq acquired around 200 BMP-1s from the USSR in 1986, while Kuwait acquired 245 around the same time. Many Kuwaiti vehicles were captured during the Iraqi invasion, but enough were evacuated to Saudi Arabia to equip at least one mechanised infantry battalion of the reformed 35th Armoured Brigade afterwards. As far as is known, all were equipped with 9M111 Fagot ATGMs (ASCC/NATO-codename 'AT-4 Spigot') and painted in the same cardboard brown colour that rapidly bleached in the sand and sun. No markings are visible on any Iraqi BMP-2s photographed in Kuwait in 1990 or 1991. Subsequently, surviving Kuwaiti BMP-2s received a black 'inverted V' on their turrets, and three wide 'invasion stripes' in white on their sides and the rear doors. (Artwork by David Bocquelet)

The BMD-1 was an armoured troop carrier designed to be airdropped along with paratroopers and to offer them some protection against small arms. Only about a dozen were acquired by Iraq by 1990: all were operated by either the 3rd or the 16th Special Forces Brigade, RGFC. This example is shown in company of a Land Rover from either one of the Republican Guards airborne units, or one of such units of the Army – as obvious from the insignia applied on the door side: this included a hawk in red with a parachute in yellow. (Artwork by David Bocquelet)

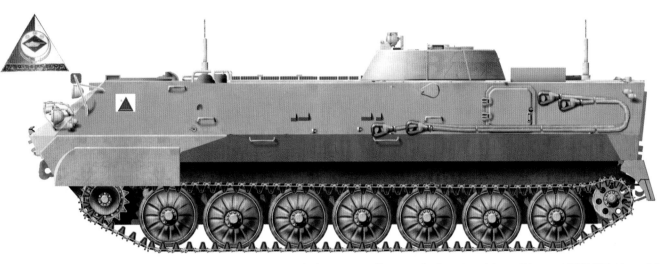

Iraq acquired a sizeable number of MT-LBu armoured command vehicles – essentially a stretched version of the well-known MT-LB APC. Most of these were assigned to the RGFC-units and many were sighted on the streets of Kuwait City in early August 1990. As usual, all were painted in carboard brown colour overall: most received a small red triangle, outlined in green and applied against a white 'background' as identification insignia: red was the colour choice of the RGFC, the official crest of which is shown in the inset. (Artwork by David Bocquelet)

The 2S1 Gvozdika was a self-propelled howitzer based on the MT-LBu multi-purpose chassis, mounting the 2A31 122mm howitzer. Iraq acquired about 300 by 1990 and they formed the backbone of the self-propelled artillery in all armoured divisions of the RGFC, and most armoured divisions of the Army. Visible on the side of the hull is the tactical insignia: the Iraqis used an elaborate system of tactical insignias, whichwill be described in detail in Volume 2. It is sufficient to note here that this sign consists of a blue-grey circle with red-blue-red bar (for artillery of the 3rd 'Salahaddin' Armoured Division), Arabic letters 'Q-X' in black at the top (for 'Qadisiyah Xaddam'), and white number 110 (for 110th Artillery Regiment). (Artwork by David Bocquelet)

Equipped with the 152mm 2A33 howitzer installed on the Object 303 tracked chassis, the 2S3 Akatsiya was the Soviet equivalent to the US-made M109. Only 35 are known to have been acquired by Iraq and they served with self-propelled artillery units of two or three armoured divisions of the RGFC. Like most other Soviet-manufactured armoured vehicles acquired by Iraq, they were all originally painted in green FS34102 overall, but received a coat of the cheap, locally manufactured 'desert sand' colour, which was slightly darker than BS381C/361 light stone, and tended to chip along the edges of all surfaces, and bleach under the sun. (Artwork by David Bocquelet)

18 M551A1 Sheridan armoured reconnaissance and airborne assault vehicles of the 2nd Brigade of the 82nd Airborne Division, deployed to Dhahran AB on 9 August 1990, were the first US Army tanks ever in Saudi Arabia. Ultimately, 33 additional Sheridans of the 82nd were to follow. Their primary armament consisted of a 152mm M81E1 rifled gun (firing caseless HEAT ammunition), which could also launch MGM-51 Shillelagh ATGMs. Most of the vehicles also received the ACAV set, consisting of a large steel shield around the commander's .50-cal (12.7mm) machine gun, allowing it to be fired with some level of protection. M551A1s and their weaponry saw only limited service during Operation Desert Storm: some six MGM-51s are known to have been fired at Iraqi bunkers and a a single Type-69 MBT was destroyed. (Artwork by David Bocquelet)

The 24th Infantry Division was the heavy unit of the US Army's rapid reaction force – the XVIII Airborne Corps - and also a unit with a history of being deployed in diverse crises abroad: amongst others, during the US intervention in Lebanon in 1958. After undergoing extensive training in desert warfare, it was the natural 'first choice' for deployment in Saudi Arabia, where it began arriving on 17 August 1990 while still equipped with M1 Abrams tanks armed with the 105mm cannon. Upon their disembarkation at the port of ad-Dammam, the Abrams MBTs were quickly re-painted with desert tan (FS33446) 'Chemical Agent Resistant Coating' (CARC) colour overall at the small shop run by civilians from Alabama's Anniston Army Depot. Furthermore, they received a simple set of identification markings, including an 'inverted V' (common for all the Coalition vehicles), and a set of tactical markings identifying vehicle's assignment to specific companies, battalions and regiments. (Artwork by David Bocquelet)

Combat vehicles based on the chassis of the M113 APC were in widespread use in 1990. The left profile shows one of about 200 M113A1 of the KLF, equipped with a launcher for the BGM-71 TOW ATGM, while the profile to the right shows a M163 of the 1st Battalion, 3rd Armoured Cavalry Regiment, US Army. As far as can be said, both vehicles were painted in similar colours, though the M163 received a coat of desert tan CARC applied in a great rush and thus had a strong green tint. (Artworks by David Bocquelet)

The KAF received a total of 18 Mirage F.1CKs, one of which crashed shortly after delivery. All of these, as well as all of the F.1BK two-seat conversion trainers, were painted in sand FS33303 and tan FS30219 on top surfaces and sides, and FS26408 on undersurfaces. They wore a bare minimum of national markings, including fin-flashes and serials applied on the fin. As of August 1990, Kuwaiti Mirages were usually armed with a pair of wing-tip mounted R.550 Magic Mk.1 or Magic Mk.2 air-to-air missiles and two internal 30mm DEFA cannons only: Matra Super 530Fs, followed by Sycomore chaff and flare dispensers and Barax ECM-pods began appearing only on aircraft evacuated to Saudi Arabia when the KAF was re-formed as the Free Kuwait Air Force in late 1990. (Artwork by Tom Cooper)

All Kuwaiti A-4KUs and TA-4KUs received the same camouflage pattern consisting of tan FS30219 and light stone FS33448 on top surfaces and sides, and light sea grey FS36307 on undersurfaces. On 2 August 1990, their typical armament consisted of one multiple ejector rack (MER) with 5-6 Mk.82SE bombs installed on the centreline. Later on, triple-ejector racks (TERs) installed either under the centreline or on inboard underwing hardpoints became more common, although the weapons hung on them remained largely the same: either Mk.82SEs, or Mk.7 CBUs. As with the Mirages, they wore only a bare minimum of national markings and serials: the title Free Kuwait Air Force was applied on aircraft evacuated to Saudi Arabia only in late 1990. (Artwork by Tom Cooper)

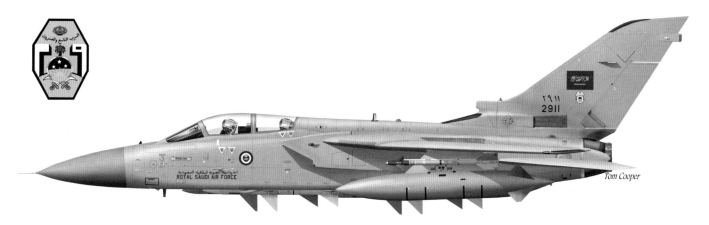

The Tornado ADV was the export variant of the Tornado F.Mk. 3 long-range interceptor made for the RAF, equipped with the powerful Foxhunter radar, and armed with up to four Skyflash medium-range air-to-air missiles and four AIM-9L Sidewinder air-to-air missiles. The first ADVs reached Saudi Arabia only on 9 February 1989, and the first unit operating them – No. 29 Squadron – was still working up, while the second – No. 34 Squadron – was still a detachment of the first. Nevertheless, they flew several dozen CAPs along the border with Kuwait during the critical weeks in early and mid-August 1990. All the Saudi Tornado ADVs were pained in barley grey (BS381C/626) on top surfaces and sides, and light aircraft grey (BS381C/627) on undersides, while their radomes were in medium sea grey (BS381C/637). Unit insignia (shown in inset) was applied on the fin, together with individual serial. (Artwork by Tom Cooper)

In 1989, No. 79 Squadron, IrAF deployed two of its Mirage F.1EQ-5s to Jordan, from where these flew a series of reconnaissance sorties along the armistice lines with Israel: equipped with Harold pods containing an oblique camera, they were capable of taking a look up to 50 kilometres deep inside Israel. During that mission, the F.1EQ-5s retained their camouflage pattern in Brun Café (FS30475) and Khaki (FS36134) on top surfaces and sides, and light blue grey (FS35189) on undersurfaces, but received Jordanian markings in order to disguise them as F.1Es operated by the Royal Jordanian Air Force. F.1EQs deployed in support of Umm an-Nidaa, the invasion of Kuwait, retained their usual set of markings, including large, four-digit serials starting with 4, as shown in the inset on the example of the F.1EQ-5 serial number 4572. Their armament consisted of wing-tip-mounted R.550 Magic Mk.1s, Super 530Fs installed on inboard underwing pylons, and Remora ECM-pods carried on their own adapters under the outboard part of the wing. (Artwork by Tom Cooper)

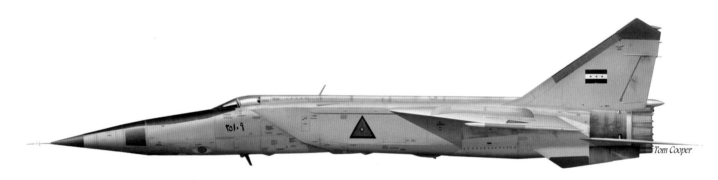

By far the most important reconnaissance platform of the IrAF as of 1990 was the MiG-25RB: a big and powerful jet capable of accelerating to speeds above Mach 2.3 and operating at altitudes of 21,000m (68,897ft). All were painted in the same light grey colour overall (FS26073, though often as dark as BS381C/626, depending on the wear): only the lower surfaces and sides of the engine nacelles were left in 'neutral steel'. Their dielectric panels were in dark gull grey (FS26231) and the anti-glare panel in flat black (FS27030). Iraqi national insignia was applied in the form of fin-flashes, and in six positions on the wing and intakes. Notably, this example – serial number 25109 – was one of very few IrAF MiG-25s still missing housings for improved RWRs, usually installed on the intake-sides. (Artwork by Tom Cooper)

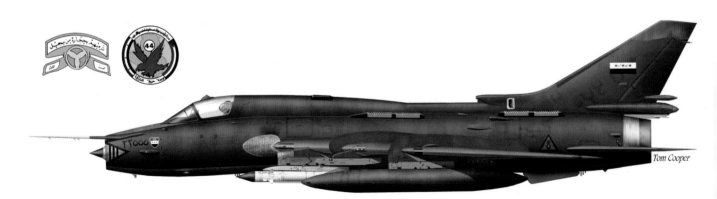

Attrition from the long conflict with Iran reduced the number of the IrAF's 'war horse' of that war – the Su-20/22 series – to 18 Su-20s and 68 Su-22M-2/M-3 and Su-22M-4Ks. Indeed, the latter variant, the most advanced available, was also the most numerous. The majority of IrAF Su-22M-4Ks were painted in diverse variants of the pattern illustrated here, consisting of dark green and chocolate brown on top surfaces and sides, and light admiralty grey (BS381C/388) on undersurfaces. Between 1988 and 1990, the IrAF introduced a new serialling-system, consisting of five digits: the first two denoting the type, the third the variant, and the last two individual aircraft. This example – serial number 22555 – was assigned to either No. 5 or No. 109 Squadron, each of which had a SEAD-detachment, qualified to deploy older Kh-28/AS-9 or Kh-10MP/AS-10 ARMs. Insets show the insignia of two other units equipped with the type: No. 5 and No. 44 Squadrons. (Artwork by Tom Cooper)

Some of the first US combat aircraft deployed in reaction to the Iraqi invasion in Kuwait were those of CVW-5 – the US Navy air wing embarked on USS Independence (CV-62). Remaining on station for the first 90 days of Operation Desert Shield, this wing included two units equipped with the F-14A Tomcat, including this example (modex NK101) from VF-154. (US DoD)

While F-14s from USS Independence were flying CAPs over the central Persian Gulf, the US Navy demonstratively moved its nuclear-powered aircraft carrier USS Dwight D Eisenhower (CVN-69) from the Mediterranean Sea through the Suez Canal into the Red Sea. This passage was widely publicised in the international media, in order to impress Baghdad. (US DoD)

AV-8Bs from the US Marine Corps' attack squadron VMA-513 as seen during their deployment to Jubail airfield in Saudi Arabia. Designed to operate from the small decks of amphibious assault ships and under austere conditions of forward operating bases ashore, the AV-8B proved an ideal platform for providing close air support to the first USMC and US Army units deployed in the theatre. (US DoD)

During the first two months of Operation Desert Shield, General Schwarzkopf emphasised the deployment of large troop contingents instead of heavy equipment. He considered this measure necessary to impress the Iraqis and thus deter them from launching an invasion of Saudi Arabia. This unit of US Marines was photographed while in the process of embarking a Boeing 747 airliner requisitioned by the MAC and bound for Saudi Arabia in September 1990. (US DoD

Amongst dozens of tactical combat units of the US Air Force that converged on Saudi Arabia in August and September 1990 was the 4th Tactical Fighter Squadron of the 388th Tactical Fighter Wing from Hill AFB, F-16Cs of which can be seen on this photograph. The unit was to see intensive action during Operation Desert Storm, too. (US DoD)

Technically, the F-117A was the most sophisticated combat aircraft deployed by the USAF to Saudi Arabia during Operation Desert Shield. More than 30 Nighthawks from the 37th TFW were based at Khamit Mushayt AB by December 1990. (US DoD)

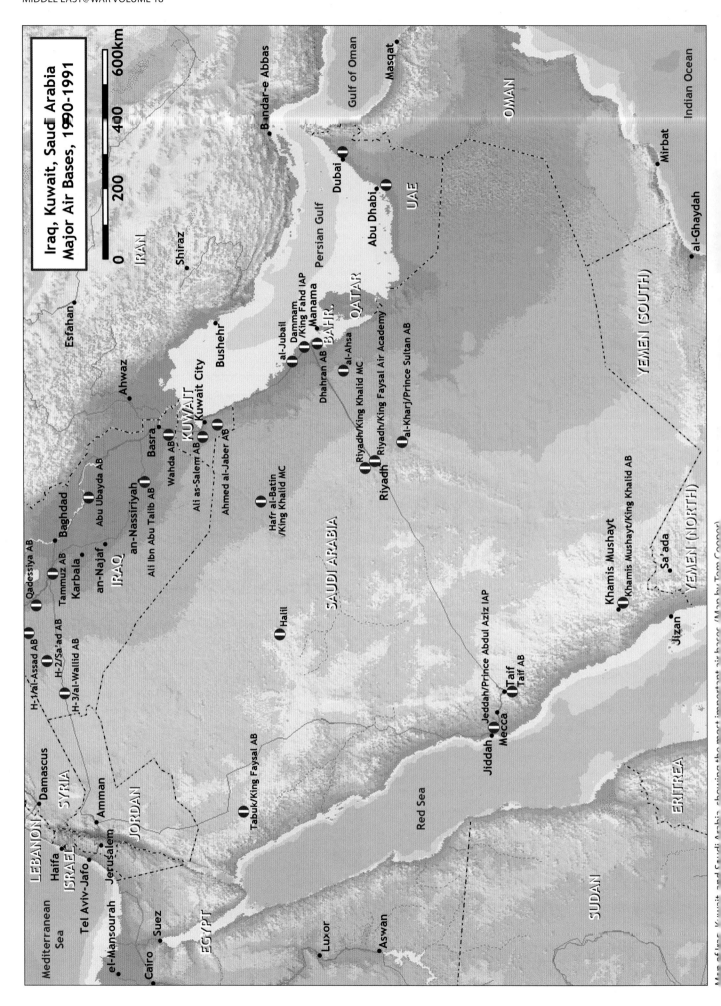

Iraq, Kuwait, Saudi Arabia
Major Air Bases, 1990–1991

600km 400 200 0

Mediterranean Sea
el-Mansourah
Cairo
Suez
EGYPT
Luxor
Aswan
Red Sea
SUDAN
ERITREA

LEBANON
Haifa
Tel Aviv-Jafo
Jerusalem
ISRAEL
Damascus
SYRIA
Amman
JORDAN
Tabuk/King Faysal AB
Jeddah/Prince Abdul Aziz IAP
Jiddah
Mecca
Taif
Taif AB
SAUDI ARABIA
Khamis Mushayt
Khamis Mushayt/King Khalid AB
Jizan
Sa'ada
YEMEN (NORTH)
YEMEN (SOUTH)
al-Ghaydah
Mirbat

H-1/al-Assad AB
H-2/Sa'ad AB
H-3/al-Wallid AB
Qadessiya AB
Tammuz AB
Baghdad
Karbala
an-Najaf
Ali Ibn Abu Talib AB
an-Nassiriyah
Abu Ubayda AB
IRAQ
Basra
Wahda AB
KUWAIT
Kuwait City
Ali as-Salem AB
Ahmed al-Jaber AB
Hafr al-Batin/King Khalid MC
Halil
Esfahan
Shiraz
IRAN
Ahwaz
Bushehr
Bandar-e Abbas
Gulf of Oman
Masqat
OMAN
Indian Ocean
Persian Gulf
al-Jubail
Dammam/King Fahd IAP
Manama
BAHR.
Dhahran AB MC
al-Ahsa
QATAR
Riyadh/King Faysal Air Academy
Dubai
Abu Dhabi
UAE
Riyadh/King Khalid MC
Riyadh
al-Kharj/Prince Sultan AB

Map of Iraq, Kuwait and Saudi Arabia, showing the most important air bases. (Map by Tom Cooper)

Cheerful troops of an RGFC unit seen while loading their equipment onto a train at the start of a fateful trip south in July 1990. (Albert Grandolini Collection)

BRDM-2 armoured scout cars, from a unit of the Republican Guards, seen while unloading from a train that brought them close to the border of Kuwait. (Albert Grandolini Collection)

in sand-box war games, while some disguised officers conducted personal reconnaissance inside Kuwait while accompanying the military convoys still permitted to use that country's port facilities.

SPEED IS LIFE

Kuwait is rather like a dagger with the blade 'edge' along the western frontier and a handle or shaft pushes into Saudi Arabia. The terrain consists of largely flat to slightly undulating sandy and stony desert, with dunes in the extreme north-east as well as parts of the centre and the south. The broad northern plain is some 90 kilometres wide, dotted with sabkhas (salt flats) and minor watercourses, gradually rising to an elevation of about 150 metres through south-west Kuwait. Along the 'shaft', there is a coastal plain some 45 kilometres wide and stretching all the way down to the Saudi border. The most significant terrain-feature is the al-Mutlaa Ridge in the north-west: running roughly north to south, this commands a shallow pass on the northern approaches to Kuwait City. In the east, marking the tri-state border since 1913, is the Wadi al-Batin. This is the largely dry remnant of an ancient river system which used to cross the northern Arabian Peninsula, running north-east to south-west. Wadi al-Batin is some 12 kilometres wide and down to 280 metres deep. At the head of the wadi, about 90 kilometres from the border, at the point through which the Tapline Road passes, is the Saudi town of Hafar al-Batin.

By 1990, all the major roads in Kuwait were paved. The principal was the four to six-lane autobahn-style Highway 80, running south from the border with Iraq at Abdaly, through al-Mutlaa and to al-Jahra, where it swings eastwards to follow the southern coast of the bay into Kuwait City and its six ring-roads. Further east is Highway 801, which runs from the Iraqi port of Umm Qasr along the coast to join Highway 80 at al-Jahra. From al-Jahra, Highway 70 runs south-west through al-Atraf to Markaz Hudud as-Salmi, and crosses the border at the Saudi town of ar-Ruqi, where there is another 306-metre high elevation. Another branch of Highway 70 runs southeast of the Ali as-Salem AB, and a few kilometres southeast of this base the highway is joined by a smaller paved road that runs northwest across the Wadi to the Iraqi town of Uglat al-Udhaybah. South of Kuwait City are the inland Highway 40 and the coastal Highway 30, with the latter joining the former south of al-Ahmadi and al-Fuhayhil as it runs down the coast past the Ras al-Qulayh naval base (near Mina as-Saud) to cross the Saudi border just north of the town of al-Khafji.

Project 17 was essentially a huge race designed to occupy Kuwait as rapidly as possible, with mechanised columns moving at around 20 km/h, surprising the Kuwaitis who would be decapitated by Special Forces brought in by 3 Wing IrAAC. As the commander of 17 Guards Armoured Brigade observed: "Speed was the most important factor to achieving surprise and surprise was the most important factor in achieving mission success."[10]

INVASION FORCE

For the invasion the RGFC units were organised into two groups, the aim of which was to envelop the main body of the KLF in the al-Jarrah area. The main force on Kuwait's northern border consisted of the Tawakkalna ala Allah Mechanised Division, the Hammurabi Armoured Division, and the al-Faw and Nebuchadnezzar Infantry Divisions, and was to push down Highway 80 while supported by elements from the 3rd and 16th Special Forces Brigades inserted by helicopters. Simultaneously, the Medina Manarwah Armoured Division, followed by the Adnan and Baghdad Infantry Divisions, would cross the Wadi al-Batin to enter western Kuwait, drive down Highway 70 and by-pass the Ali as-Salem AB. The northern group of forces was then to swing into Kuwait City and secure the IAP, while the western force would drive down the 'shaft' along the Saudi border, secure the Ahmed al-Jaber AB, and then defend the newly won territory.

In the tactical plan, Hammurabi would drive down Highway 80 to take Kuwait City, where each battalion was given a specific objective, followed by Nebuchadnezzar which was responsible for the city's occupation. Al-Faw would drive down Highway 801

and take Bubiyan Island. Tawakkalna on the right would take Ali as-Salim AB and, after being relieved by Medina, it would drive south of Kuwait City to take the southern part of the country to the Saudi border. The western task force would cross the desert north of the mouth of the Wadi al-Batin, then Madina would secure the Ali as-Salim AB before swooping south of Kuwait City to take the al-Ahmadi area followed by Adnan and Baghdad which would help Tawakkalna secure the south of the country. The 3rd Special Forces Brigade RGFC was to be deployed by helicopters to seize the Mutlaa Ridge, while the 16th Special Forces Brigade was to infiltrate along Highway 80 to secure the road between al-Jahra and Kuwait City. Finally, additional elements of the Guard's special forces units were to be flown into the Kuwaiti capitol by helicopters to decapitate the leadership and secure vital installations. Based upon wartime experience it was decided that the armoured divisions would each receive a Guards infantry brigade from the infantry divisions to secure the rear while the Hammurabi Division commander Major General Qais Abd al-Razaq, decided to use his 130mm gun batteries to fire illumination rounds at ranges of 5 kilometres to help the division advance rapidly at night.[11]

The IrAAC would support this operation with the whole 3rd Air Wing, including two gunship squadrons equipped with Messerschmitt Bölkow Böhm (MBB) Bo.105s and Mil Mi-25s, two transport squadrons equipped with Mil Mi-8/17s, and an assault squadron equipped with Bell 412STs – a total of 96 helicopters. Finally, with the 'Israeli threat' providing the necessary smokescreen, on 1 August, the 223rd and 224th Missile Brigades were ordered to re-deploy to western Iraq, while the 225th moved towards the south, and the headquarters of the SSMD conducted a war-game to simulate a response to an Israeli air strike. Overall, Saddam thus committed about 95,000 troops with 570 MBTs of the RGFC to this operation.[12]

VITAL SUPPLIES

The Guards were supremely confident and decided to be self-sufficient for the offensive with all supplies carried by divisional assets, major logistical support following after 24 hours. Short-falls were to be made up by exploiting civilian facilities including petrol stations. Another major problem for the Guards was the fact that August is the hottest month of the year in Kuwait, which meant there was a serious threat from heat-stroke, especially in vehicles of Soviet origin which were designed to keep personnel warm in the fierce Russian winters. To protect his troops Major General Qais Abd al-Razaq, the Hammurabi Division commander, ordered extra water tanks welded to the AFV's hulls next to the external fuel tanks and similar precautions were probably taken in other formations.

AERIAL PLANNING

With hindsight, the Iraqi planning for the invasion of Kuwait was 'almost perfect'. It did contain two major flaws, though: early planning by the Special Forces Division envisaged raids on Kuwait IAP, the Ali as-Salem Sabbah AB, and Ahmed al-Jaber AB. However, these were cancelled when the inexperienced IrAF Commander, Lieutenant-General Hassan, informed Saddam his airmen could keep the skies clear for the Army's helicopters by bombing runways and missile batteries. Whatever doubts the Guards' commanders might have had, they could not change Saddam's mind. Their commandos now focussed upon decapitating the Kuwaiti government and supporting the troops on the ground. Correspondingly, although not informed about the coming invasion, the IrAF was ordered to bolster the 3rd ADS in the south with additional strike squadrons from the centre

Table 10: Iraqi Republican Guards Forces Command's units involved in Umm an-Nidaa, 2 August 1990

Divisions	Brigades
Adnan Infantry Division	12th and 21st Commando and 31st Infantry Brigades RGFC
Baghdad Infantry Division	4th, 5th, 6th and 7th Infantry, and 11th Commando Brigades RGFC
al-Faw Infantry Division	24th, 25th, 27th and 28th Infantry Brigades RGFC
Hammurabi Armoured Division	8th and 17th Armoured, 15th Mechanised Brigades RGFC
Medinah Armoured Division	2nd and 20th Armoured, 14th Mechanised Brigades RGFC
Nebuchadnezzar Infantry Division	19th and 20th Special Forces, 22nd and 23rd Infantry Brigades RGFC
Tawakkalna Mechanised Division	9th Armoured, 18th and 29th Mechanised Infantry Brigades RGFC
Independent forces	3rd and 16th Special Forces Brigades RGFC; 440th Naval Infantry Brigade (Iraqi Navy)

Table 11: IrAF Units involved in Umm an-Nidaa, 2 August 1990

Unit	Base	Aircraft Type	Tasks
No. 6 Squadron	Ali Ibn Abu Talib AB	MiG-29	air superiority
No. 29 Squadron	Ali Ibn Abu Talib AB	MiG-23BN	ground attack
No. 49 Squadron	Ali Ibn Abu Talib AB	MiG-23BN	ground attack
No. 79 Squadron	Ali Ibn Abu Talib AB	Mirage F.1EQ-2/-4	air superiority
No. 87 Squadron	Ali Ibn Abu Talib AB	MiG-25RB	reconnaissance
No. 115 Squadron?	Ali Ibn Abu Talib AB	Su-25K	ground attack
No. 5 Squadron	Wahda AB	Su-22M-4K	ground attack
No. 109 Squadron	Wahda AB	Su-22M-4K	SEAD & ground attack

and the north of the country: during July, it sent two squadrons of Su-22s, two of MiG-23BNs, and one each of MIG-29s, Mirage F.1EQs, and Su-25s – a total of 120 fighter-bombers – to Ali Ibn Abu Talib AB, outside Nassiriyah, and to Wahda AB, outside Basra. Their task was to establish air superiority over Kuwait through limited strikes on KAF air bases, provide CAS, and fly reconnaissance. The balance of the IrAF was put on alert to shield around 200 installations around Iraq from anticipated Israeli air strikes.[13]

FINAL MOVES

On 31 July 1990, the brigade and battalion commanders of the RGFC units involved were informed about Project 17 and that Operation *Umm an-Nidaa* was to start at 0400 (Iraq time) on 2 August. It was only on the following day, a mere 24 hours before the invasion, that Lieutenant-General Salah Aboud Mahmoud – commander of the Basra-based III Corps of the Iraqi Army – was alerted of the forthcoming operation and informed his units were to act as a reserve, foremost in the form of moving the 5th Mechanised Infantry Division to az-Zubayr, and the 6th Armoured Division to Safwan, where they were to prepare to drive down Highway 801. Worse yet, it was also only on 31 July that the commander of the Iraqi Navy, Rear Admiral Ghaib Hassan was informed not only of the invasion, but also of his task of taking Faylakah Island and the Ras al-Qulayh Naval Base.

Meanwhile, the summer heat had a significant impact upon Kuwaiti defensive plans. August was usually the period when most Kuwaitis went on holiday – and the armed forces were no exception. Certainly enough, the Emir placed his forces on full alert in response to Saddam's threats from 17 July, but when the situation eased a week later, 75% of the troops were stood down. As of 25 July 1990, there were no contingency plans or preparations, and the sole 'activity' of the entire KAF and the KLF were border patrols by small detachments – all of which could clearly see the Iraqi troops north of them. Indeed, the Kuwaiti Land Forces continued their peacetime routine with most of the equipment remaining in storage, the majority of officers and NCOs on leave, and as little as a single battalion per brigade on duty. Overall, perhaps as few as 8,000 of the KLF's troops were with their units: of these, only small elements of the 6th Mechanised Brigade were deployed north of the Mutlaa Ridge to reassure the nervous Border Guards.[14]

Another unit that had something like a battalion of troops on hand was the 35th Armoured Brigade, home-based about 35 kilometres south of the ridge. Within Kuwait City was the battalion-sized Amiri Guards, the 15th Armoured Brigade was concentrated within its home-based at al-Ahmadi, in the south.[15]

The 2,200-strong KAF had all of its 21 remaining Mirage F.1CK/CK-1 and F.1BK/BK-1s, together with 8 transports and 32 helicopters at Ali as-Salem Sabbah AB, while all the 29 A-4KU/TA-4KU Skyhawks, and all the Hawks, were at Ahmed al-Jaber AB. The air force also had an AN/TPS-63 battlefield radar operated by a team from the Westinghouse Corporation deployed in northern Kuwait near the frontier: between 2200hrs and 2300hrs on 1 August, this reported the approaching Iraqis, prompting the Ministry of Defence in Kuwait City to issue an alert. However, with most of the crucial officers on leave, the result was chaos, and it was only at 0230hrs that the Emir, the cabinet and some senior leaders met in the Dasman Palace. Amid constantly failing communications, it proved impossible for them to find out exactly what was going on – which in turn created a sense of panic and prevented any kind of coordination of the defences. For all practical purposes, whatever KAF and KLF commanders were with their troops, they were left on their own.

HELIBORNE ATTACK

The first act of the Iraqi invasion was for several commando companies of the Republican Guards to take over the lightly-manned border posts and nearby police stations – usually without bloodshed. As each of the tasks in question was completed, green flares marked the success. Around 0300hrs, the RGFC then drove across the border in force, its troops informed they were entering the country to help Kuwaitis who wished to replace the corrupt regime. The excellent road system of Kuwait made for rapid progress: with lead mechanised formations moving at 30km/h they approached al-Jahra – only 18km from the HQ of the KAF and even closer to Ali as-Salem AB – within only three hours.

T-55s of the 5th Mechanised Division from the III Corps, as seen on a march in the direction of az-Zubayr in early August 1990. Saddam kept even top commanders of the Iraqi Army in the dark regarding his intentions about Kuwait. (Albert Grandolini Collection)

At 0425hrs – 20 minutes late due to the confusion caused by the blanket of secrecy – the helicopters of the 3rd Wing IrAAC took off to deploy 900 troops of the two special forces brigades to the Mutlaa Ridge and into Kuwait City. That was when what had been promised to be a bloodless walk-over turned into a very different scenario – primarily due to the IrAF's failure to clear the skies, as promised by Lieutenant-General Hassan: his interceptors were unable to take off because of the fog over their base. In a post-war analysis, Ali Hassan al-Majid – better known as 'Chemical Ali' – lambasted the inexperienced IrAF commander by asking pointedly:

> You did not think that maybe there will be a change in the weather that affects the airports in Iraq…meanwhile there is good weather in Kuwait?[16]

Of course, the big formation of Iraqi Army helicopters was detected by multiple Kuwaiti radars, and the ADOC promptly scrambled four Mirages at 0455hrs: these reached the north of the country as the pilots of IrAF's interceptors were still sitting in their cockpits on the ground, covered by vapour. One of the Kuwaitis even briefly locked his radar on to the IrAF's Boeing 727 ELINT-gatherer that was already at its station, but lacked top cover: nevertheless, the KAF pilot turned around and joined the fight further south, instead.[17]

To say that the IrAAC's rotorcraft then suffered from air force's failure to plan more carefully would be an understatement: many of the wounds were self-inflicted, and caused by the lack of training in formation flying by night, and even more so by the lack of night vision equipment. Unsurprisingly, several helicopters collided with power lines, or because their pilots misjudged their height while entering landing zones in which rotors created swirling clouds of dust. The chaos within the landing zone at the Mutlaa Ridge was further compounded by the arrival of two KAF Mirages: their pilots

launched a total of four R.550 Magic guided air-to-air missiles first and then returned to attack with 30mm cannon fire, claiming eight helicopters shot down in the process. It was a tribute to the training and courage of the Guard's special forces that its troops emerged from the chaos to seize the ridge and the nearby I-HAWK SAM-site – shortly after this claimed one of the helicopters as shot down. The Iraqis confirmed the loss of 'only two or three of their' machines.[18]

The helicopters carrying elements of the 16th Special Forces Brigade RGFC into Kuwait City – a formation of about 30 Mi-8s and Bell 412Sts followed by at least one Mi-25 – appear to have experienced even bigger problems. No fewer than nine were claimed by the two I-HAWK SAM-sites protecting the capital commanded by Captain Abdullah al-Asfoor, the site at Ras al-Jalayb reportedly fired three missiles to claim a big Iraqi helicopter as shot down. The site at al-Adourmi reported at least 12 engagements in which it claimed one Iraqi fighter-bomber and eight helicopters as shot down by a total of 14 missiles. Five additional helicopters were claimed as shot down by KAF Mirages, and one by the SA.342 Gazelle flown by Lieutenant-Colonel Fayez Abdullah ar-Rasheedi. Finally, according to unconfirmed reports, the formation may have been attacked by six BAe Hawks from No. 12 Squadron, KAF that – flown by instructor-pilots – claimed as many as two Mi-8s and three Iraqi SA.342 Gazelles before flying away to the safety of Bahrain (where one, serial number 142, was damaged on landing). A pair of IrAF Mirage F.1EQs scrambled from Ali Ibn Abu Talib AB was late on the scene: they swooped high above Kuwait City before requesting permission to attack, but this was granted only once the Kuwaiti fighter-bombers were already south of the border. While most of the Kuwaiti claims in question were subsequently officially confirmed and credited to the pilots in question (for those claimed by Mirage F.1CK/CK-2-pilots, see Table 12), they seem to have been highly optimistic, for the Iraqi sources indicate no such massacre to have taken place. On the contrary, most of the special forces appear

Wreckage of an Iraqi Mi-8 or Mi-17 assault helicopter, shot down during the assault on Kuwait City. (KAF)

Gazelle attack and scout helicopters led both of major formations of the 3rd Wing IrAAC into the opening attacks of the invasion of Kuwait. At least one example from No. 88 Squadron IrAAC is known to have been shot down by Kuwaiti air defences on the morning of 2 August 1990. Its pilot, Captain Mohammed Abdel Aziz Tabra, was killed. (Albert Grandolini Collection)

to have landed safely. The relative success of this landing resulted in no walk-over though: the attempt to storm the Dasman Palace was thwarted by the vigilant Amiri Guard, supported by several Saladin armoured cars. As the commandos began to work their way around the building, a convoy of limousines extracted most of the Sabbah family and the cabinet to the Ali as-Salim Sabbah AB, from where they were flown out to Saudi Arabia on board several KAF Gazelles (including the example previously flown in combat by ar-Rasheedi, who returned to Ali as-Selem Sabbah AB with the intention to refuel and re-arm, minutes before), Pumas and Super Puma helicopters. Elsewhere, the commandos were more successful in capturing the

Communications Complex, the National Council, the Cabinet premises, the Ministry of Planning, and the main base of the Amiri Guard – before pressing on towards the Dasman Palace.[19]

However, the renewed assault upon the isolated palace had to await the arrival of the tanks of the 17th Armoured Brigade RGFC: due to the fierce resistance by the Kuwaiti Guards it did not fall until 1400hrs, and even then only after a two-hour battle in which the Emir's younger brother Sheikh Fahd al-Ahmed as-Sabbah was killed, and the Iraqi special forces suffered up to 60 casualties – on the top of losses suffered by the 3rd Wing IrAAC, which might have included up to 40 helicopters, or about 40% of those committed.[20]

While large elements of the 3rd and 16th Special Forces Brigades of the RGFC were deployed with the help of helicopters, the balance of both units followed on the ground – some of them driving Soviet-made BMD-1 airborne infantry fighting vehicles. (Albert Grandolini Collection)

A pair of BMD-1s as seen while entering Kuwait City, early on the morning of 2 August 1990. (Albert Grandolini Collection)

MAIN THRUST

Meanwhile in northern Kuwait, the main thrust down Highway 80 saw the armour roll through the night, screeching and clanking, leaving dense columns of dust but hearing nothing on their radios. Indeed, the commander of the 17th Armoured Brigade, Brigadier-General Ra'ad Hamdani, later observed 'My staff officers began to believe that the whole mission was cancelled and that our brigade was the only one on the way to Kuwait City'.

However, that was just the wrong impression of over-concerned officers. The al-Faw Division was speeding down Highway 801 but also thanks to deploying one of its commando companies to quickly seize the bridge to Bubiyan and an amphibious operation before it could reach the island itself encountered little resistance. In its path was the base of the 6th Mechanised Brigade, and elements of Colonel Salem as-Srour's 35th Armoured Brigade, both of which were hives of activity following telephone alerts from Kuwait City and calls to individual officers and other ranks to report to the bases. Deputy Chief of Staff KLF, General Jaber, tried to direct his forces with help of a cellular phone as he drove his Mercedes sedan and while finding brief sanctuary in a bunker, outside of which Iraqi tanks were parked as they paused in their advance. As the troops began to arrive, they formed ad-hoc units which refuelled and armed their vehicles at frantic speed: eventually, only minor elements of each brigade – including 10 Chieftains of as-Srour's 8th Tank Battalion – were able to deploy south of the Mutlaa Ridge before the Hammurabi Armoured Division RGFC arrived.[21]

The Kuwaitis believed the Iraqi vanguard was merely a reconnaissance force and engaged them at a distance of 300 metres, hitting one of the T-72s on the front, but Hamdani and ar-Razzaq reacted by outflanking the defenders from the north. The result was the quick collapse of the 6th Brigade and the capture of its shaken commander. According to Hamdani the defenders panicked and abandoned their vehicles, 'leaving most of their tanks with their engines running behind them.' However, as-Srour would remain a thorn in the Iraqi side, for he withdrew his weak battalion southeast towards Kuwait City, picking up the 7th Tank Battalion with 26 Chieftains and 7 M109 self-propelled howitzers as he went.[22]

By this point in time, the western Iraqi force was supposed to envelop the remaining defenders or at least to prevent their withdrawal. However, Medinah lost its way during the long trip across the desert, and then its radio network collapsed, compounding the problem. Instead, the spearhead of this division then fought a prolonged but indecisive battle with the 35th Brigade, that ended only when the second armoured brigade arrived to renew its advance. The situation of the Nebuchadnezzar Armoured Division was nothing better. This should have swept into southern Kuwait behind Hammurabi, but was delayed – foremost by the ineptitude of its commanders – and reached the city only late in the afternoon. This failure resulted in thousands of Kuwaiti residents and troops managing to escape across the Saudi border, and left enough time for the KAF to first continue its operations and then evacuate its air bases.

IRAQI AIR STRIKES

The IrAF was not only late in getting airborne due to the fog that morning, but then also missed the chance to intercept any of the helicopters evacuating the Kuwaiti rulers to Saudi Arabia. Its radars did detect the retreating Kuwaitis and the first two Mirage F.1EQs scrambled from Ali Ibn Abu Talib AB shadowed these for a few minutes. However, their pilots were ordered to hold fire. The two Mirages also failed to react to the appearance of two Kuwaiti Mirages that were scrambled to support the I-HAWK battery on Faylaka Island whose AN/MPQ-50 Pulse Acquisition Radar (PAR) was being jammed by an Aerospatiale SA.321 Super Frelon helicopter from No. 101 Squadron (a unit operationally assigned to the Iraqi Navy) in support of a landing by Iraqi naval infantry. A Magic missile fired by Major Taher at-Taher (his wingman was Lieutenant Bassam al-Jounid) shot down

A BMP-1 IFV (foreground), T-72 MBT, and three BMP-2s of the Republican Guards as seen on the outskirts of Kuwait City. By the time they reached the Kuwaiti capitol, many of the Iraqi heavy vehicles were crucially short on fuel and had to be refuelled from local petrol stations. (Albert Grandolini Collection)

A BMP-2, MT-LBu (a stretched command variant of the well-known MT-LB APC), and T-72 from one of RGFC's armoured brigades as seen on the northern edge of Kuwait City. (Albert Grandolini Collection)

T-72s of the 17th Armoured Brigade (Hammurabi Armoured Division, RGFC) rolling down an avenue in Kuwait City early on 2 August 1990. (Albert Grandolini Collection)

A Chieftain MBT of the 35th Brigade, KLF. Activated and deployed in a great rush, Kuwaiti Chieftains played the role of speed-bumps for elements of two armoured divisions of the Iraqi Republican Guards. (Albert Grandolini Collection)

this helicopter and killed the crew including Captain Hassan Younes and Lieutenant Abdul Salam Hassan Khalil, before the Kuwaiti Mirages returned to Kuwait City, all the time shadowed by two F.1EQs, whose pilots respected the order of their ground controller not to engage. Taher and Jounid thus went on and claimed three additional Iraqi helicopters as shot down over their capital.[23]

The pilots of the two Iraqi interceptors were next ordered to provide top cover for three formations of six Iraqi fighter-bombers each as these approached northern Kuwait. Strangely enough,

although having extensive experience from battling I-HAWK SAMs during the war with Iran, and knowing how to effectively counter these with Caiman-equipped Mirage F.1EQs and SPS-141-equipped Su-22s, the IrAF seems to have not taken any related precautions. Instead, the Iraqi air force reacted only after suffering its first losses. The leading formation of MiG-23BNs from No. 49 Squadron, led by the commander of that unit, Lieutenant-Colonel Mazen Saleh Kitan ash-Shawi, was approaching the joint of the borders between Iraq, Kuwait and Saudi Arabia when engaged by the Kuwaiti I-HAWKs. A SAM proximity fused near Shawi's aircraft as this was underway at a very low level, causing it to hit the ground, instantly killing the pilot. Almost the same happened to the formation of Su-22M-4Ks from No. 69 Squadron that was approaching Kuwait from the north-eastern direction: the aircraft flown by captains Zayd Qalaf Hayder and Riyadh Kamel Ali were both shot down by direct hits. It was only at that point in time that the third Iraqi formation, the SEAD-section consisting of Su-22M-

Lieutenant-Colonel Mazin Kitan Saleh ash-Shawi was the commander of No. 49 Squadron, IrAF and pilot of the MiG-23BN shot down by a Kuwaiti MIM-23B I-HAWK SAM on the morning of 2 August 1990. He thus became the first officer of the IrAF killed in this war. (via Ali Tobchi)

Captain Zayd Qalaf Hayder (left) and Captain Riyadh Kamel were two pilots from No. 69 Squadron's formation that were shot down by Kuwaiti MIM-23B I-HAWK SAMs on the morning of 2 August 1990. (IraqiAirForceMemorial.com)

Wreckage of the British Airways Boeing 747, registration G-AWND, destroyed during the Iraqi airstrike on Kuwait International early on 2 August 1990. (Albert Grandolini Collection)

A rare, pre-1990-War photograph of a Kuwaiti BAe Hawk training jet from No. 12 Squadron. Reportedly, this unit flew six combat sorties and claimed at least one kill against Iraqi helicopters on the morning of 2 August 1990, before being evacuated to Bahrain. (KAF)

4Ks from No. 109 Squadron, returned fire in the form of a single Kh-25MP anti-radar missile. Reportedly, this forced the I-HAWK site on Bubiyan to shut down its main radar.[24]

Surviving Iraqi fighter-bombers continued their mission. One formation each bombed the runways and taxiways of the Ali as-Salem and Ahmed al-Jaber ABs, rendering them non-operational. At least two of the KAF Mirages at the former had taken heavy damage too: indeed, the F.1CK with serial number 712 was reduced to little more than the remnants of the rear fuselage and fin, while another – unknown – example was rendered non-operational by splinter damage. A third Iraqi formation then bombed Kuwait IAP where it destroyed a British Airways Boeing 747 – registered as G-AWND – on the ground. Finally, one of the Su-22M-4Ks deployed the laser-homing variant of the Kh-25 missile to destroy the Umm al-Haiman telephone exchange in Kuwait City – thus finally knocking out the Kuwaiti military communications. The damage caused by Iraqi air strikes to the two major KAF air bases was sufficient to force the crews of all six Mirage F.1CKs that were still airborne to land on a narrow road running along the perimeter of Ahmed al-Jaber AB:

although 2,700m long, this was only 4.5 metres wide, thus offering barely enough space for the landing of the aircraft. Nevertheless, as soon as the aircraft stopped, the ground crews rushed to refuel and re-arm them.[25]

Meanwhile, two KAF Skyhawks led by Lieutenant-Colonel Majed al-Ahmad and vectored by a ground controller that was still holding out inside the tower at the Ali as-Salem Sabbah AB – meanwhile all but surrounded by Iraqi troops – attacked the columns of the Medina and Baghdad divisions along both the Abdaly and Salmi roads. They first released five Mk.82 bombs each and then strafed, causing additional casualties to the unprepared Iraqis, until Ahmad's aircraft was damaged by an Iraqi MANPAD and the pilot forced to return to al-Jaber AB. Once there, the aircraft proved irreparable due to the absence of foreign technicians.[26]

AMPHIBIOUS ASSAULT
Around 0600 hrs, the small Iraqi Navy task force – consisting of two Osa fast missile boats, with 150 Marines embarked – was finally about to approach the Kuwaiti coast. Hardly had they reached the

area when they came under fire from two enemy patrol boats, only to find out that the guns of one of their vessels broken down, while the other Osa lost its radar. The Kuwaitis fired quite precisely, and despite Iraqi zig-zagging, scored a hit on the command cabin of the second vessel. Left without a choice, the remaining Iraqi Osa – the one carrying the commander of 440th Marine Infantry Brigade, Colonel Muzahim Mustafa and 75 of his troops – then pressed its attack home, irrespective of enemy fire. Once inside the main Kuwaiti Navy facility at al-Qulayah, the Iraqi troops quickly disembarked and overwhelmed the light resistance: by 0745 hrs, Mustafa and his troops had captured 271 Kuwaiti sailors (including an astounded base commander, who thought the entire action an unannounced exercise) and 213 foreign contractors, three large and three light missile boats, three supply ships and eight smaller vessels – all of this at the cost of one Osa written off, one marine killed and several wounded.[27]

EXODUS

With the Iraqis preoccupied with their futile assault on the Dasman Palace and securing Kuwait City, what was left of the Kuwaiti military found a few hours to recover from the first shock. At Ali as-Salem AB, ground crews found an intact section of the runway long enough for two Mirage F.1CKS to launch at 0630hrs. Finding no Iraqi interceptors in the air, their pilots swooped low over Kuwait City, where they claimed two additional Iraqi helicopters as shot down, before diverting for al-Jaber AB to re-arm and refuel. By then, the writing was already on the wall: over the next three hours, ground crews of the KAF managed to dispatch 15 Mirages to Saudi Arabia: one of them claimed an additional Iraqi helicopter, thus bringing the total for No. 18 and No. 61 Squadrons to 15, as listed in Table 12. Following the example of the air force, nearly all of the personnel and equipment of the 15th Mechanized Brigade were evacuated to Saudi Arabia, having started already during the morning.[28]

Untouched by Kuwaiti air strikes, the main force of the Hammurabi Division approached the urban area surrounding the international airport aided by the green and blue road signs that guided the troops to their objectives on the tourist maps – before splitting up. The 'Faris' Regiment of the 17th Armoured Brigade took the 5th Ring Road towards Shiyukh Port and Ra'as ar-Rad, while the rest continued along the 6th Ring Road towards Kuwait IAP. As the latter column approached the area known to the Iraqis as the 'Pilgrim Rest House', it came under what the Iraqis described as 'ineffective Kuwaiti fire', before continuing its advance without further delay. The force firing at Hamdani's tanks consisted of Chieftains of the 35th Brigade, KLF: most of their shots missed – possibly because their sights had not been set before the vehicles

moved out. Of course, the Kuwaitis claimed 'dozens' of Iraqi vehicles knocked out: actually, the Iraqis lost not a single tank, but a few trucks and a trailer carrying a self-propelled howitzer were destroyed, and some prisoners were taken. The Division's 15th Mechanised Brigade was also engaged against scattered KLF units. However, overall, if there was any kind of a problem for the Iraqis then it was the mass of cars full of panicking civilians in front of them. By 0830hrs the roads were nearing gridlock, hindering the Guards' advance and their thirsty vehicles consumed ever more fuel until they began to choke into silence. The crowds made it difficult to reach the petrol stations to refuel until the Iraqis coerced the police to open paths through the crowds to the petrol stations. Once refuelled, the Hammurabi Division drove on to take its objectives, Hamdani distributing tanks at every intersection to support road blocks which arrested every real or imagined government official, army officer or person of importance. Pockets of resistance continued and the television station was not taken until that night. Indeed, the Hammurabi Division reached its official objective – the Masila Hotel Beach Resort – only late during the night.[29]

THE END OF THE 35TH BRIGADE

Late during the morning of 2 August, the situation of whatever was left of the Kuwaiti armed forces was rapidly deteriorating. At 1100hrs, Sorour learned of an armoured force approaching Kuwait City from the west. Hoping this might be the GCC's Peninsula Shield Force from Saudi Arabia, he dispatched an officer to meet it. Fortunately, the latter identified the approaching column as Iraqis – indeed, vehicles of the Baghdad Division RGFC – and radioed a timely warning, allowing parts of the 35th Brigade to set up an ambush. After losing a few vehicles, the Baghdad Division withdrew some three kilometres to regroup at a truck-weighing station: just as it was joined there by the vehicles of the 14th Mechanised Brigade of the Medina Division, RGFC, the area came under artillery fire from M109s of the 51st Artillery Battalion, attached to Sorour's force. The Iraqis retaliated accurately, one of their rounds landing near the Kuwaiti field HQ, wounding Sorour's artillery commander, Lieutenant-Colonel Fahad Ashush, and forcing M109s to scatter further south and east. Nevertheless, soldiers brought replacement ammunition in their private cars, thus allowing the self-propelled howitzers to remain in action and cover the withdrawal of the 35th Brigade to the south of the Salmia Road, thus avoiding a clumsy envelopment attempt by of the Medina Division, covered by Chieftains of the 7th Battalion. The Kuwaitis thus extracted themselves just in time to avoid an assault by no less than two Iraqi brigades.[30]

Once underway, Colonel Sorour received the order to move to the base of the 15th Brigade, where his troops could replenish their depleted ammunition – but, also to act at his own discretion, because the High Command had no clear picture of the battlefield, and communications were tenuous at best. Left on his own, the Kuwaiti commander decided to withdraw all the way to the Saudi border in order to keep his flanks safe. Actually, such threats were hollow for the Iraqi entry into Kuwait City caused a total traffic collapse: as thousands of civilians attempted to flee to Saudi Arabia, while others attempted to

Table 12: Officially credited Air-to-Air Victories by KAF Mirage F.1-Pilots		
Pilot	**Claims**	**Weapon**
Captain Mohammed ad-Dossari	2 helicopters	Magic Mk.1
Lieutenant Habis al-Mutairi	2 helicopters	Magic Mk.1
Lieutenant Abdullah Suwaillin	2 helicopters	Magic Mk.1
Lieutenant Ali al-Anzi	2 helicopters	Magic Mk.1
Major Taher at-Taher	3 helicopters	1x 30mm cannon & 2x Magic Mk.1
Lieutenant Bassam al-Jouaid	1 or 2 helicopters	unclear
Captain Ayman al-Mudaf	2 helicopters	unclear
Lieutenant Faysal al-Hamoud	1 helicopter	unclear

Another MT-LBu of the RGFC as seen parked on a cross-road inside Kuwait City. Clearly visible is the insignia of the Republican Guards, applied on a white field on the forward upper hull. (Albert Grandolini Collection)

withdraw their money from banks or simply to see what was going on outside, the roads filled with traffic, and the police just watched. The resulting chaos blocked the Iraqi advance for hours.

It was only outside the city that the 10th Armoured and the 14th Mechanised Brigades of the Medina Division, followed by the Tawakkalna gradually extracted themselves from the traffic jams and pushed through towards the south. Even then, traffic jams and lack of fuel caused the Medina to reach its final objective – Mina al-Ahmadi – only at 0130hrs on 3 August 1990. Srour kept ahead of them before going into bivouac during the night and sending a party south to inform the Saudis he intended to cross the border. The next morning, the 35th Brigade evacuated into Saudi Arabia: shortly after, its vacated position was hit by an Iraqi air strike.[31]

SKYHAWKS AS REAR GUARD

At 1220hrs on 2 August, the IrAF delivered its second air strike against both of the Kuwaiti air bases. Nothing is known about the composition of the fighter-bomber formations and their attack appears not to have left any kind of lasting impressions upon the KAF airmen still at al-Jaber AB. Although there are reports about the use of runway denial sub-munitions, the Kuwaitis subsequently managed to launch seven additional A-4s. At least a pair of these was vectored into attacks on Iraqi ground forces in the al-Muthana area: although narrowly bracketed by the Iraqi anti-aircraft fire, both disengaged safely and flew away to Saudi Arabia. Flying another A-4, Lieutenant Adnan Abdul Rasool even ran into an Iraqi helicopter, turned around and claimed his opponent as shot down by 20mm cannon fire. Several pilots of IrAF's Mirages and MiG-29s that were airborne over Kuwait by this point in time reported sighting KAF Skyhawks, but no air combats took place: due to the distance from the nearest Iraqi radars and poor radio

communications, their ground controllers experienced significant problems with recognising friendly from enemy aircraft and refused to grant permission to open fire.[32]

Less lucky was the enterprising Lieutenant-Colonel Rasheedi. Left back at Ali as-Salem Sabah AB after his Gazelle helicopter was used to evacuate members of the royal family early in the morning. Together with 1st Lieutenant Dia'a as-Sayagh, 1st Sergeant Kamil R. Jaber, and Lance Corporal Hassan T. al-Fadagh, he eventually managed to prepare a single SA.330H Super Puma helicopter for a sortie to al-Jaber AB, in an attempt to evacuate KAF officers trapped there. However, shortly after taking off, their Super Puma was engaged by the MIM-23B I-HAWK SAM-site positioned near al-Adourmi and shot down, killing everybody on board. Three Gazelle helicopters armed with HOT ATGMs that took off from Ali as-Salem Sabah AB to attack Iraqi armour were all reportedly shot down too.[33]

Few of the KAF's Skyhawks remained in the country after that point in time. They continued operating from one of the highways in southern Kuwait until the morning of 3 August, by when at least two had to be abandoned after they overshot and ended in soft sand, while a third crashed during a take-off by night. By then, the total losses of the KAF – approximately half of these to enemy action – included up to 8 Mirages, 4 Skyhawks, 5 Gazelles (three shot down by the Iraqis and two shot-up on the ground), and all 4 Super Pumas (except for the one mentioned above, three others were lost on 3 August, see the next sub-chapter). Nevertheless, up to 80% of its aircraft and crews – including 6 BAe Hawks, 3 L-100-30s, and most of the helicopters – had reached sanctuaries in Saudi Arabia and Bahrain, where they were quickly re-organised as the Free Kuwait Air Force. Behind them, the Iraqis subsequently claimed to have captured intact up to 14 Mirages, 5 Skyhawks, 6 BAe Hawks and

Table 13: Known Officially credited Air-to-Air Victories by KAF A-4KU-Pilots		
Pilot	**Claims**	**Weapon**
Major Ala'a as-Sayegh	1 helicopter	20mm cannon
Major Hussein al-Qattan	1 helicopter	20mm cannon
Lieutenant Adnan Abdul Rasool	1 helicopter	20mm cannon
details unknown	2 helicopters	

one L-100-30, together with between 180 and 240 Matra R.550 Magic air-to-air missiles: Western sources confirmed the capture of 5 Mirage F.1CK/CK-2s and 3 F.1BKs. Also lost were all the I-HAWK SAM-sites, all SA-8s, and one of the brand-new Skyguard batteries. The Iraqis evacuated all the Mirages to Abu Ubaida AB, but found their equipment was inferior to their own F.1EQs. Therefore, they were relegated to training purposes or used as sources of spares. The Kuwaiti Hawk jet trainers proved of better use: indeed, the IrAF is known to have wanted to acquire this type in the 1980s, but the related negotiations failed. Thus, all were transferred to Rashid AB, in Baghdad, where they were used for training.[34]

In Saudi Arabia, the surviving KAF aircraft and helicopters were concentrated at King Abdul Aziz AB, outside Dhahran. According to unconfirmed reports, the Mirage F.1CKs then flew a few sorties over Kuwait on 3 August, before being withdrawn to al-Ahsa AB, outside Hufuf. Subsequently, commercial enterprises from the USA and France were contracted to maintain and service surviving A-4s and Mirages, respectively.

FAIT ACCOMPLI

Late in the night of 2 August 1990, as the Iraqi columns finally reached southern Kuwait, Sabawi Ibrahim Hassan at-Tikriti – the newly appointed chief of intelligence for Iraq's 19th Province – informed Rawi that the Kuwaiti Crown Prince would be leading a two-brigade counter-offensive from the Saudi border. The Guards' officers were sceptical: Hamdani observed that the Crown Prince had been unable to resist for an hour during the morning, and was openly wondering about his ability to organise an offensive needing 18 brigades to counter 8 Iraqi divisions in Kuwait. Thus, this intelligence was ignored and on the next day the RGFC tightened its grip in the south. During the morning the Medina Division moved down to the al-Qulayah Naval Base: due to the secrecy surrounding the entire operation, its HQ was not informed about this being already secured by the 440th Naval Infantry Brigade. Thus, the Guards nearly opened fire upon the troops protecting the facility: a major fratricide incident was avoided when the latter raised the Iraqi flag.[35]

Skirmishes with scattered remnants of the KLF continued throughout 3 August, as the defenders attempted to hold the Ali as-Salem AB and several road junctions in the south. When the Super Puma helicopters attempted to transport ammunition and supplies to pockets of resistance left at the encircled air base, one of them exploded on landing while two others were destroyed in the ensuing conflagration. The fighting died down as the remnants of the Kuwaiti troops – all meanwhile out of ammunition – were pushed across the border. Due to the lack of fuel, they abandoned most of their equipment: thus, while up to 7,000 KLF troops reached the safety of Saudi Arabia, they were short on almost everything.[36]

By the noon of 4 August 1990, the Medina, Tawakkalna, Baghdad and Adnan Divisions established a wide cordon about a kilometre short of the Saudi border: this was to serve as Saddam's demonstration that he had no further territorial ambitions. Even so, the border was not completely sealed for a week longer. The exact number of Iraqi casualties by that point in time remains unknown, but was probably at about 660, including 300 dead. The Kuwaitis suffered up to 4,000 casualties, and had several additional thousands taken as prisoners.[37]

Meanwhile, Baghdad officials were busy explaining it entered Kuwait at the request of the local population that wished to

Despite repeated IrAF air strikes on both air bases of the KAF, a small number of Kuwaiti A-4KUs remained operational and continued fighting through the morning of 2 August, effectively serving as a rear-guard for units withdrawing into Saudi Arabia. This example was photographed following its evacuation to the latter country. (Albert Grandolini Collection)

An AS.332 Super Puma helicopter of the KAF: one such helicopter was shot down by a Kuwaiti MIM-23B I-HAWK SAM-site, killing all four occupants. (US Army photo)

Later during the morning of 2 August, a major obstacle for the Iraqi advance into Kuwait City became the ever denser civilian traffic. This MT-LBu was photographed while navigating between civilian cars down one of the ring-highways around the city. (Albert Grandolini Collection)

overthrow the Emir, that it had established a new government under Ala'a Hussein Ali, and that it would withdraw troops whenever he would issue a corresponding request. However, on 7 August 1990, Baghdad then announced an annexation of Kuwait as its 19th Province, and 'demotion' of Hussein to the position of provincial governor. Finally, on 12 August 1990, Saddam Hussein – knowing full well that this would never happen – announced he would withdraw from Kuwait only if Israel would withdraw from Palestinian territories, the Golan Heights and Lebanon, and if Syria would also withdraw its forces from Lebanon.[38]

GUARD'S LESSONS

From the standpoint of the RGFC's commanders, the invasion of Kuwait was often compared with the final operations from the war with Iran, especially Operations *Tawakkalna 2*, *3* and *4*, and thus seen as 'an overwhelming success at a light cost'.[39] Actually, the operation was anything other than 'flawless': even the involved commanders couldn't avoid the conclusion that many of the attacks within Kuwait City were uncoordinated and based on an underestimation of the scale of Kuwaiti resistance, while the IrAF's operations especially were rather haphazard by nature. It was foremost the complete chaos in the Kuwaiti chain of command that resulted in the KAF and the KLF relying largely upon the self-sacrifice of a few isolated men to save the country's government – and thus its future. A much

ZIL-trucks of the Tawakkalna ala Allah Armoured Division (recognizable by the insignia applied on cabin doors) towing D-30 howitzers and ZPU-4 anti-aircraft machine guns along the coastal highway. (Albert Grandolini Collection)

A T-72 of the RGFC passing by two Chinese-made 37mm Type-74 twin-barrel flak-guns positioned inside Kuwait City. (Tom Cooper Collection)

less-well-known fact – especially so in Iraq – is that in the aftermath of the occupation, much of the Guards' discipline declined, and its troops began stealing food and bedding from the locals, in turn causing further friction with their Kuwaiti 'brothers'.[40]

Moreover, the invasion of Kuwait stunned not only the word but even the Iraqi Army. Khazraji learned of Uum an-Nidaa in the morning when his secretary general, Lieutenant-General Ala'a al-Jenabi, telephoned him and asked him to immediately come to the HQ. When he arrived, al-Jenabi informed him, 'We've completed the conquest of Kuwait'. Shanshall heard the news 15 minutes later when he arrived in the Defence Ministry in Baghdad. Khazraji then sought a meeting with Saddam, only to be informed by the latter that he selected the RGFC for this operation because they were responsible to him and not the army, and could therefore guarantee secrecy.[41]

A T-72 of the Iraqi Republican Guards positioned to control the coast west of Kuwait City. (Albert Grandolini Collection)

The crew and the infantry squad of this BMP-2 of the RGFC were photographed while taking a break after their quick advance into Kuwait. (Albert Grandolini Collection)

THE OCCUPATION OF KUWAIT

The Iraqi invasion of Kuwait was no 'Anschluss': few Kuwaitis wanted to 'rejoin the fatherland'. Unsurprisingly, by early October 1990 more than half of the native Kuwaitis had left the country: they joined a whole-scale exodus of up to 1 million of foreigners. Those Iraqis that moved into their abandoned homes usually preferred to loot these – just like they looted the central bank, gold and gem markets of Kuwait City (renamed al-Qadhima on 28 August 1990), while the treatment of facilities like banks, schools and hospitals was reminiscent of what the Soviet troops did in post-war Eastern Europe: the equipment was removed together with its contents. As far as they did not manage to flee to Saudi Arabia, most of the

Westerners were rounded up and transferred to Baghdad, ostensibly as guests of the Iraqi government. In reality, they were used as human shields. Foreign embassies in Kuwait City were besieged by Iraqi troops and their staff gradually forced out by power- and water-supply outages. A few Kuwaitis waged a guerrilla war in the form of night-time hit-and-run attacks – which the Iraqis countered with ill-treating the population on a large-scale. Any insurgents that were captured were usually tortured before being executed. While firm figures remain unknown, it has been estimated 1,000 Kuwaiti civilians died during the Iraqi occupation and 600 disappeared. Only the remains of about 375 were subsequently found in mass graves laid by the Iraqis.[42]

Having narrowly avoided capture, the Kuwaiti government reorganised itself in exile and started operating from Saudi Arabia: indeed, it continued operating its foreign petroleum refining and marketing business in Western Europe and controlling substantial foreign assets. In early September 1990, it pledged US$2.5 billion to the United States to help cover the cost of its military operations in the Gulf and another US$2.5 billion to other countries – including Jordan, Egypt, and Turkey – which had sustained the greatest economic damage from an economic embargo imposed by the United Nations upon Iraq. Iraq's overseas assets were quickly frozen and in late October 1990 the UN Security Council approved a resolution declaring Iraq responsible for all damage and personal injuries resulting from its occupation of Kuwait – thus laying the groundwork for the eventual seizure of overseas assets.

SAUDI REACTION

The Saudis went onto full alert within an hour of the invasion and although Defence Minister Prince Sultan Bin Abdul Azizwas was in Morocco (recuperating from a knee operation) the Higher Officers Committee met immediately and prepared to reinforce the commanders of the Eastern and Northern Military Regions, Major-Generals Salih al-Muhaya and Abd al-Rahmanal-Alkami, respectively. A Joint Forces Command was established at noon of 10 August 1990, under the commander of the RSADF, General Khaled, to control the northern border.[43]

Just like the Egyptian president Mubarak, the Saudi King Fahd was outraged by the invasion which he regarded as a personal betrayal. Together, they initiated numerous reactions by the Arab League. Only Iraq's closest traditional ally – Jordan – and the PLO showed reluctant in condemning Saddam, and this despite receiving substantial Saudi largesse in the past. Together with (North) Yemen, all were subjected to economic sanctions, and thousands of their expatriate workers expelled from Saudi Arabia. Moreover, King Fahd became convinced of a potential threat to his realm and thus soon began seeking US and British military support. At an Arab League meeting in Cairo, on 9 August, the only opposition to an invitation for Western military support and deployment of foreign troops to regain Kuwait came from the PLO and Libya, while Algeria and Yemen abstained. Saudi Arabia reacted by expulsing thousands of Yemeni workers and reinforcing its economic sanctions, causing severe and long-lasting consequences for the local economy. Actually, the Iraqis treated Saudi Arabia with extreme caution: when their troops accidentally crossed into the southern part of the former Neutral Zone, they immediately withdrew and apologised to Riyadh. Similarly, the Saudis still in Kuwait were treated with deference.[44]

However, none of this mattered: on the contrary, it was the response of the USA which was of greatest importance for subsequent developments. By the time Saddam met Ambassador Glaspie, Washington had perceived Iraq as a threat to Kuwait. Thus, by 2 and 3 August, it became obvious that the USA would lead the 'response'.[45]

US REACTION

As discussed earlier, Washington had been monitoring the continuous growth in Iraqi military capabilities with ever growing concern for years. As the barrage of rhetoric emitted from Baghdad was followed by reports of Iraqi troop concentrations along the border with Iraq, not only the intelligence services and Washington, but even the US military became active. CENTCOM was informed that two Iraqi divisions had deployed near the Kuwaiti frontier on 19 July 1990. Two days later, the intelligence reports were updated by notation that an armoured division had moved into a position just north of Kuwait, which in turn prompted Schwarzkopf to run the above-mentioned war-game evaluation of the existing Oplan 1002-90. The same day the British military attaché to Baghdad reported to his US contacts the movement of about 3,000 military vehicles southwards and the CIA then warned that there was a 60% chance that Iraqi forces would invade. Correspondingly, and since all other intelligence services confirmed an Iraqi build-up and warned of a possible Iraqi military action, the DIA started reporting on the related developments twice per day. On 24 July, satellite intelligence revealed much of the scale of the Iraqi build-up; however, the DIA noted weakness in the Iraqi logistic artillery and logistics train, and a bare 2:1 advantage in tank strength, and thus concluded that the prospects of an immediate military action were 'low'. Instead, it described this deployment as 'intimidation' before concluding in time-honoured way of bureaucratic face-saving; 'These forces could initiate military operations against Kuwait at any time with no warning'.[46]

By 26 July 1990, the US intelligence services assessed Iraq as having 120,000 combat troops deployed in the southeast of the country, in turn prompting Schwarzkopf to make a series of proposals for quickly boosting the US military presence in the region. All of these were ignored because Arab states were replying with optimistic reports about the prospect of a diplomatic settlement, and proved anxious to avoid a rise in the US presence. Indeed, the UAE even disapproved the US request for permission to base Boeing KC-135 tankers in the country. Ultimately, the diplomats' failure to avoid the conflict was because they were unwilling to believe Saddam would take the military option and though that the crisis would blow itself out, indeed President Bush made a response to the Glaspie meeting which was almost obsequious.[47]

On 31 July 1990, Schwarzkopf notified the White House that the forward movement of the RGFC's concentration was that of reaching jump-off lines for an invasion, and thus the latter was imminent. The following day both the CIA and the DIA agreed with this interpretation, and Schwarzkopf then repeated his conclusion in a meeting with Secretary of Defence, Richard B. 'Dick' Chaney, and the Joint Chiefs of Staff. However, he underestimated the Iraqi intentions and announced they would halt at the 30th Parallel, thus taking only the Kuwaiti part of the Rumaila oilfield and Bubiyan Island. To dissuade them, he also presented a detailed plan for air and sea strikes which included vulnerable, high-value targets, such as military headquarters, power plants, and factories and also discussed the latest version of Oplan 1002-90 and options to respond to a possible Iraqi attack. By then, it was too late.

With the invasion under way on 2 August 1990, the Americans tried to catch up with a situation now beyond any hope of their control. After President Bush condemned the invasion at a press conference and called for 'the immediate and unconditional withdrawal of Iraqi forces', he and the members of the National Security Council (NSC) were briefed by Schwarzkopf and the Chairman of the Joint Chiefs of Staff, General Colin L. Powell. Meanwhile, the Security Council of the United Nations adopted its Resolution 660, also condemning the invasion and demanding an unconditional Iraqi withdrawal.

On 3 August 1990, the NSC meet again with Powell and Schwarzkopf, and the latter two presented military options aimed to demonstrate the US resolve in the crisis, and – if necessary – punishing Iraq for the invasion of Kuwait. At the same meeting, Bush observed that an Iraqi attack on Saudi Arabia would be a cause

Chairman of the Joint Chiefs of Staff, General Colin L. Powell (left) with General Schwarzkopf. (US DoD)

for war and decided to put CENTCOM on alert. Correspondingly, Schwarzkopf's command was assigned numerous units of the US Air Force (USAF) and the US Navy (USN), and the CVBG centred on the aircraft carrier USS *Independence* (CV-62) was ordered into the Persian Gulf, which it entered two days later.[48]

Early on 4 August, during a meeting at Camp David, Schwarzkopf briefed the president on plans for deploying a defensive force to Saudi Arabia, and suggested an offensive might be possible within 8-12 months. Bush ordered him to prepare for an offensive based on Oplan 1002-90, but only after a formal request for assistance from Saudi Arabia. At that point in time, the White House received a message from King Fahd, requesting a briefing by the US military. Correspondingly, a team was put together including the commander of the 3rd Army, General John J Yeosok – who was summoned from the dinning table that evening.[49]

Two days later, Vice-president Cheney led a delegation including Schwarzkopf, Yeosock and Horner to Jeddah, for a meeting with King Fahd – who, no doubt, was relieved at the prospect of US forces to offset the perceived Iraqi menace. The Saudi ruler then quickly agreed to invite American forces to help protect his country – to a level where Horner remained in Riyadh to set up the Forward Headquarters CENTCOM in the basement of the MDOA. Cheney, Schwarzkopf and Yeosok returned to the USA to prepare the transfer of up to 250,000 military personnel to Saudi Arabia. The spearhead of this force was to be composed of the USMC and the US Army's strategic reaction force – the XVIII Airborne Corps – which since July had been commanded by the former commander of the Special Operations Command, Lieutenant-General Gary E Luck. This corps included the 82nd Airborne Division, the 101st Airborne Division, and the 24th Infantry Division (Mechanised)

with 216 M1 Abrams MBTs. All of these units then received the order to deploy to Saudi Arabia.[50]

7

PREPARING FOR THE MOTHER OF ALL BATTLES

Alarmed by the Iraqi invasion of Kuwait, the USA and Saudi Arabia scrambled to react. Negotiations quickly revealed the obvious: despite all the investment of the proceeding decades, the desert kingdom was unable to protect itself. Therefore, the decision was taken to rush several carrier battle groups, dozens of combat aircraft, and entire units of the US Army and the US Marine Corps to the scene. As US allies from Europe and abroad followed in fashion, the biggest military build-up in the last two decades of the 20th Century came into being. Meanwhile, along the borders between Iraq, Kuwait and Saudi Arabia, each side observed the other closely, and anxiously, took counsel of its fears and prepared for what Saddam eventually declared 'The Mother of All Battles' (Umm al-Ma'arik).

SAUDI PROBLEM

Through mid-August, the US-led coalition feared Saddam would strike along the coastal highway to take the vital Eastern Province oil fields. This fear was further increased when US intelligence over-assessed the whole Iraqi Army at '1 million troops in 63 divisions and 275 manoeuvre brigades with 5,700 MBT, some 3,400 guns, 300 MLRS and the IrAF at 733 combat aircraft'. The Iraqis were deemed, purely on the basis of their order of battle, to have 540,000 troops, 4,280 MBT and 3,110 guns in what came to be called the

Kuwait Theatre of Operations (KTO). These figures remained in the public domain although the intelligence later reduced them to 336,000 men with 3,475 MBTs and 2,475 guns.[1]

The situation was considered even more critical because the Iraqis deployed strong forces along the 221-kilometre long Kuwaiti-Saudi frontier, while Saddam's assurances that he had no further territorial ambitions rang as hollow as those by Adolph Hitler in 1939, especially in view of several of his earlier U-turns. The Saudi forces were a slender reed, but would man the frontier with Northern Area Command: based at King Khaled Military City near Hafr al-Batin, this included the 8th and 20th Mechanised Brigades RSLF as well as the Gulf Peninsula Shield Force which was barely a light brigade. The brigades each nominally had 5,000 men and 35 tanks (compared with 4,500 men and 105 tanks in an armoured brigade), but they were under-strength and dependent upon foreign technical support – much of which consisted of people anxious to quit and leave what was likely to become a war zone. Of the two Pakistani brigades under Saudi operational control, the one at Tabuq was sent south to counter any moves by the Yemenis, while the 7th Pakistani Armoured Brigade later reinforced the Saudi National Guard brigade in the northeast.[2]

In addition to the Regular Saudi Army and the Pakistanis there was also the 2nd SANG Brigade, which would become the backbone of the Saudi operations, but even then: the total strength was probably under 15,000 men with 70 MBTs. Support from friendly foreign powers was thus considered as 'urgently needed'.

OPERATION *DESERT SHIELD*

The Americans were the first to respond and on 7 August General Powell, Chairman of the JCS, ordered the ready brigade of the 82nd Airborne Division, Maritime Prepositioning Squadrons (MPS) from Guam and Diego Garcia, the CVBG with USS *Dwight D Eisenhower* (CVN-69) and the battleship USS *Wisconsin* (BB-64) – that carried BGM-109 Tomahawk land-attack missiles – 12 squadrons of combat aircraft, and three equipped with E-3 Sentry AWACS and tankers, to the Arabian Peninsula and surrounding waters. The code-name of this operation, formally introduced on 8 August 1990, became *Desert Shield*; this was initiated with the landing of Colonel Ron Rokosz's 2nd Brigade of the 82nd 'All-American' Airborne Division at Dhahran AB.[3]

The 2nd Brigade quickly moved northwards and took three days to assemble in its new positions. Lacking artillery and anti-armour munitions the unit could do little but to serve as a 'trip-wire' force early on. Nevertheless, its quick deployment was a powerful demonstration. Moreover, much more was to follow and by the end of the first week of *Desert Shield*, more than 4,000 US Army soldiers had deployed to Saudi Arabia, together with 15 AH-64A Apache helicopter gunships, 8 OH-54 Kiowa scout helicopters, 18 M551A1 Sheridan light tanks, 56 BGM-71 TOW anti-tank missile systems, 12 towed 105mm howitzers, and two M270 multiple launch rocket systems.[4]

On the morning of 9 August, the entire staff of CENTCOM's Forward Headquarters arrived in Riyadh. Initially, this was under General Horner, who was dual-hatted as acting commander CENTCOM and Central Command Air Force, until 28 August

The first 'tanks' of the US Army to reach Saudi Arabia were 18 thinly armoured M551 Sheridans from the 2nd Brigade of the 82nd Airborne Division, deployed to Dhahran AB on 9 August 1990. (US DoD)

Hard on the heels of the two CVBGs deployed in reaction to the Iraqi invasion of Kuwait was the battleship USS Wisconsin (BB-64) – the first of two ships of the Iowa-Class to see action during Operations *Desert Shield* and then *Desert Storm*. (US DoD)

A long row of AH-64A Apache helicopter gunships of the US Army, as seen in January 1991: designed to provide crucial close air support for ground troops in Central Europe, the type initially experienced significant problems caused by the Saudi sand and weather. (US DoD)

The warships of the US and allied navies also played a crucial role in enforcing an international blockade of Iraq. This photograph shows the interception of the Iraqi merchant *Zanobia* by the destroyer USS *Goldsborough* (DDG-20) in the Persian Gulf. (US DoD)

when Schwarzkopf and his Marine Chief of Staff, Major-General Robert B Johnston, established their HQ.

TRANSPORT PROBLEM

Deployment of further ground forces proved a major problem. Limited availability of transport aircraft and facilities available in the host nations in the always fluid situation in the Middle East meant that Yeosock hoped to first deploy aviation units, then air defence systems, and then anti-armour weapons, with heavy forces arriving in the second echelon. Indeed, the US had a formidable air transport organisation in the form of the Military Airlift Command (MAC, which included Air Force Reserve and Air National Guard elements), equipped with 127 Lockheed C-5 Galaxy and 270 Lockheed C-141 StarLifter transports. Indeed, by 15 August up to 93% of the former and 73% of the latter were supporting *Desert Shield*. However, in turn this forced the MAC to cancel all of its other sorties. The last two reserve squadrons equipped with C-5s were mobilised on 3 September but by then the strain upon the US strategic airlift capability was such that on 19 August the Strategic Air Command (SAC) pressed up to 20 of its McDonnell-Douglas KC-10A Extender tankers to serve as cargo aircraft.[5]

To ease the MAC's burden, President Bush then ordered the first phase mobilisation of the Civil Reserve Air Fleet on 17 August 1990 (followed by a second, on 16 January 1991): the thriving US civil aviation market eventually provided 115 Boeing 707, 727, 747, 757, and 767s, Lockheed L-100/1011s, and Douglas DC-8s and DC-10s. Although always reluctant to seek assistance in such cases, on 26 August Washington then accepted the offer to use two Boeing 747s of Kuwait Airways at no cost), then the services of Evergreen Airliners – which hauled cargo starting in early October – and, finally, two Boeing 747s from South Korea. It was only on 12 December 1990, that the Pentagon took the decision to authorise contracting additional airliners from countries that were NATO members.

Thus, the next troops to arrive in Saudi Arabia were those of the 7th Marine Expeditionary Brigade (MEB) under Major-General John I Hopkins, starting from 14 August 1990. This, nominally more powerful force of 16,500 men, rather illustrated an extremely unpleasant fact, for the American action reflected in the old adage 'for want of a nail…the battle was lost': on their arrival, the Marines were shocked to discover that their tanks aboard MPS in the port of al-Jubail wouldn't start because their batteries had not been charged up. For several days, they had to scour shops looking for replacements. Even when that problem was overcome, there was another caused by the fact that many tanks lacked oil, and also by the necessity to calibrate weapons and weapon-control systems – while the Saudis refused to allow them to conduct live firing exercises. However, such an influx of power reflected Schwarzkopf's priorities, for in order to buy time, he insisted on a maximum build-up of combat power to deter an Iraqi advance – by providing an illusion of power – instead of sustainment.[6]

To further confuse the Iraqis, the troops were sometimes clandestinely floated out of Saudi bases, and then returned to be shown to the World's media. The plot generally worked well: although one British press-photographer noted he had earlier photographed the same soldier carrying a guitar over his shoulder, once he discovered the truth he remained silent. However, the fundamental flaw of Schwarzkopf's philosophy was that the build-up of manpower was at the expense of heavy equipment and this may have undermined the defence of eastern Saudi Arabia if the Iraqis decided to attack: in that respect it left the coalition forces resembling a turkey that swells in size to dissuade predators, which could have proven counter-productive. Fortunately, the Iraqis did not exploit their early numerical advantage.

Eventually, between August 1990 and March 1991, the airlifters would bring nearly 500,000 men and women to Saudi Arabia: more than 64% of these arrived in civilian aircraft, as did nearly 27% of about 488,000 tonnes of supplies and equipment flown in (see Table 14). In turn, the harsh environment and living conditions meant that sick or injured troops had to be airlifted out: by New Year's Day 1991, no fewer than 1,644 had been flown to Europe, and 1,522 to the USA.

BATTLEWAGONS TO THE RESCUE

The first US combat aircraft to reach the theatre were those of the Carrier Air Wing 5 (CVW-5), embarked on board the aircraft carrier USS *Independence*. Together with her escorts, this ship was ordered into the Persian Gulf on 2 August, and reached its required station within range of Kuwait just two days later, thus becoming the first aircraft carrier that operated inside the Persian Gulf since 1977: she remained in the area for the next 90 days. The second carrier battle group, the one centred on USS *Eisenhower* (CVN-69) – with CVW-7 on board – moved closer to the scene, followed by USS *Saratoga* (CV-60) – with CVW-17 – both of which remained in the Red Sea. Subsequently, the number of available aircraft carriers of the US Navy fluctuated

The massive deployment of troops and equipment during Operation *Desert Shield* required the full mobilisation of the MAC, including nearly all of its huge Lockheed C-5A Galaxy transports. This example was photographed after landing in Saudi Arabia in January 1991. (US DoD)

US Army troops disembarking a Lockheed C-141 StarLifter of the Military Airlift Command, USAF, at an airfield in Saudi Arabia in September 1990. (US DoD)

Table 14: Desert Shield/Desert Storm Strategic Airlift

Month	USAF			Civilian			Total		
	Sorties	Tonnes	People	Sorties	Tonnes	People	Sorties	Tonnes	People
Aug	1,430	39,468	40,411	198	8,117	32,559	1,628	47,585	72,970
Sep	1,582	48,952	21,231	305	12,701	37,274	1,887	61,653	58,505
Oct	1,189	36,430	9,993	259	9,731	39,779	1,448	46,161	49,772
Nov	1,230	32,917	7,320	237	8,493	13,111	1,467	41,410	20,431
Dec	2,149	58,763	33,048	577	24,879	85,126	2,726	83,642	118,174
Jan	2,481	70,653	45,242	793	30,392	69,874	3,274	101,045	115,116
Feb	2,175	58,556	14,794	807	30,483	29,699	2,982	89,039	44,493
Mar	465	11,337	6,583	213	6,946	13,583	678	18,283	20,166
Total	12,701	357,076	178,622	3,389	131,742	321,005	16,090	488,818	499,627

Sources: Survey Vol 5 Table 22. Tonnage is converted from US short tons to metric tonnes .
Note: C-141 flew 8,536 sorties to move 93,126 troops and 144,661 tonnes.

A trio of C-5As unloading urgently needed equipment and supplies at an air base in Saudi Arabia. (US DoD)

(see Table 15 for details).

The aircraft carriers of the US Navy were reinforced by battleships USS *Wisconsin* (BB-64), starting from 24 August, and then USS *Missouri* (BB-63) in November 1990. These vessels' 16-inch (406mm) guns could be directed with the help of unmanned aerial vehicles (UAVs), but they also carried RGM-109 TLAMs. A total of nine cruisers, four destroyers, and two submarines that escorted the carriers and battleships also carried Tomahawk cruise missiles.

M198 howitzers of the 5th Battalion, 11th Regiment of the 1st Marine Division as seen after their arrival in Saudi Arabia. (US DoD)

Table 15: US Navy Aircraft Carrier Deployments into the Arabian Theatre		
Ship	Hull Number	Deployment dates
USS *Independence*	CV-62	2 August – 4 November 1990
USS *Eisenhower*	CVN-69	8 August – 24 August 1990
USS *Saratoga*	CV-60	21 August – 21 September 1990; 23 October – 9 December 1990; 6 January – 11 March 1991
USS *John F Kennedy*	CV-67	6 September 1990 – 12 March 1991
USS *Midway*	CV-41	2 November 1990 – 14 March 1991
USS *Ranger*	CV-61	13 January – 19 April 1991
USS *America*	CV-66	15 January – 4 March 1991
USS *Theodore Roosevelt*	CVN-71	14 January – 20 April 1991

BUILDING UP AIR POWER

The first US combat aircraft to arrive in Saudi Arabia were 23 F-15Cs from 71st TFS. They landed at Dhahran AB on the afternoon of 8 August 1990, after flying – fully armed – for 15 hours over 12,800 kilometres non-stop from Langley AFB, Virginia, with the help of multiple in-flight refuellings. A stream of USAF aircraft were followed by US Marines, whose VMFA-451 Hornets arrived in Shaik Isa, Bahrain, on the afternoon of 23 August. The emphasis upon precision attack meant that in addition to the normal F-15s, F-16s and A-10s, a wing of F-111F with bomb laser-guidance systems rather than the 'dumb' F-111E were deployed, while on 23 August Schwarzkopf requested a LANTIRN-equipped F-16 squadron from Europe (for strengths see Table 16) and he also received F-117A Nighthawk stealth fighters.[7]

The last of the tactical fighters arrived on 2 September. Support aircraft also arrived: indeed five E-3A Sentry AWACS just beat the 71st TFS into Dhahran AB. USAF General Dynamics EF-111A Ravens reached Taif, while Grumman EA-6B Prowlers of the USMC landed at Shaikh Isa by 5 September. There were 36 F-4G 'Wild Weasel' SEAD aircraft in-theatre as well as 6 EC-130 Airborne Battlefield Command and Control Center (ABCCC) aircraft at Sharjah. On 12 September, the last combat aircraft under Phase I of 'Desert Shield', five AC-130 gunships, landed at King Fahd IAP. Unlike the US Marine Corps and the US Navy, the USAF and its NATO allies deployed few full squadrons, usually sending squadron headquarters whose strength was made up with detachments.

Available outside of the Arabian Peninsula, but within range of Iraq, were Boeing B-52G bombers. Initially, about a squadron-worth of these was based at Diego Garcia, but on 24 August Horner

The need for transport aircraft eventually reached such proportions that SAC was forced to press its precious KC-10A Extender tankers into service as cargo aircraft. This example was photographed while waiting to load at Ramstein AFB in West Germany. (US DoD)

The quick deployment of two CVBGs of the US Navy in early and mid-August 1990, followed by a third by the end of the same month, was the first signal that Washington was taking the situation caused by the Iraqi invasion on Kuwait very seriously. This view shows the USS America (CV-66), together with a supply ship and one of the escorting cruisers during an underway-replenishment operation in the Red Sea. (US DoD)

was given operational control of Strategic Air Commands' (SAC's) strategic reconnaissance and tanker forces supporting the theatre. These were all assigned to the newly created 17th Air Division (Provisional), which subsequently began to grow in numbers as additional aircraft moved into bases in Europe, Turkey and Egypt.

Starting on 11 August, NATO also despatched aircraft. The

A pair of fully-armed F-15Cs from the 1st TFW, USAF, seen while standing alert between fortified underground facilities at Dhahran AB in September 1990. (US DoD)

An F-111F from the 48th Tactical Fighter Wing, rolling for take-off with the help of full afterburners, from RAF Lakenheath in Great Britain. This aircraft was departing for deployment to Operation *Desert Shield* in mid-August 1990. (US DoD)

GR.Mk 1A fighter-bombers from the United Kingdom. A day later, three Nimrod MR.2P arrived, while the last reinforcement consisted of four BAE Buccaneer S.Mk 2s, which arrived on 26 January 1991. Across the Channel, France despatched Mirage 2000C interceptors, Mirage F.1CR reconnaissance fighters, and Jaguar A fighter-bombers under Operation *Daguet*, starting from 16 September 1990. Later on, the French Air Force (Armée de l'Air, AdA) also deployed Mirage F.1C interceptors to Qatar. The final addition during September 1990 were a dozen Tornado IDS of the Italian Air Force, deployed under Operation *Locusta* to al-Dhafra AB in the UAE on 25 September, and 24 McDonnell-Douglas CF-18As of the Royal Canadian Air Force deployed in Qatar under Operation *Friction*.

The air forces of the USA and NATO had joined those of the air forces of Saudi Arabia, Bahrain, Oman, Qatar and the United Arab Emirates (UAE). In addition to deploying their own combat aircraft, on 7 September Washington granted permission for Riyadh to purchase 24 additional F-15C/Ds (the first of these arrived on 20 September 1990). Cairo offered combat aircraft of the Egyptian Air Force, too, but the Saudis pointed out that the skies were already crowded, and subsequently the – apparently offended – Egyptians did not respond to a Saudi request for their jets.[8]

British launched their military effort on the Arabian Peninsula on that day under Operation *GRANBY*, and by dispatching six Tornado F.Mk. 3 interceptors from Cyprus, and 12 SEPECAT Jaguar

SAC supported both US and foreign transfers by assigning 186

Table 16: Fixed-wing Air Build up in Arabian Peninsula[10]						
Service	Aircraft	Sep 1	Oct 1	Nov 1	Dec 1	Jan 1
USAF	Total	528	647	689	742	952
	Combat	308	362	366	387	528
US Navy	Total	65	148	143	156	156
	Combat	49	106	106	108	108
US Marines	Total	115	146	146	146	205
	Combat	97	118	118	118	173
NATO	Combat	40	92	106	106	126
Arab	Combat	277	277	277	277	277

tankers to support *Desert Shield*, including 44% of its KC-135 and 75% of its KC-10 fleets. By 20 December, SAC tankers had flown 13,129 sorties in support of *Desert Shield* and supplied 25,028 aircraft with 15,200 tonnes of fuel. As the prospect of an offensive operation approached, the SAC reinforced the tanker force to 224 aircraft by 13 January 1991.[9]

The strategic airlifter effort was augmented by 96 C-130 Hercules, a third of the fleet, which distributed personnel and material around the Arabian Peninsula, were later reinforced by another 35 transports. The last two squadrons arriving at Sharjah and Al Ain air bases on September 8, and were later supported by the mobilisation on 1 October of Air Reserve and Air National Guard units and the arrival of three Royal New Zealand Air Force Hercules. The American aircraft alone would deliver 300,000 tons of cargo and 209,000 troops. On October 31 the theatre's airlift forces were placed under the 1610th Airlift Division (Provisional).

COMBAT AIR PATROLS

During the days immediately after the Iraqi invasion of Kuwait, the RSAF held its interceptors – supported by Sentry AWACS' – on constant combat air patrols (CAPs) over north-eastern Saudi Arabia, 24 hours a day. These were quickly augmented by USAF aircraft. Activity of Iraqi reconnaissance and fighters during early October prompted the USAF and the RSAF to extend their

Together with dozens of combat aircraft, the USAF quickly rushed its own E-3A Sentry AWACS to Saudi Arabia. Capable of simultaneously detecting and tracking hundreds of targets underway over land and sea, while coordinating the work of friendly interceptors, fighter-bombers and support aircraft, the US and Saudi Sentries played a crucial role in the Operation *Desert Shield*. (US DoD)

Amongst the USAF's tactical aircraft rushed to Saudi Arabia quite early on were F-4G Wild Weasels of the 35th TFW – the most advanced, dedicated platform for 'suppression of enemy air defences' (SEAD) – purposes. This pair of AGM-88 toting F-4Gs was photographed on 11 January 1991. (US DoD)

Table 17: Overall Desert Shield Air Activity[12]

Date	US Air Force	US Navy	US Marines	Allies	Total (US Tac airlift)
Aug/Sep 90	2,402	396	495	407	3,700 (895)
Oct 90	2,480	261	424	565	3,730 (699)
Nov 90	2,673	518	472	1,210	4,873 (684)
Dec 90	2,215	615	453	947	4,230 (901)
Jan 91	1,768	281	296	764	3,109 (658)
Totals	11,538	2,071	2,140	3,893	19,642 (3,837)
Dates are for weeks ending during the month. January 1991 to week-ending 14 January					

One of the first Jaguar GR.Mk 1A fighter-bombers of the RAF deployed to Saudi Arabia, seen in the process of touching down after a training sortie. (US DoD)

A B-52G from the 2nd Bomber Wing as seen from a KC-135 tanker. (US DoD)

While the available military cities constructed in Saudi Arabia during the 1960-1980s provided enough space for a mass deployment of US and allied air power, their housing facilities still provided insufficient for all the staff. Correspondingly, multiple 'tent-cities' had to be erected nearby. This was the home for the airmen of the 401st Tactical Fighter Wing (USAF). (US DoD)

CAPs into western and central regions of the border with Iraq. Given the problems with the Saudi air defence command system, the USAF flew in their own to augment the host's system from 26 September, but, within a month there were potentially serious problems co-ordinating air defence: it was only on 22 December that the Saudi-based IADS had a successful test link-up with the NATO Airborne Warning and Control System in Turkey.

From early August, Coalition aircraft were extremely active (see Table 17) and while they did not fire their weapons in anger, on the morning of November 21 a US Army AH-1 Cobra attack helicopter accidentally launched a Hellfire missile into one of Horner's ammunition dumps at King Fahd IAP causing some damage. Activity focused upon maintaining a shield over the Arabian Peninsula; electronic, electro-optic and optical reconnaissance north of the Saudi border; and training.[11]

SEALIFT

On 7 August 1990, Schwarzkopf requested the release of 239 prepositioned vehicles already in Bahrain and Oman. However, sealift was the only way to bring in the sheer volume of supplies that the Americans needed: indeed, in August alone it delivered more supplies and equipment than the first three months of airlifter activity. Maintenance failures meant sealift resources metaphorically 'ran on the rocks': the eight European-built Algol-class (T-AKR 287) Fast Sealift Ships (FSS) could each carry some 25,000 tonnes and were collectively capable of carrying an armoured/mechanized division to a crisis point. However, they were maintained at reduced operating status and ready to move only with at least four days notice. Thus, although mobilised at the same time, when the time came for them to move the 24th Division, unexpected repairs meant that three of FSS suffered malfunctions in need of 10-days of repairs on average, while one – carrying that division's helicopters and support equipment – broke down in the middle of the Atlantic. The latter ship was towed to Spain, where the cargo was transhipped and thus arrived in Saudi Arabia only on 23 September, more than a month after it had departed![14]

Of the 96 Ready Reserve Fleet (RRF) ships, 64 were supposed to be underway within four days of receiving orders. However, the average age of these ships was 27 years, and some were 47 years old, 80% had century-old steam turbine technology rather than diesels, while their maintenance

Four ships of the Marine Prepositioning Squadron-1 disgorging their loads of heavy vehicles of the US Marine Corps at the Saudi port of Jubail in November 1990. (US DoD)

Table 18: Desert Shield/Desert Storm Strategic Sealift[16]

Month	Strategic Sealift		RRF/US Flag		Allied Flag		Total	
	Voyage	Tonnes	Voyage	Tonnes	Voyage	Tonnes	Voyage	Tonnes
Aug	21	229,537	-	-	-	-	21	229,537
Sep	7	51,896	25	161,525	5	15,199	37	228,620
Oct	9	85,144	30	128,738	32	82,701	71	296,583
Nov	11	74,094	15	83,078	10	30,082	36	187,254
Dec	13	108,378	34	137,490	29	77,110	76	322,978
Jan	10	104,113	54	258,052	86	260,196	150	622,361
Feb	7	60,087	24	106,176	31	103,973	62	270,236
Mar	-	-	3	7,624	4	17,059	7	24,701
Total	78	713,249	185	882,701	197	586,320	460	2,182,270

Note: Strategic Sealift included FSS, Afloat Positioning Ships, Maritime Pre-positioning Ships.

MIM-104 PATRIOT

An AN/MPQ-53 ECS of an MIM-104/PAC-2 system of the US Army as deployed in Saudi Arabia in late 1990. (US DoD)

In addition to aircraft, the US and allied air defences of Saudi Arabia were reinforced through the first combat deployment of the MIM-104 Patriot (Phased Array Tracking Radar to Intercept to Target) SAM-system.

In the US Army, the Patriot SAM-system was usually deployed in form of a battalion, commanded by a lieutenant-colonel, and consisted of up to 600 soldiers organised into the HQ-battery, a maintenance company, and between four and six 'line batteries' (the actual launching sites). Each Patriot battalion was equipped with the Information Coordination Central (ICC) – a command station designed to coordinate the combat operations of a battalion, and for networking the system with other means of air defence, foremost E-3 Sentry AWACS aircraft of the USAF, but also the US Navy's warships. Usually commanded by a captain, each line battery consisted of 70-80 troops, organized into three or four platoons (Fire Control platoon, Launcher platoon, and the HQ/Maintenance platoon), and was equipped with six launchers.

The heart of every line battery was the Electric Power Plant (EPP) – the power source. This consisted of two 150kW diesel engines mounted on a modified M977 Heavy Expanded Mobility Tactical Truck (HEMTT). The eyes and the nerve centre of the system were the AN/MPQ-53 passive, electronically scanned array (PESA) radar, the AN/MSQ-104 Engagement Control Station (ECS), and the OQ-349 Antenna Mast Group (AMG). Installed on a heavy trailer, and equipped with IFF, electronic counter-countermeasures (ECCM) and track-via-missile (TVM) guidance subsystems, the AN/MPQ-53 created a comparatively narrow but highly agile radar beam, which enabled it to detect small, fast targets. It was capable of examining the track's size, speed, altitude, and heading, and deciding whether or not it was a legitimate 'track' or 'clutter'.

If the track was classified as an aircraft, it would be shown on a display within the AN/MSQ-104 ECS, while the IFF-system 'pinged' the track to determine if it had any IFF-response. Installed inside an airconditioned and pressurized shelter mounted on the bed of a M927 cargo truck (or a Light Medium Tactical vehicle cargo truck), and containing consoles for two crewmen, the ECS included the Weapons Control Computer (WCC), connected to the Data Link Terminal (DLT), the OE-349 Antenna Mast Group (AMG, an UHF communications array), and the Routing Logic Radio Interface Units. The WCC was a multiprocessor militarized computer responsible for controlling the operator interface, calculating missile intercept algorithms, and providing limited fault diagnostics. The DLT connected the ECS to remotely operated, self-contained M901 mobile, trainable, four-round

had been woefully neglected. Unsurprisingly, the four scheduled to be available by 17 August were delayed by a week.[15]

On 10 August, orders were issued to activate 17 additional ships. However, it had already proved difficult finding US crews, and thus most had to be replaced by Filipinos. Few of the ships were modern roll-on, roll-off (ro-ro) or container carriers and most had to load individual items by crane into the holds, and their cruise speed was much slower than that of modern designs. Nevertheless, 72 were eventually activated, about a third of which moved on schedule.

The RRFs would play a major role in supporting American forces and would be responsible for moving 28% of all cargo (see Table 18), while the small American mercantile marine moved 13% in turn forcing the Pentagon had to charter 210 foreign commercial vessels (to which some of the companies involved charged double the normal rate), that moved another 26.5% of the cargo.

semi-trailer Launching Stations.

Once deployed, one site required a crew of only three to operate: the Tactical Control Officer (TCO, usually a lieutenant), the Tactical Control Assistant (TCA), and a communication system specialist. Of course, serving the TELs required two additional crewmembers, and there was a reload crew, responsible for replacing spent canisters after missiles were launched.

If the track was determined as a hostile aircraft, and engagement command obtained, the TCO instructed the TCA to engage; the TCA pressed the 'engage' switch, sending a signal to the selected launcher, and fired a missile automatically selected by the system. The AN/MPQ-53 acquired the missile and fed it interception data while illuminating the target for the missile's semi-active radar seeker. The MIM-104A had an engagement range of 70km (43 miles), and a speed of more than Mach 2.

PAC-1 UPGRADE

In the mid-1980s, the Patriot Advanced Capability (PAC-1) software upgrade was added creating two modes of operation. In addition to the original, designed to target enemy aircraft, the operator could now switch the system to the 'tactical ballistic missile (TBM) search mode', which prompted the AN/MSQ-104 ECS to search nearly vertically upwards instead low to the horizon. Furthermore, the search beams were tightened and the frequency at which they were 'shot'

was increased significantly: while resulting in a shorter detection range, this made the ECS capable of detecting and engaging ballistic missiles.

Further development resulted in the emergence of the PAC-2 upgrade: this included optimized radar search algorithms and a modified TBM-search beam protocol, and also MIM-104C missiles optimised for high-speed ballistic missile engagements. The MIM-104C missile could reach speeds of up to Mach 4.1, and had an engagement range of 96km for aircraft or about 20km high for ballistic missiles. First tested in 1987, the PAC-2 entered service with US Army units just in time for deployment within Operation *Desert Shield*.

US ARMY PATRIOTS IN SAUDI ARABIA

The US Army unit that brought PAC-2s to Saudi Arabia was the 11th Air Defense Artillery Brigade. As of 12 September 1990, this had five batteries of the 2nd Battalion 7th Air Defense Artillery Regiment and the 3rd Battalion of the 43rd Air Defense Artillery Regiment with a total of 32 MIM-104C missiles in the country. This number eventually grew to a total of 16 batteries by mid-January 1991, 15 of which were operational.

As well as PAC-2s, by February 1991, the US Army deployed 22 older and shorter-ranged MIM-23 I-HAWK SAM-sites in Saudi Arabia.[13]

An M901 Launching Station (containing four SAMs) of the US Army in position outside Riyadh. (US DoD):

LOGISTICS MAZE

Of course, there was a requirement to unload all of this cargo. Saudi Arabia's seven ports could handle 10,000 tonnes a day in 1990, with ad-Dammam and al-Jubail acting as the prime shipping points for the Western forces. Air bases at Dhahran and Riyadh could operate up to 149 C-141-sized transports and 330 tonnes a day. At ad-Dammam two-thirds of the berths were assigned to support the coalition with 15 ships arriving each day: eventually, the port there unloaded a total of 28,000 containers, 114,000 wheeled

vehicles, 12,000 tracked vehicles, 1,500 helicopters and 360,000 tons of ammunition. Unsurprisingly, for most of the period September 1990 – February 1991, a road convoy was leaving this port every 15 minutes. Meanwhile, the French, Egyptians and Syrians used the Red Sea port of Yanbu.

The Saudi road system was excellent, with all major routes having at least two – and usually more – well maintained surfaced lanes. Consequently traffic both in convoy and individual vehicles could move rapidly and the fact that the oil industry needed to transport

One of Military Sealift Command's ro-ro ships unloading heavy vehicles of the US Army in the port of Jubail in December 1990. (US DoD)

heavy equipment to various sites meant there were many heavy equipment transporters (HET) as well as tractor-trailer cargo trucks to move the large US equipment, such as MBTs, including 333 HETs, 680 fuel and water tankers, and 12,150 trucks. Unfortunately, the flow of material and the limited logistics organization meant that although 17,540 vehicles, 450 aircraft and 1,521 containers had been unloaded by September, supplies were clogging up the ports because of an inadequate organisation to assign and move them.[17]

During the Second World War it was observed that the desert would be a 'tactician's paradise and a quartermaster's hell' which made logistics (supplies) vital to success. *Desert Shield* only confirmed such experiences; each US division had a daily requirement of 345,000 gallons of diesel fuel and 50,000 gallons of aviation fuel, while during the subsequent Operations *Desert Storm* and *Desert Sabre*, a single division required 2.4 million gallons of diesel – in turn needing 475 tanker trucks, each carrying 5,000 gallons. Yeosock had appointed the extremely capable logistics specialist Major General William G 'Gus' Pagonis on 7 August. He was another ROTC graduate of Pennsylvania State University and served as deputy chief of staff for logistics at Forces Command. He had impressed Yeosock during one of the earlier REFORGER (Return of Forces to Germany) exercises, a few years before.[18]

Pagonis would eventually be supported by a staff of 2,291 – which relied less on computers and much more on paper records than might be expected. Nevertheless, this proved surprisingly efficient, even if there were numerous problems including the fact that the Saudis would only deal with high-ranking officers and ignored the NCOs. The solution to this issue was quite simple: US Army NCOs of Pagonis' command wore officers' insignia during any negotiations. Much more problematic was the fact that many shipping containers included loads for several 'customers' or

were supported only by vague documentation, in turn forcing the Americans to check the loads of 28,000 containers by opening and personally inspecting every single one. The key Saudi figures in this logistics maze were Brigadier-Generals Abd al-Aziz al-Hussein (Western forces) and Salem al-Uwaymer (Arab forces). Khaled later concluded:

I had to create a staff to enable the insatiable American logisticians to work closely with my logisticians so as to tap the tremendous resources of the kingdom. The relationship worked smoothly, although not without some moments of tensions, which was hardly surprising considering the herculean efforts deployed and the vast sums of money disbursed.[19]

Starting from 6 September 1990, the Saudis helped to solve some of Pagonis' potential problems by agreeing to provide 15 million gallons of water and 86 tonnes of ice every day, together with 181,000 gallons of petrol, 120,000 gallons of diesel, 52,000 gallons of jet fuel, and 20 million meals. On top of that, the Saudis provided 500 HETs to the Egyptians and Syrians, and Riyadh supplied another 1,000 and 250 to the Americans and then the British, respectively. This was of particular importance of the US Army that, although it deployed nearly 75% of its truck-transporting companies to the theatre, they only had 112 such vehicles and were thus was still short on HETs for their bulk loads, while the Marines had a mere 34. However, it was fuel that was the key to the entire campaign. With the two US Army corps that eventually deployed in Saudi Arabia consuming about 4.5 million gallons a day, the Saudis were forced to not only increase their refinery output, but also to buy petrol, oil and lubricants (POL) worth US$700 million – and stock this at sea, as a contingency in the case their refineries were attacked. Furthermore they constructed a 240km pipeline from the as-Safaniya refinery to the brand new King Fahd AB north of Dhahran and a 645-kilometre pipeline to the bladder farm at al-Qaisuma. Finally, more than 2,500 commercial fuel tankers were deployed to carry fuel forward from the refineries to several bladder farms (POL terminals), each of which contained 200-300 bladders.[20]

WESTERN ALLIED FORCES

The US allies in Europe and the Pacific were quick to provide forces, despite some problems. Paris had become very close to Baghdad during the Iran-Iraq War and Saddam owed the French up to US$6 billion alone for military equipment and services. Unsurprisingly, while President Francois Mitterand supported an intervention with French involvement, his Minister of Defence, Jean-Pierre Chevènement was fiercely pro-Iraq: he shared the Iraqi view that the entire affair was engineered by Washington to rein-in Saddam by encouraging him to invade Kuwait and insisted on micro-managing the subsequent deployment, causing numerous issues with the Saudis. Deployed within the frame of Operation *Salamandre*, the French task force began arriving through the Red Sea port of Yanbu from 26 September (its movement originally required 42 ships). Initially, *Salamandre* included a helicopter regiment of the French Army Aviation (Aviation Légère de l'armée de Terre, ALAT) commanded by Lieutenant-General Michel Roquejeoffre, which arrived on 6 September. Eight days later, Paris announced the deployment of a 3,500-strong demi-brigade of the 6th Light Armoured Division (6e Division Légère Blindée, DLB), reinforced by a further helicopter regiment: this arrived on 19 September. Eventually, the French deployment grew into Operation *Daguet*, which saw the 6e DLB under Major-General Jean-Charles Mouscardès moving into the area south of Hafr al-Batin, between 14 and 17 October 1990.[21]

The British response was almost a kneejerk in the light of experiences from 1961, or during the Falklands War of 1982, but Prime Minister Margaret Thatcher was quick in ordering the RAF to Saudi Arabia, while Brigadier General Anthony Cordingley's 7th Armoured Brigade, the 'Desert Rats', brought with it 140 Challenger

1 MBTs and 24 artillery tubes to reinforce the 1st MEF between 16 October and 20 November 1990. Relations between the British, French and the Saudis were generally good.[22]

Canada, Italy and New Zealand dispatched air contingents, while Czechoslovakia sent a chemical-decontamination unit with 198 troops, which arrived on 11 December. All these contingents were operating under US command, together with about 1,500 medical personnel from Honduras, Hungary, the Philippines, Romania, Sierra Leone, Singapore, South Korea and Sweden.

ARAB AND OTHER ALLIED FORCES

Multiple Arab and allied nations followed the example (see Table 19), although most of their governments insisted that their forces operate only under Saudi command.[23] Correspondingly, the GCC Peninsula Shield Force was broken up, with the Omani and

An AMX-30 MBT and other vehicles of the 6e DLB in a camp south of Hafr al-Batin. (US DoD)

A Vickers Victor tanker of the RAF as seen at Jubail airport during Operation *Desert Shield*. (US DoD)

A pair of Tornado GR.Mk 1A fighter-bombers of the RAF seen during a training flight over Saudi Arabia, in the course of Operation *Desert Shield*. (US DoD)

Bahraini units ending being assigned to the 8th Saudi Mechanised Brigade, and the Emirati and Qatari units to the 10th Mechanised Brigade RSLF. The Kuwaiti 35th Brigade provided the cadre for the emerging Free Kuwaiti Army, staffed by escapees and recruits that formed its second mechanised infantry battalion, and equipped with Yugoslav-made M84s. The 15th Brigade was also reformed, and two new, battalion-sized units – Haq and Khulud – were activated, but they proved to have very limited capabilities.[24]

The Moroccans deployed their 6th Mechanised Battalion – much

of which consisted of special forces troops (which the Saudis rated highly) – in August – while Niger and Senegal followed with an infantry battalion each in October 1990. These three units all lacked equipment and were thus initially deployed in three strongpoints protecting key routes and oil installations (the Niger troops near Hafr al-Batin and the others north of Ras Mishab). Later on, the Saudis provided them with 200 redundant Panhard AML-90 armoured reconnaissance cars. Bangladesh provided the 1st East Bengal Regiment and an engineer battalion, while a force of Afghan

Table 19: Arab and Allied Forces deployed during Desert Shield/Desert Storm, 1990-1991			
Country	Arrived	Type	Total
Afghanistan	Unknown	Ground	308
Bahrain	-	Air and ground	223
Bangladesh	October	Ground	2,231
Egypt	August	Ground	33,677
Kuwait	-	Air and ground	9.643
Morocco	August	Ground	1,327
Niger	September	Ground	481
Pakistan	-	Ground	6,406
Oman	-	Air and ground	957
Qatar	-	Air and ground	1,581
Senegal	September	Ground	496
Syria	August	Ground	14,300
UAE	-	Air and ground	1,497
Source: Khaled pp.248-249, 253-258, 260, 420.			

Table 20: Total Arab and Allied Troop Deployments, August 1990 – January 1991[28]				
Country	26 Aug	21 Oct	12 Nov	21 Jan
Bahrain	100	100	100	100
Bangladesh	-	2,000	2,000	2,000
Egypt	5,000	14,000	29,000	33,600
Kuwait	7,000	7,000	7,000	7,000
Morocco	1,300	1,300	1,300	1,300
Niger	-	450	450	450
Oman	500	500	500	500
Pakistan	2,000	6,000	6,000	6,000
Qatar	500	500	500	500
Senegal	-	500	500	500
Syria	1,200	4,000	14,300	14,300
UAE	800	800	800	800
Total	18,400	37,150	62,450	67,050

Mujahideen also arrived to serve as military police.[25]

However, by far the biggest contingent of additional Arab troops arrived from Egypt. The 1st Ranger Regiment of the Egyptian Army had already arrived on 11 August, and this was followed by the 3rd Mechanised Division (including 200 M60A3 MBTs). When the Egyptians indicated their preparedness to do more, Riyadh agreed and this resulted in the arrival of the 4th Armoured Division with 560 M60A3 MBTs and 140 artillery pieces. The Egyptian troops were experienced, well-trained and disciplined troops, and many of their senior officers possessed combat experience from the October 1973 Arab-Israeli War. The Americans, who helped equip and train units like the 3rd Mechanised and 4th Armoured Divisions, and regularly exercised with them, had great hopes and were looking forward to working with them.

Politically important was the deployment of the Syrian Arab Army's (SyAA) contingent. On one hand, it reflected the concern of Iraq's neighbours about Saddam's invasion and annexation of Kuwait. Unsurprisingly, the SyAA was quick in deploying two of its divisions to the border with Iraq. Furthermore, President Hafez al-Assad of Syria was a long-time staunch enemy of Saddam and thus it did not take long for him to dispatch General Ali Aslan to Saudi Arabia, to see what assistance might be necessary. The 45th Commando Brigade SyAA followed just a few weeks later. However, Washington's staunch pro-Israeli stance made the Syrians wary of operating together with, or under, US command. Therefore, it took extra negotiations with Major-General Ali Habib – Commander of Syrian Forces in the Arabian Peninsula – to prevent any such possibility. The result was that when the 9th Armoured Division (commanded by Major-General Naidm Farris Abbas) with its 235 T-62M MBTs and 90 artillery tubes arrived in Saudi Arabia, later on, it was not subordinated to the XVIII Airborne Corps of the US Army as originally planned: instead, the Saudis found a solution by replacing it with the Egyptian 4th Armoured Division and moving the Syrians about 55km behind the front.[26]

The deployment of Egyptian and Syrian contingents proceeded anything but flawlessly: both expected the Saudis to provide all the necessary transport. However, with the Americans chartering every ship they could put their hands upon, it took time for Riyadh to find the necessary cargo space. Furthermore when the first echelon of the Egyptian 3rd Mechanised Division was finally embarked, its voyage over the Red Sea was promptly disrupted: not informed

Training of fresh volunteers of the Free Kuwait Army in the Saudi Desert, September 1990. Quickly overrun by the Iraqi armed forces, the small kingdom could do little but scratch only enough troops to establish two full brigades and two battalion-sized units. (Albert Grandolini Collection)

about a convoy departing Egyptian ports, the US Navy deployed combat aircraft to make low-level inspection passes – which the convoy commander interpreted as an attack, and promptly ordered all the ships to return.[27]

FLOW OF REINFORCEMENTS

As August turned into September, Operation *Desert Shield* continued through the arrival of ever larger contingents from the XVIII Airborne Corps, which still served as the major fighting formation. Major-General James H Johnson commanded the 82nd Airborne Division, Major-General J. H. Binford Peay the 101st Airborne Division, and Major-General Barry McCaffrey the 24th Infantry Division (Mechanised). Johnson's first troops marched to their aircraft under a North Carolina thunderstorm on the evening of 6 August, departing only 36 hours after being alerted. Still, it took a whole week for his first brigade to arrive, while his last was not completely ready in Saudi Arabia until 24 August, by when the 82nd Airborne was reinforced by an advance party of the 5th Special Forces Group (Airborne) of the 1st Special Forces Regiment. The deployment of McCaffrey's units was plagued by numerous factors – in addition to those related to transport. Originally, his unit was to include the 48th Infantry Brigade of the Georgia National Guard, but by the time this received its order for deployment,

M60A3 MBTs of the 4th Armoured Division of the Egyptian Army, as seen during an exercise in Saudi Arabia later in 1990. (US DoD):

Amphibious assault ship USS *Iwo Jima* (LHP-2), one of the helicopter carriers carrying the 4th MEB, seen underway in the Persian Gulf in November 1990. (US DoD)

which arrived between 6 and 14 September.

WAS THERE AN IRAQI PLAN FOR THE INVASION OF SAUDI ARABIA?

Ever since the Iraqi invasion of Kuwait, there has been a big question mark over the issue of possible Iraqi intentions to continue their advance into north-eastern Saudi Arabia. As described above, the Americans and the Saudi royal house were quickly convinced that the strongman in Baghdad had such ambitions. Correspondingly, they launched Operation *Desert Shield* in an attempt to either prevent an Iraqi invasion of Saudi Arabia, or bolster defences in the case the deterrent resulting from the deployment of US and allied troops failed.

Whilst there were plentiful assessments, very little evidence has been published supporting the thesis that Saddam actually planned such an attack. Theoretically, the situation should have changed after the official Iraqi documentation became available in 2003; however, whatever was left of the same showed that the emergence of the Coalition consisting of the USA, Saudi Arabia and numerous allies rather left Saddam Hussein facing a dilemma: if he bowed to the international pressure – even that from his closest aides – his self-perceived status as an Arab champion against Israel would be ruined; even his grip upon power might be in jeopardy. Thus, the strongman in

the politicians had decided not to mobilise the National Guard. Instead, McCaffrey was assigned the brigade-sized 3rd Armoured Cavalry Regiment – troops of which arrived in September, but, due to delays, heavy equipment only on 17 October 1990. A similar problem was subsequently encountered by the 1st Cavalry Division, whose 'round-out' formation, the 155th Armoured Brigade of the Mississippi National Guard had to be replaced by the 1st 'Tiger' Brigade from the 2nd Armoured Division.[29] Ground troops were further reinforced by the deployment of the 12th Aviation Brigade from the V Corps of the US Army, which arrived on 2 October 1990.

From 14 August, the 1st MEB was reinforced by the first elements of the 7th Marine Expeditionary Brigade (commanded by Major-General John I Hopkins), and finally completed its deployment to Saudi Arabia on 12 September, by when it was reinforced by the 1st Marine Expeditionary Force and the 3rd Marine Air Wing (MAW). However, on 12 September both brigades were put under the control of the 1st Marine Division commanded by Major-General James M Myatt.[30] In preparation for a possible amphibious landing in Kuwait, the USMC created an amphibious force, the 4th MEB,

Baghdad was neither willing to take greater risks, nor to withdraw. Indeed, he ignored his entourage's proposals to press into Saudi Arabia immediately after Kuwait was overrun – at least because the deployed divisions of the RGFC lacked logistic and support forces, if not because originally he never planned such an action.[31] According to Israeli sources, on or around 11 August, Saddam would then have changed his mind and ordered Rawi to prepare the plan for Operation *Spirit of Victory* (*Rooh an-Nasr*), the aim of which would have been a seizure of oilfields in north-eastern Saudi Arabia. Accordingly, a committee of representatives from the Directorates for Planning, Operations, Intelligence, the Chemical Corps, and the IrAF would have been set up to run related preparations. According to this version of events, the General Headquarters (GHQ) in Baghdad went as far as to approve the resulting plan – supposedly including the use of chemical and even biological weapons – at an unknown date.[32]

Certainly enough, on 16 August, Saddam issued an order for the mobilisation of 35 divisions, 'to demonstrate national resolve', and then a switch of the II Corps of the Iraqi Army, deployed on the border with Iran, to Kuwait. However, and while Iraq is known to

A view of the forward deck of the amphibious assault ship USS Nassau (LHA-4), showing a densely packed row of Boeing-Vertol CH-46 Sea Knight, UH-1 Huey, and AH-1W Sea Cobra helicopters of the US Marine Corps, and a single AV-8B in the process of taking off. (US DoD)

have had 1,232 bombs and 13,000 artillery shells filled with mustard gas, and 8,320 122mm rockets filled with nerve agents as of August 1990, Iraqi documentation indicates that Saddam was ready to use them *only* if there was a *direct threat to his government*.[33]

Unsurprisingly, informed about Iraqi re-deployments, Horner concluded that the Iraqis adopted a, 'clearly defensive posture' between 12 and 14 August. Even though warning that the continued Iraqi defence activity on the border to Saudi Arabia left them with an option 'to defend or attack with little or no warning', the next day he noted that the Guards were being replaced by less well-equipped infantry divisions, and on 22 August he reduced the prospect of a surprise attack, even though there were still elements of three 'heavy' divisions on the border. While generally considered as 'optimistic' by those surrounding him, Schwarzkopf did not share Horner's conclusions: on 23 August 1990, he was alarmed about reports indicating the appearance of tanks containing decontamination materials near two Iraqi artillery battalions, and feared this might indicate preparations for an (offensive) deployment of chemical weapons. His point of view remained unchanged as of 1 September: while confirming the Iraqis were digging in, he claimed they could (still) launch an attack within just 18 hours. Two days later, he admitted the absence of artillery and logistical preparations, and that the available assets could support little more than a short raid. Indeed, the further expansion of the Iraqi forces in the KTO continued to cause him worries: on 11 September, Schwarzkopf noted that with 16-17 divisions in the country, the enemy was still capable of launching an offensive within 12 to 24 hours. Even the reports about the withdrawal of the RGFC from Kuwait, on 14 September, only slowly increased the confidence of CENTCOM's commander: one week later, although agreeing that this was the least likely course of action, he still insisted that the 18 Iraqi divisions deployed in the KTO could launch an offensive within 36-48 hours.[34]

On the contrary, as far as is known about the planning of the RGFC, this only included a series of what could be described as 'spoiling attacks' towards al-Khafji and Ras al-Mishab – some of these probably related to the GMID's report from 29 August, that contained the warning about the US policy of 're-alienating Iraq from Kuwait' and that if the USA failed to achieve this with an economic embargo, they would certainly 'expand into military aggression'. While the same report also contained a weak recommendation that Iraq, 'uses its forces accordingly', once again, Saddam did not order any kind of an invasion of Saudi Arabia.[35]

Finally, even if there was any kind of serious planning for offensive operations, this was all but abandoned when Saddam ordered the Guards to withdraw from Kuwait, on 7 September 1990. The reason for this withdrawal was that instead of continuing to pursue

A CH-46 Sea Knight helicopter (left, foreground) and AH-1W Sea Cobras as seen after their disembarkation to a forward operating base in Saudi Arabia. (US DoD)

T-55 or Type-69 MBTs of the Iraqi Army in position in the Kuwaiti desert in late August 1990. (Albert Grandolini Collection)

designs for an invasion of Saudi Arabia, the GHQ was meanwhile ordered to develop a defence-in-depth plan, in which the RGFC was returned to its old duty: that of serving as an operational-level-reserve shielding Basra and ready to counter-attack. Unsurprisingly, the same day the US intelligence services had reported the creation of a defensive belt running from the northern shore of Kuwait Bay around to the north-western corner of the country, backed up by a counterattack force of five RGFC divisions.[36] According to this plan – entirely based upon experience of fighting Iran, and thus a gross underestimate of the Coalition's eventual strength and capabilities – the only offensive operation was a possible counterattack towards al-Mishab. Moreover, the same plan prompted an expansion of the RGFC through the establishment of four major units – including the an-Nidaa Armoured Division, and al-Qods, al-Abed and al-Mustafa Infantry Divisions – of which one was to be deployed in the north, and the others in the south.[37]

Indeed, 'instead' of sending the RGFC into Saudi Arabia, the Ministry of Defence and the GHQ quickly mobilised conscripts born in 1961-1966, followed by those born 1953-1960, and then even those born 1972-1973 (the youngest recruits ever in the Iraqi Army) to fill-out 15 divisions held at cadre status, and re-establish 14 divisions.[38] The majority of these troops were rushed into the KTO, where two corps-level operational HQs came into being, codenamed Jihad and Gulf. As the Iraqi engineers frantically fortified not only the border with Saudi Arabia but the entire territory, a mass of material that was to act as decoys was also rushed to Kuwait – including 500 decommissioned or destroyed tank-wrecks, some 200 damaged or captured AFVs, and 211 obsolete guns, which were dispersed among existing equipment, or replaced the equipment that was moved.[39]

Finally, by the end of October, the Coalition's intelligence noted the construction of oil-filled trenches in Kuwait – result of Project Tariq: at Saddam's suggestion, these were to be set on fire so to obscure targets in both the visible and thermal imaging ranges of aircraft and missiles. The dot on the I was provided through the deployment into the KTO of the entire 225th and 226th Missile Brigades, and through the re-deployment of several units of the Iraqi Navy equipped with Chinese-made Hai Ying HY-2 anti-ship missiles (ASCC/NATO-codename CSSC-2 Silkworm) to the area around the Kuwaiti port of al-Qulayah and on the Faw Peninsula in southern Iraq.[40]

KHARZRAJI'S DISMISSAL

Ultimately, it appears that the available evidence for a possible Iraqi invasion of Saudi Arabia as of August 1990 is meagre at best. Indeed, considering the standpoints of commanders that survived the following 14 years, it is rather unlikely that such an operation was seriously considered. It is a matter of fact that the professional Iraqi officers viewed the prospects of a clash with the US-led coalition with alarm. On 28 August, Chief-of-Staff of the Army, Khazraji, and the Head of the Military Industries Authority, Lieutenant-General Amer Muhammad Rashid, presented reports backed by the RGFC's commander and by chief of the DMI, Hussein Kamel, that warned of an inevitable war and that this would be lost alone due to superior Western technology. On 18 September, Saddam convened a meeting at the GHQ, during which Khazraji outlined his case and added that the Iraqi military was exhausted after the war with Iran. The strongman angrily interrupted him, dismissed his concerns about a war with the West and ended the meeting. Two days later, Khazraji was dismissed and replaced by his Chief of Operations, Lieutenant-General Hussein Rashid Muhammad – who in turn was replaced by Lieutenant-General Sultan Hashim Ahmad (former Chief of Logistics). Immediately afterwards, a committee under the new director of the DMI (and former officer of the IrAF), General Muhammad Rashid – and including Rashid's new Chief of Operations, General Hashim Ahmad, and the Chiefs of Operations of the IrAF and the GMID – was established with the task of examining strategic threats. The airmen, a delegation of which hasd meanwhile toured Libya with the aim of learning about local experiences from US strikes on Tripoli and Benghazi in 1986, promptly expressed concerns that the Coalition's air power would quickly wreck the Kari IADS. The rest of the committee 'noted with concern' the large concentration of Iraqi armour in southern Kuwait, where this was vulnerable to encirclement, and recommended some of this to be transferred north. Finally, the committee produced plans for revenge attacks against Israel and air support for the forces deployed in the KTO.[41]

FROM DEFENSIVE INTO OFFENSIVE POSTURE

The initial requirement for the US and Coalition forces arriving in the Middle East was to protect Saudi Arabia's Eastern Province and its vital oilfields (containing 20% of the World's oil reserves), the Saudi capital of Riyadh, and thus also Bahrain's and Qatar's oil and gas fields. Correspondingly, the Saudis and their allies deployed along the frontier do a depth of 75 kilometres.

The most obvious route for an Iraqi offensive was down the coastal highway through al-Khafji and al-Jubail to Dhahran. The second was along the Wadi Hafr al-Batin down the Tapline Road: together with the coastal highway, the latter forming an area the Americans called the 'Triangle', with an-Nuayriyah and Manifah Bay in the north, and Abu Hadriyah in the south. This is why, upon its arrival in Saudi Arabia, the 2nd Brigade of the 82nd Airborne Division first created a defensive perimeter around Dhahran AB. In that area, the road was bounded by *sabkhas* – passable for infantry and light vehicles, but not for MBTs and large trucks. Its defensive plan, Operation *Dragon I*, envisaged engaging the incoming enemy armour with air power, then attack helicopters, artillery, and anti-tank missiles. As additional troops and equipment arrived, the scale of this plan was expanded into *Desert Dragon II*, on 12 August, and then *Desert Dragon III*, on 3 September. This was further refined and war-gamed by the CENTCOM staff on 4 October, by when even Schwarzkopf admitted, he was now planning for an offensive. Indeed, during a war-game testing the final draft of *Desert Dragon III*, on 14 November, he presented the first outline of an offensive plan designated 'Combined OPLAN for the Defence of Saudi Arabia'.[42]

Meanwhile, with most of its forces in position, the Saudi Eastern Area Command (commander Major-General Saleh Bin Ali al-Mohayya) soon had a total of 267 MBTs and 140 artillery pieces.[43] Of course, this was not enough to resist a serious Iraqi incursion and could act as little more than a trip wire. Correspondingly, during the conference in Washington on 20 August 1990, the JCS and Schwarzkopf estimated that by 25 September CENTCOM would only be capable of defending eastern Saudi Arabia with a high degree of confidence, while remaining unable of switching to the offensive before 5 December.[44] Indeed, even Powell initially encouraged Schwarzkopf only to plan defensive operations, claiming the President was reluctant to support an offensive to regain Kuwait: CENTCOM also worked on a scenario that even once all of the III Corps of the Iraqi Army had deployed into the KTO, an Iraqi offensive might still punch through all the way to Riyadh, with the RGFC acting as a follow-on force and reserve. Moreover, Schwarzkopf was happy to claim in public that he was only planning defensive measures, and thus avoided giving the Iraqis an excuse for a possible pre-emptive strike.[45]

Ultimately, the XVIII Airborne Corps' 763 MBTs and 1,494 AFVs, 444 artillery pieces, 81 MLRS', 227 attack helicopters and 368 ATGM-equipped vehicles were in Saudi Arabia by 5 November, and deployed right behind the JFC East and North. The 3rd Cavalry was screening the West, the 24th Division held the centre; while the

1 MEF – reinforced by the British 7th Armoured Brigade – held a 25-kilometre wide arc on the coastal plain around al-Jubail, about 75 kilometres behind the forward line. Behind them were the 1st Cavalry Division and the 82nd Airborne. The plan for the case of an Iraqi attack was a general withdrawal combined with erosion of the Iraqi strength through air- and ground weaponry, until the enemy reached the positions of the 24th Division, in front of which the main killing zone was established. So far, what the Americans and their allies were doing strongly resembled the Iraqi tactics from the war with Iran. As so often when it comes to US military, tensions began to develop between the US Army and the USMC, primarily related to the lack of armour. The latter had only 123 old M60s, and an entirely different defensive philosophy (based upon mines and demolitions aimed to force the enemy off the road and into killing grounds for air power and naval gunfire), while the Army's fall-back plan for a withdrawal down the Tapline Road was threatening to expose the western flank of the Marines. To prevent this from happening, Luck re-deployed the 3rd Cavalry to act as a major barrier against an armoured thrust.

INTELLIGENCE GATHERING

In addition to receiving satellite imagery, CENTCOM also benefitted from a wide variety of platforms to probe behind the enemy lines.[46] The first USAF aircraft used were SAC's Boeing RC-135 Rivet Joint, which began Burning Wind SIGINT missions on 9 August and within two days were providing 24-hour coverage. On 29 August SAC's Lockheed U-2 very high altitude photo-reconnaissance aircraft and Lockheed TR-1 tactical reconnaissance with side-looking radar began operations as imagery was clearly vital, and on 8 September the first medium-altitude photographic reconnaissance missions were flown by McDonnell-Douglas RF-4Cs. By 2 December Horner's reconnaissance arm had flown 469 tactical, 421 strategic and 2,800 ELINT sorties, while AWACS – which both supported the shield and monitored IrAF activity – had flown 253 sorties. One reconnaissance system which was late to the table was the Joint Surveillance Target Acquisition System (J-STARS) – an airborne battlefield surveillance radar system with a range of 150 kilometres, installed into a modified Boeing 707, re-designated as the E-8A. Schwarzkopf requested its deployment as early as of 10 August but in early September the Joint Chiefs rejected the request arguing, '*Desert Shield* is not suitable in time or place for introduction of J-STARS'. Only at the last minute did the Pentagon change its mind: the two available aircraft arrived on 12 January 1991, together with six ground stations and four support vehicles that provided 44 remote terminals.[47]

Conventional reconnaissance aircraft seem to have been not the only ones deployed by the US-led Coalition to monitor developments inside Iraq and Kuwait. Late during the evening of 16 December 1990, the crew of an Iraqi Airways Boeing 747 led by Captain Remzi (former fighter pilot with a long career of flying Sukhoi Su-7BMKs and Su-20s during the war with Iran) reported sighting an F-117A fighter close to the left wingtip of their aircraft – and that while underway over Najaf. As far as is known, this was the first-ever encounter between an Iraqi pilot and the shadowy stealth fighter of the US Air Force: it remains unknown to this day what exactly the latter was doing only 200 kilometres southwest of Baghdad at that point in time.[48]

ISSUES WITH THE INTELLIGENCE

By October 1990, the principal issue for both sides became one of determining the other side's capabilities and intentions. Ironically,

M1A1 MBTs of A Company, 3rd Battalion, 32nd Armoured Regiment of the 1st Cavalry Division, lining up prior to a live-firing exercise in Saudi Arabia. (US DoD)

An M1A1 of the 3rd Cavalry navigating the desert of north-eastern Saudi Arabia in November 1990. At the time, the unit was serving as a major barrier against a possible Iraqi armoured thrust. Deployed in a great rush, many of its vehicles retained their European-style camouflage colours. (US DoD)

both were largely dependent upon electronic means of intelligence-gathering (COMINT, SIGINT and ELINT), and upon imagery from manned and unmanned aircraft and satellites. As much as the latter quickly filled target folders for major Iraqi defence lines in the KTO, air bases and even most of the strategic facilities inside Iraq, and enabled the Army Intelligence and Threat Analysis Center (ITAC) to create daily-updated maps (showing the location of every Iraqi division down to every single vehicle, gun pit and command post), it could not provide many missing crucial details. Even so, the key factor was not actually the acquisition, but the assessment and distribution of intelligence.[50]

COMINT proved a valuable source of intelligence, but the US military in general was suffering a dreadful shortage of Arabic speakers. Moreover, following the discovery of an Israeli tap on the land line connecting the H-3 complex of air bases in western Iraq with Baghdad, Saddam banned the use of either wireless or land-line telephones, while radio communications were subjected to tight communications security. Indeed, to ensure security, Saddam demanded written or even verbal messages to be delivered by liaison officers, despite the immense problems this caused – for example to units that had to stand still as a grave in well-camouflaged positions when satellites were expected to pass overhead.[51]

The result was that the Coalition could mark the flow of formations into the KTO, but not assess their actual strength.

it was in this regard that the Coalition failed again, as observed by Khaled:

> The areas of uncertainty were vast. Above all, uncertainty about Saddam's intentions remained a persistent source of anxiety throughout this period…I suspect…that in most cases the U.S. was as much in the dark as we were… (and thus) …. There was a paradox: the Coalition was at one and the same time, all-seeing and yet extraordinarily ignorant.[49]

Indeed, neither the Americans nor the Saudis had any significant human intelligence (HUMINT, i.e. 'spies') presence in Iraq and

In reaction, it assumed the 'worst case scenario' – which in turn resulted in the size of the Iraqi ground forces being massively exaggerated. For example, by late February 1991, CENTCOM estimated that the Iraqi Army had 43 divisions in the KTO with 42 'heavy' (armoured or mechanised) and 83 'light' brigades, while the actual strength included 52 divisions with 43 'heavy' and 131 'light' brigades – most of which were well under their nominal strength: while US intelligence assessed the Iraqis having 540,000 troops, actually there were between 360,000 and 422,000. Furthermore, the Coalition entirely failed to detect five corps-sized commands deployed in south-western Iraq.[52]

On the other side, Iraqi intelligence proved at least as inadequate

Although requested by Schwarzkopf early during the Operation *Desert Shield*, Boeing E-8A J-STARS were a later-comer in the theatre: ultimately, although still available in prototype form only, the type was to prove its value beyond any expectations. (US DoD)

From 9 August 1990, SAC's RC-135 Rivet Joint COMINT/SIGINT/ELING-gathering aircraft ran Operation Burning Wind, in the course of which they began snooping on all sorts of electronic emissions from the Iraqi armed forces, thus significantly increasing the situational awareness of the US and allies. (US DoD)

According to unofficial Iraqi reports, USAF F-117A Nighthawk fighter-bombers seem to have flown reconnaissance sorties deep within Iraqi airspace at least as of December 1990. For sure, the same also served the purpose of testing IrAF's air defences. This F-117A is seen in similar position to the one reported by Captain Remzi: his sighting startled the commanders of the IrAF, forcing them into the conclusion that they lacked the means to effectively combat the most advanced US combat aircraft. (US DoD)

tactical intentions. However, they lacked the ability to intercept high-level decisions passed via troposcatters and microwave systems, or those emitted in the upper ultra-high (UHF) and super high frequency (SHF) ranges – and thus proved unable to determine longer-term enemy intentions. Nevertheless, COMINT proved to be the key source that helped the Iraqis monitor the Coalition's build-up, even though if it repeatedly proved vulnerable to deception.[55]

Finally, the Iraqis deployed their two equivalents to the British Special Air Service (SAS) – Units 888 and 999 – to run deep reconnaissance in Saudi territory: the former was responsible for intelligence gathering and the latter for long-range observation. Combined, by November these sources provided them with a reasonably accurate picture of the Coalition's order of battle, even though not its deployment.[56]

as that of the Coalition. The GMID was over-reliant on the information provided by the PLO, whose sources might have been polite and ephemeral, but unreliable, too. For example, on 9 August, they reported that the Americans and the Israelis were about to attack missile facilities around Baghdad. That said, and just like the Iraqis themselves, the PLO correctly forecasted an aerial bombing campaign that would concentrate upon the SSMD's sites, even though it expected an Israeli participation in the same. Moreover, the Palestinians claimed that the Israeli air and ground forces had been deployed to Saudi Arabia, and that Israel was preparing a nuclear strike upon Iraq.[53]

Much of the remaining Iraqi 'intelligence' was collected from the Western media, which the Iraqis almost picked like beggars on a dump: indeed, after the war, some of them concluded that this was their most accurate source of information at both the operational and strategic levels, and that their actual problem was to work themselves through the sheer bulk of information in order to sort the wheat from the chaff. For example, in November 1990, the GMID was said to report that while Washington was serious about attacking Iraq, '…we have not received any evidence that enables us to identify the right timing for that attack.' In another case, on 23 August, it warned that the Army should focus its defences along the main roads, which the enemy would have to use due to the harshness of the desert and moving sand. Overall, reporting from even such top Iraqi services was as vague as a gypsy's warning.[54]

As already during the war with Iran, the work of the Iraqi COMINT and SIGINT intelligence units proved far more useful. The majority of these were concentrated within the Technical Equipment Directorate of the Logistics and Organisational Branch of the Armed Forces GHQ controlled by the Army, even if several units were directly linked to the IrAF's ADOC. During the war with Iran, they demonstrated the capability to use these effectively to identify Iranian ground forces, track deployments, and determine

Table 21: Known Iraqi Electronic Warfare Units, 1990-1991[57]

Unit	Base
4th Warning and Control Regiment	Balad
22nd Warning and Control Regiment	Kirkuk
23rd Warning and Control Regiment	Amarah
32nd Warning and Control Regiment	Mosul
Unit 113	Basra
Unit 114 (COMINT)	Baghdad
Unit 115	Amarah
Unit 116	unknown
Unit 117	Kirkuk
Unit 118	unknown
Unit 120	unknown
Unit 128 (communication jamming)	Rashid AB (Baghdad)
Unit 600	Basra
Unit 620	unknown
Unit 621	unknown
Unit 622	Amarah
Unit 623	unknown
Unit 624	Dohuk-Erbil

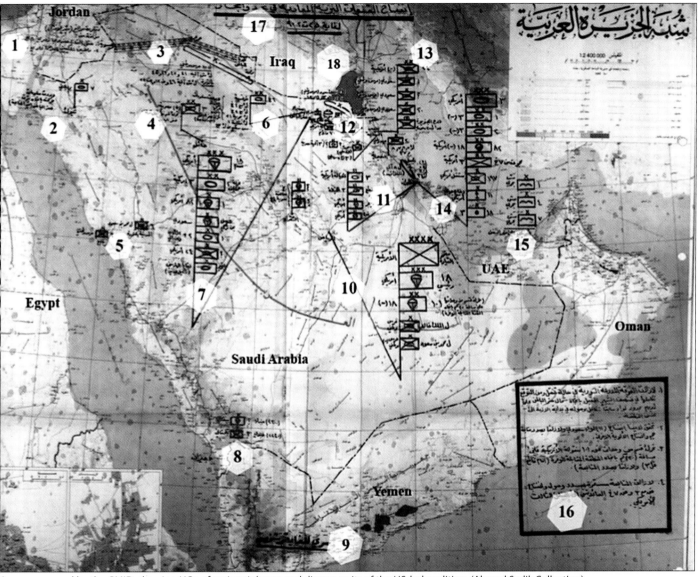

A map prepared by the GMID, showing HQs of major air bases and diverse units of the US-led coalition. (Ahmad Sadik Collection)

LACK OF MAPS

Both sides were plagued by a shortage of accurate maps of the terrain – especially the western desert in Iraq. General Luck is known to have had to rely upon reports by special forces and videotapes taken by his Apache helicopter gunships. The Iraqi Directorate of Military Surveying had 'spent' all of its 16 obsolete 1:250,000 scale maps of Saudi Arabia during the preparations for the invasion of Kuwait, and subsequently lacked sample maps and aerial photographs of the country, and also the ability to produce new ones in 1:50,000 or at last 1:100,000 scale. The GMID did attempt to acquire SPOT images in October 1990, but this time Paris dragged its feet, forcing Baghdad to modify large-scale tourist maps. The paucity of tactical intelligence was a problem for both sides, and while it might be blamed on ignorance on the Iraqi and Saudi side, on the Coalition's side it was hindered by the absence of XVIII Airborne Corps' aerial collection battalion. This was committed to counter-drug-smuggling operations in Latin America and replaced only in mid-October. Similarly, the Joint Imagery Processing Centre – capable of producing annotated images – arrived only in December. Moreover, corps intelligence battalions all failed to develop and distribute information to divisional level and below, while the Defense Intelligence Agency – the JCS' crucial intelligence arm – was neither equipped nor organised to meet such needs. Finally,

although the HQ of the XVIII Corps was equipped to download satellite images, that of the VII Corps was not: this is why it proved of advantage to conduct tests of the J-STARS during Operation *Desert Shield*, after all. The arrival of the two E-8A prototypes was followed by a similar French development: an SA.330 Puma helicopter equipped as Investigative Helicopter-carried Coherent Radar Observatory (Observatoire Radar Coherent Heliporte d'Investigation, Orchidée).[58] Left without such aids, the USMC and the VII Corps made use of platoon of five AAI RQ-2 Pioneer unmanned aerial vehicles (UAVs) that arrived only on 26 January 1991, and flew their first sortie over the KTO on 1 February.[59]

INTEGRATED EXERCISES

Training was vital to strengthening aircrew skills not only for combat but also for combat-support units, and in improving co-ordination between allied air forces. The first joint exercise was Operation *Arabian Gulf*, launched on 10 August. On 6 September, a small-scale electronic combat exercises began, followed two days later by integrated-package training. The integrated strike package would be the means of prosecuting the air war against Iraq in 1991: its essence was a combination of strike fighters and support aircraft. Initially, training involved only single services in ever-growing packages: gradually, this was developed to the multi-service and then multi-

A view of at least 10 KC-135 tankers of the US Air Force at a base in Saudi Arabia. The entire Operation *Desert Shield*, as well as the subsequent war against Iraq, would be essentially impossible without the availability of the huge fleet of tanker-aircraft operated by the SAC as of 1990. (US DoD)

President Bush, with General Schwarzkopf, during a visit to US troops deployed to Saudi Arabia. (US DoD/National Archives)

control. It involved more than 300 simulated combat and 200 other sorties in support of 18 air packages involving some 40 coalition air units.

From the end of October, training exercises were used to deceive the IrAF with aircraft approaching close to the border then turning back at the last minute both to test enemy reactions and to get them used to seeing approaching formations.[60] By mid-November the airmen were planning exercises to simulate the ATOs for D-Day plus 1 with '*Imminent Thunder*' involving 1,000 coalition aircraft flying 4,000 sorties. The Tactical Air Control Centre (TACC) was re-organised on 17 December, as preparations for an offensive continued, including changing aircraft call signs. From 12 January, the airmen began the transition to operational flying with aircraft being armed, as sorties dropped by 60%, while on the eve of the air offensive USAF serviceability had reached 94%.

President Bush's November decision to reinforce the theatre led Cheney, on 16 November, to order the despatch of 283 aircraft,

national level, with Saudi aircraft joining a USAF package on 18 September, so that by early October multi-national packages of up to 50 aircraft were the norm. On 24 October a three-day exercise, *Initial Hack*, began, simulating the 'first day' air tasking order. This included pre- and post-strike in-flight refuelling, simulated attacks on air bases, air defence, close air support and command and

Table 22: Ground Forces under US Control[67]

Country	26 Aug	18 Sept	21 Oct	12 Nov	21 Jan
US	40,000	140,000	20,000	210,000	450,000
UK	-	6,000	6,000	11,000	35,000
France	-	3,500	3,500	8,500	9,500

Table 23: Total US Manpower in the Gulf Region, 1990-1991[68]

Date	Total	Army
1 September 1990	95,965	31,337
7 November 1990	266,096	124,704
15 January 1991	422,041	245,290
22 February 1991	533,608	296,965

Table 24: Arrival Dates of US and Allied Divisions, 1990-1991[69]

Formation	Arrival Date	Completed
VII US Corps		13 January 1991
XVIII US Airborne Corps	9 August 1990	1 September 1990
1st US Armored Division	11 January 1991	21 January 1991
1st US Infantry Division	6 January 1991	26 January 1991
1st US Cavalry Division	11 September 1990	23 October 1990
1st US Marine Division	6 September 1990	Activated
1st British Armoured Division	5 December 1990	9 January 1991
2nd US Marine Division	14 December 1990	17 January 1991
3rd US Armored Division	15 January 1991	6 February 1991
24th US Mechanised Division	16 August 1990	24 September 1990
82nd US Airborne Division	9 August 1990	8 September 1990
101st US Airborne Division	28 August 1990	9 October 1990
3rd Egyptian Mechanised Division	21 September 1990	6 October 1990
4th Egyptian Armoured Division	19 December 1990	11 January 1991
9th Syrian Armoured Division	1 November 1990	31 December 1990

Table 25: Coalition Ground Equipment Build-up, 1990-1991[70]

Service	Equipment	1 Sep	1 Oct	1 Nov	1 Dec	1 Jan
US Army	MBT	118	241	712	712	838
	IFV/APC	140	586	1,378	1,361	1,484
	Artillery	65	248	420	446	516
	MLRS	13	37	63	63	90
US Marines	MBT	42	140	145	145	225
	IFV/APC	92	301	300	320	492
	Artillery	28	106	106	98	160
British	MBT	-	-	140	140	117
	IFV/APC	-	-	72	75	75
	Artillery	-	-	24	24	24

many from NATO bases. The Phase II air deployment began with the arrival on 29 November of F-111F at Taif AB, Saudi Arabia and by the beginning of 1991 Horner had almost all of the USAF's precision attack aircraft, most of the Nighthawks and 75% of Wild Weasels.[61] To ease command of both tactical fighter and combat support aircraft, including AWACS and reconnaissance aircraft, Horner formed the 14th and 15th Air Divisions (Provisional), the former under Glosson and the latter under Brigadier General Glenn A. Profitt.

TURKEY AND IRAN

Like the Syrians, Turkey deployed 50,000 of its troops along the border to Iraq in August 1990, and then doubled that figure to more than 100,000 a month later. While the bulk of Coalition air

An SA.342 Gazelle helicopter of the ALAT, as seen during an exercise in the Saudi Desert during Operation *Desert Shield*. (US DoD)

The planning for an offensive operation against Iraq required the re-deployment of additional assets of the US armed forces to the territory of operations. Correspondingly, in November 1990, three CVBGs of the US Navy were ordered in the direction of the Middle East. Amongst these was the was one centred upon the aircraft carrier USS *Ranger* (CV-61), seen here during an underway replenishment operation, in company of a supply ship and the Dutch Navy frigate *Jacob Van Heemserck* (F-812). (US DoD)

of an advance *Proven Force* party to Incirlik AB and later an increase in USAF strength to 157 combat and combat support aircraft.[62]

In addition there were 1,200 Coalition combat aircraft on the Arabian Peninsula and 320 either in the surrounding waters or foreign bases as the 'cold' war prepared to go 'hot' in the Arabian Peninsula. Another 80 USAF combat/combat support aircraft would arrive by 1 February. In the New Year of 1990/1991 the Coalition gradually built up the number of combat and support sorties close to the whole Iraqi border. The final preparations were completed and H-Hour was selected as 0300 on 17 January 1991 because it was assessed that that would be the time when the Iraqi defences were at their weakest.

On the contrary, Tehran openly condemned the Iraqi invasion of Kuwait. However, while putting its military on alert it only deployed smaller contingents to the border and then declared its neutrality – prompting a rather astonishing U-turn by Saddam: on 3 August, he wrote a letter to Iran's leaders, proposing a 'quick peace' and abandoning all of his objectives of the earlier war. Sensing the desperation of the strongman in Baghdad, Tehran remained non-committal even when Saddam, on 15 August, pledged he would return almost all the land seized in the Iran-Iraq War, and followed this announcement with action.

and troop activity took place around the Arabian Peninsula, Turkey remained concerned about the implications of the Kuwaiti invasion and NATO aircraft strengthened Ankara's air defences, before staging Exercise *Display Determination 90* in September. As early as 4 September General Robert C. Oaks, commander of the US Air Force in Europe, proposed a second air front from Turkey and by 12 October he had begun detailed planning aided by Ankara's agreement, in mid-October, to retain some aircraft deployed for Exercise *Display Determination 90* at Incirlik AB. On 20 December, Turkey officially requested NATO to reinforce the Turkish Air Force, and three days later General John Galvin, US Commander in Europe, established Joint Task Force *Proven Force* as a Turkey-based aerial deterrent under Oaks' Operations Chief, Major General James L. Jamerson. On 7 January 1991, Ankara approved the deployment

Three days later, Iraqi forces withdrew from the last parts of Iran that they had captured and held at such a terrible cost during eight years of war. Encouraged, the Iranians opened negotiations and on 10 September the two countries announced plans to resume diplomatic relations just four days later. Finally, on 24 September 1990, Tehran pledged to abide by UN sanctions imposed upon Iraq, only to permit the smuggling of some 150 tonnes of food and medicine to Baghdad.[63]

DESERT SHIELD II

The data acquired and provided by the two E-8As, the sole Orchidée, and the RQ-2s proved essential for planning the more CENTCOM began to consider an offensive operation. Indeed, it became a crucial issue once President Bush ordered a major reinforcement of the deployed troops in order to enable the recovery of Kuwait with a minimum loss. Correspondingly, on 8 November 1990, Operation *Desert Shield II* was initiated, with the aim of bringing 150,000 additional soldiers, marines, airmen and sailors of the US armed forces to the Arabian Peninsula, and thus enable a two-corps offensive. The majority of US Army troops came from the German-based VII Corps, and whilst first element of this corps to reach Saudi Arabia was the 2nd Armoured Cavalry Regiment on 22 December 1990 the bulk reached Saudi Arabia only during mid-January 1991. Moreover, this decision emboldened the British to send not only another armoured brigade, but also the HQ of an armoured division. Finally, France decided to send another 6,000 troops, including a regiment of 44 AMX-30B2 MBTs. This required 25 ships to haul about 75,000 tonnes of equipment and supplies, combined with troops already in Saudi Arabia, it bolstered the strength of the 6e DLB to a total of 9,500 troops, supported by 60 Gazelle attack helicopters, 72 Puma transport helicopters, and 18 artillery pieces.[64]

This renewed build-up of ground forces resulted in an increase from 160 MBTs and 106 artillery tubes and MLRS that CENTCOM had in Saudi Arabia as of early September 1990, to 997 MBTs and 613 artillery pieces and MLRS by early November alone. Overall, the total US manpower in Saudi Arabia grew from 104,304 on 3 September 1990 (alternative figures are provided in Table 23), to 200,079 (including 32,333 from the USAF) on 10 October; 235,215 (including 30,981 from the USAF) on 15 November; and 271,127 (including 34,163 from the USAF) on 15 December.[65]

During the same time, the US military alone transferred 1,800 aircraft, 12,435 tracked and 117,157 wheeled vehicles, 41,000 containers, 1,633,000 tonnes of cargo, 317,500 tonnes of ammunition, and 350,000 personnel to Saudi Arabia. Within the theatre, 3,568 truck convoys covered 56.3 million kilometres. This effort was supported by two battalions of the Egyptian Army (total of 1,000 troops), who ran forward supply points at an-Nuayriya and al-Qaisuma, and proved highly skilled in handling munitions and fuel, while two Bangladeshi supply companies operated from Damman.[66]

COMMAND AND CONTROL

As the Coalition forces continued to grow, organising the command and control of the force became the next issue – and then one posing complex and delicate problems. At least initially, there was an informal arrangement in which Schwarzkopf commanded US and NATO-forces, while General Mohammed Saleh al-Hammad (Chief of the Royal Saudi General Staff) commanded the Saudi, Arab and allied forces – with the leaders of specific national contingents reporting directly to their respective governments. The Americans further established the Coalition Coordination Communication Integration Centre, supervised by Yeosock's deputy, Major-General Paul R Schwartz. This not only served as a model for Saudi staff officers, and gave American planners easier access to the Saudi command system, but also improved international staff work.[71]

However, ultimately, it was CENTCOM that became the arbiter and deviser of the grand strategy and policy, and its commands acting as executive and operational commands – even though the Saudi, Arab, and allied forces acted under its direction, but not its control. For this purpose, already on 10 August 1990, the Saudis created an autonomous Joint Forces Command (JFC). This authority commanded by former chief of Air Defence, Lieutenant-General Prince Khaled bin Sultan (a graduate of Sandhurst and the US Air War College, and former project manager for the acquisition

and installation of Chinese-made surface-to-surface missiles), with Major-Genral Majid Tilhab al-Otaibi as deputy, was not recognized by Saleh al-Hamad and his unit commanders. Khaled thus had to battle quite hard to establish himself. The ultimate solution was to create two forward command bodies: the Joint Forces Commands (JFCs) East and North, under Major-General Sultan Adi al-Mutairi and Suleiman al-Wahayyib, respectively. The JFC East and JFC North became responsible for operations, while regional area commanders remained responsible for logistics and administrative support.[72]

Khaled's good relations with Schwarzkopf – who radiated optimism from the moment he arrived – and the NATO commanders, ensured fairly smooth arrangements. Indeed, Schwarzkopf, Khaled, Hine and Roquejeoffre met daily, wile CENTCOM and the Saudi General Staff were located in neighbouring facilities in Riyadh.[73]

INSTANT THUNDER: FROM IDEAS TO THE PLAN

The US Air Force (USAF) began planning its reaction to the Iraqi invasion even before the first Americans arrived on the Arabian Peninsula following Schwarzkopf's request of 8 August. Because Horner's staff was initially busy just planning and conducting the assembly of US air power on the Arabian Peninsula, offensive planning was assigned to Colonel John A. Warden; the Pentagon's leading authority on air power. He was also the USAF Deputy Director of Plans and assembled a staff dubbed 'Checkmate' in a Pentagon basement office. They produced *Instant Thunder*, which emphasized attacks upon strategic targets such as Iraqi command and control, the oil industry, electricity, communications, strategic offensive and defensive forces. This reflected Warden's belief in striking enemy 'centres of gravity' and, despite giving a low priority to attacks on enemy ground forces, Schwarzkopf approved it on August 10, with the proviso that it included forces based in Turkey. But when Powell was briefed the next day he questioned whether there were the resources to meet the objectives and directed that *Instant Thunder* become a joint plan with greater emphasis upon attacking enemy armour.[74]

Warden revised the plan between 11 and 17 August adding the goals of winning air superiority over the KTO and striking both command and control as well as armour within the theatre, while adding chemical weapon stocks to the target folder. He presented it to Schwarzkopf on August 17 and as he did so Schwarzkopf scribbled the outline of a four-phase campaign, *Desert Storm*, incorporating *Instant Thunder*, the suppression of air defences in Kuwait, the halving of enemy ground forces and ground attack. Although *Instant Thunder* still assigned attacks on ground forces a low minor priority he approved the plan and sent Warden to brief Horner in Riyadh.

Since 12 August, Horner had planned an air campaign to meet an Iraqi offensive and this focused upon interdiction of troops, including the use of B-52s, achieving air superiority (counter-air), and then planning for D-Day: a Coalition ground offensive. On 17 August, Horner asked Brigadier General Buster C. Glosson, Deputy Commander of Joint Task Force Middle East, to prepare for both a strategic and tactical air campaign. This was drafted over the next three days as the 'D-Day Game Plan' with enemy forces remaining the priority, although there was a strategic element against targets which supported ground forces (this was actually an operational level objective). Horner felt Washington was interfering by calling in Warden, whose briefing on August 20 was received with disdain, partly for personal reasons and partly because of the low priority assigned to striking ground forces. Horner pointedly requested three of the staff planners to remain in theatre but Warden was sent home.

Forward deployed from Tonopah AFB, to Khamis Mushayt AB in Saudi Arabia, where this photograph was taken, the F-117A Nighthawk fighter-bombers of the 415th and 416th TFS (37th TFW) were to play a crucial role in collapsing the Kari IADS and thus opening the way for the integrated aerial offensive against Iraq. (US DoD)

A row of F-15E fighters from the 336th Tactical Fighter Squadron/4th Tactical Fighter Wing, seen on the apron of al-Kharj AB in Saudi Arabia. The type was to play a crucial role and fly some of most dangerous combat operations of Operation *Desert Storm*. (US DoD)

campaign. Here too planning was hindered by intelligence problems, in part self-made because the USAF operational forces showed little interest in distributing data even though planning depended upon precision strikes.[75]

The phases were:
a) strategic campaign,
b) achieving air superiority over the KTO,
c) reducing enemy forces and chemical weapon delivery systems, and
d) supporting the liberation of Kuwait.

Horner and Glosson viewed it as sequential, but overlapping and simultaneous. Following presentations to Cheney, the Joint Chiefs, and Powell, between 25 August and 12 September and then developed with greater focus upon destroying up to half of the KTO enemy ground forces before the ground offensive. Planning involved other members of the Coalition only informally from September, with the RAF formally joining the following month, and the Saudis late in November. The revised plan, which made the Guards a priority, was then presented to the Joint Chiefs on 10 October.

Following major reviews on 8 and 14 November, the ultimate plan was presented by Horner to Cheney and Powell on 20 December 1990, although there was tinkering right up to 17 January. However, when Horner briefed Schwarzkopf on the revised air plan, on 15 January 1991, 'Stormin Norman' was furious. Schwarzkopf wanted simultaneous phases with the full weight of air power falling upon Iraqi ground forces in the KTO. This meant last minute changes to the air plan and in particular the detailed 300-page Air Tasking Orders (ATO) which were difficult to prepare and distribute, especially when the two corps commanders wanted a week of sustained air attacks to erode enemy strength along their line of advance from G-Day, the day the land offensive would begin. No-one knew when this would be, but as their targets were constantly changing they were ignored.

Horner and Glosson were distinguished combat airmen who were determined to avoid the mistakes of *Rolling Thunder* over North Vietnam in 1965-1968. 'Chuck' Horner, aged 54, had joined the USAF Reserve through the University of Iowa and had flown 110 Wild Weasel (electronic support) missions and would retire in September 1994 having flown 5,300 hours. Glosson, aged 48, would retire with 3,600 hours and had been the USAFE deputy chief of staff for plans and programmes until September 1988.

On 22 August, Horner asked Glosson to draft an outline offensive air campaign and he created the Special Planning Group or *Black Hole* which met in a basement storage room in RSAF headquarters in Riyadh. Heavily influenced by the Israeli 1982 air campaign in the Lebanese Bekaa Valley, it incorporated *Instant Thunder* in a four-phase plan including a more surgical strategic bombing

PROBLEMS, SHORTAGES AND UPGRADES

Eventually, huge stocks of materials would arrive in Saudi Arabia, including 9,500 body bags (officially designated 'human remains pouches'). Still, many units found themselves short of such key equipment as desert uniforms, chemical warfare suits, radios, vehicles, ammunition, and body-armour. Moreover, the troops deployed during *Desert Shield* experienced similar conditions to those deployed during *Vantage*, 30 years before: the searing heat in daylight and freezing temperatures at night were endurable, but sand was a huge problem that made maintenance difficult – especially for US Army helicopters. It tended to erode leading edges of rotor blades, clog fuel lines and particle separators, and pit windscreens, distorting the vision of crews wearing night-vision goggles (NVGs). All of this required such adaptations as the use of special paint for rotor blades and improved particle separators. Still, heat effected engine coolants and seals, warped metal and plastic arts, while dust and sand proved deadly for electronic components like radios and computers.[76]

There were also critical shortages of ammunition and the quality of many vehicles left much to be desired. The US forces undertook a programme to ensure that older models of the M1 Abrams were replaced by later M1A1s with the 120mm gun and an improved NBC system, and in the case of the M1A1(HA) greatly improved armour. Similarly, M60A1s of the

Some of the US troops ordered to deploy to Saudi Arabia during Operation *Desert Shield*, arrived there only after that enterprise was over, and the Operation *Desert Storm* began. The same was true for this element of the 101st Airborne Division, about to embark a transport aircraft that would fly them to the combat zone on 26 February 1991. (US DoD)

Even once the necessary heavy vehicles and associated equipment arrived in Saudi Arabia, they nearly always required additional maintenance to become combat-ready. All vehicles also needed camouflage colours better suited to the local circumstances. This civilian employee was photographed while applying a thick coat of sand colour onto an M1A1 shortly after its arrival in Saudi Arabia. (US DoD)

USMC required an upgrade through the installation of explosive reactive armour (ERA). Eventually, the US Army deployed 783 M1A1 Abrams with the 120mm guns to Saudi Arabia, but even these were found not to be in the best condition: just one battalion of the US Army's 2nd Armoured Division's 1st 'Tiger' Brigade was forced to replace the gun tubes on 21 out of 58 of its tanks, put new sets of tracks on 24 tanks, and replace 430 road wheels. Ultimately, the Army Material Command (AMC) upgraded a total of 1,032 Abrams tanks and equipped hundreds of these with mine ploughs; upgraded all the M2A2 Bradley IFVs deployed in the theatre with Kevlar spall

liners; issued dozens of Armoured Combat Earthmovers (ACEs) to units; and gathered and deployed to Saudi Arabia 1,059 HETs from their own reserves and training units, and 270 from the former Warsaw Pact countries.

Unsurprisingly, US Army stockpiles in Europe were 'drained' to support Operation *Desert Shield*, including the shipment of 220,000 rounds of armour-piercing ammunition for the 120mm guns of M1A1 Abrams tanks alone (ultimately, only 3,600 of these were expended, primarily thanks to superior fire discipline).[77]

An M1A1 Abrams MBT seen shortly after arrival in Saudi Arabia. The deployment of this variant, up-gunned with the 120mm cannon, was necessary to enable offensive operations for the liberation of Kuwait. (US DoD)

IRAQI PLANNING

When Saddam and his GHQ learned that President Bush had authorised a massive reinforcement of US forces in the Arabian Peninsula, they reacted by mobilising 250,000 additional troops.[78] Furthermore, the GMID and other Iraqi intelligence services updated their assessments about the enemy capabilities and intentions. By January 1991, they anticipated a month-long aerial offensive, with the Coalition ground forces then sweeping up the Wadi Hafr al-Batin to isolate Iraqi forces in the KTO, combined with airborne and amphibious assaults in northern Kuwait. However, with Saddam being entirely unaware of the qualitative superiority of the Coalition forces, his idea for the defence of Kuwait was that of drawing the Americans, especially, into a bloody war of attrition. He became anxious to convert Kuwait City into a new 'Stalingrad' through construction of extensive defences, with focus upon resistance against an amphibious assault and the creation of an urban battle. On 1 November 1990, he appointed Hussein Kamel, a commander RGFC (under supervision of Ali Hassan al-Majid), with the order to achieve exactly that goal.[79]

At the operational level the Iraqis recognised that they faced threats which included an amphibious assault, an advance up the Wadi al-Batin, large airborne operations as well as the possibilities of a second front through Turkey and even from Iran. One of their reactions was to reinforce troops responsible for the defence of Wadi Hafr al-Batin, on 26 August (and again in December).[80] Over the following weeks ever more comprehensive Iraqi measures for the defence of Kuwait were introduced. The Iraqi Army Engineer Corps was fully committed to building defences, facilities and communications to a degree where even civilian authorities – like the Ministry of Construction and Housing – had to be mobilised to construct 2,000 kilometres of roads and by-passes, and 150 kilometres of rail line form Umm Qasr. The original, corps-based logistic system was replaced by four lines-of-communication areas (Mintaqa al-Muwasalat) – a concept first employed during Iraqi operations against Israel in 1973 – with one for the south and one for the west. This enabled the rapid deployment of huge stockpiles of ammunition and supplies. With the Kuwaiti water-desalination plants proving insufficient to supply the troops, additional wells were dug or reactivated, and a 100-kilometre pipeline laid from Iraq.[81]

Never satisfied, on 10 November 1990, Saddam ordered the

Table 26: US Estimates of Iraqi strength in the KTO	
Date	Total Divisions
17 August	8
7 September	14
21 September	22
20 October	25
17 November	27
17 December	32
15 January	35
Based on Survey Vol 5 Chronology	

establishment of several committees to evaluate results and report within two days. These concluded that the Iraqi forces in the KTO were too far forward and advocated the return to the defence-in-depth concept. This was implemented by Saddam's directive from 18 November, which also demanded counter-attacks from concealed positions. On 20 and 21 November, Muhammad discussed this directive with his corps commanders and adopted tactics similar to that of the German Army during the winter of 1916-1917: manning of forward positions was halved, while the main defence line was based upon battalion-sized battle groups augmented by tanks and ATGMs, with most of the troops in each division actually being assigned to act as a reserve. To further bolster this new policy, seven divisions from northern and eastern Iraq were re-deployed into the KTO, starting from 22 November: all of them were deployed within the second echelon.[82]

Even then, the Army's and RGFC's leadership remained pessimistic about the prospects of a prolonged battle. This in turn prompted another series of reshuffles between top commanders. On 12 December, Defence Minister Shanshal (now aged 70) was replaced by the Inspector General of the Armed Forces, Lieutenant-General Sa'adi Touma Abbas. Furthermore, Saddam appointed his deputy, Izzat Ibrahim ad-Duri, as the Deputy Commander-in-Chief of the Armed Forces – a position last held by late Khairallah. Through this act, Muhammad's role became akin to that of General Wilhelm Keitel, head of the German Armed Forces High Command (Oberkommando der Wehrmacht) in the Second World War: like the Führer before him, Saddam thus directed planning of the defence of Kuwait and became the arbiter of strategic decision-making, while

Muhammad was responsible for the military to follow his orders.[83]

In a last-ditch attempt, Saddam made several efforts to avoid the looming confrontation, but mutual intransigence left him without the choice. On 14 January 1991, he placed the Iraqi armed forces on high alert.[84]

IRAQI AIR FORCE'S ACTIVITIES

The Iraqi Air Force, followed by the GMID, was probably the first branch of the Iraqi armed forces to recognize the scale of the potential threat. Unsurprisingly, already on 6 August 1990, both began considering the option of transferring some of their combat aircraft abroad to avoid being caught at their bases by a surprise US attack.[85]

Saddam ignored such concerns early on, but granted permission for Hassan to dispatch a team of officers to Libya, to study local experiences from confrontations with the US air power in 1986. Whether the resulting report really prompted General Hussein's Deputy Air Defence, Lieutenant-General Shahin Yassin Muhammad, to not only launch an upgrade of the Kari IADS by of de-centralizing it, but also to issue specific additional orders remains unclear. Certainly enough, he devolved the control to four existing ADSs and their SOCs. Furthermore, Hussein's Deputy Operations ordered the Air Force Intelligence Directorate to provide a list of potential targets for offensive and defensive operations to each of four ADS-commanders, who in return were to provide their related planning for approval. On the basis of the replies he received, Shahin decided to establish the 5th ADS, responsible for air defence of the 19th Province – Kuwait. However, subsequent developments were to show that he had either failed to warn all of his commanders to expect a vigorous attack on their radars with anti-radar missiles, or that not all of these listened to his advice. Eventually, Saddam expressed confidence that the IrAF could protect all 160 major installations in Iraq, including those related to nuclear, biological, and chemical warfare.[86]

Hussein's Deputy Operations developed plans for supporting an Iraqi offensive in the direction of Dhahran. For these purposes, Mirage F.1EQ-2s equipped with reconnaissance pods flew several sorties over Saudi Arabia in August 1990. In at least two cases, they had to be turned back by RSAF F-15s while already well inside Saudi airspace. However, further attempts of this kind were abandoned as soon as the IrAF recognized that an offensive into Saudi Arabia was unlikely to take place. Instead, between September and November, the Directorate of Operations then began considering limited offensive operations – primarily against desalination plants, air bases and oil refineries in Saudi Arabia. However, neither the IrAF nor the GMID were prepared for such an option: the scarcity of information in the target folders and the probability of high losses led to the conclusion that such operations could not be realized. Similar conclusions were drawn from a study for a possible attack on one of US Navy's aircraft carriers in the Persian Gulf.[87]

Instead, in October 1990, the Directorate of Operations drew a new plan for a massive air strike upon Israel. Envisaged to include more than 50 combat aircraft – including all of the brand-new Su-24MKs – this was based on intelligence collected during reconnaissance operations over Jordan in 1989, and intended to first punch a hole in Israeli air defences with the help of Mirages equipped with Caiman offensive jammers and Soviet-made anti-radar missiles, and then target the Dimona nuclear complex in conjunction with SSMD's al-Hussein missiles. As far as is known, at least one related exercise was undertaken later the same month.[88]

Around the same time (and again in early November 1990), some

In attempt to develop the two Adnan-2 AEW-aircraft to a standard suitable for combat operations, the Directorate of Military Industries of Iraq and the IrAF ran a series of intensive tests and rehearsals: to no avail. The type continued suffering from radar-related problems and – although being shown in public accompanied by MiG-29 interceptors, as in this photograph from a parade in 1989 – it never officially entered service. (via Ali Tobchi)

Further improvisations applied and flight-tested by the IrAF in 1990 included the conversion of an Ilyushin Il-76 transport into a makeshift tanker for Mirage F.1EQ-4/5/6s, as shown in this photograph. A similar modification was applied to one of the surviving Tu-16 bombers. Of potential use for an attack on Israel, which was considered by IrAF's planners in October 1990, neither ever saw combat application. (Albert Grandolini Collection)

shallow penetrations of Saudi airspace by IrAF aircraft did occur, but otherwise the air force limited itself to regular reconnaissance sorties along the border. These began on 2 November and sometimes included the sole Faw-727. On 16 November, the USAF's AWACS detected a mission by one of the Adnan-2s that were still undergoing testing. Another such sortie was tracked on 2 December 1990, when the modified transport passed through Jordanian airspace. The highest number of Iraqi reconnaissance sorties – five – were registered on 28 November, by when it became clear that the involved IrAF's Mirage F.1EQ-2s and MiG-25RBs had become the 'eyes' of the Iraqi armed forces, that were actively searching for signs of ground activity. Two or three such sorties were flown continuously until at least 13 January 1991.[89]

Meanwhile, the IrAF was monitoring the build-up of the Coalition's armada with ever growing concern. During the week ending with 30 August, it flew up to 197 sorties a day (only those observed by US and Saudi AWACS aircraft were counted), while the Coalition flew an average of 74. However, just a week later, the average Iraqi sortie count dropped to about 80 a day, while that of the Coalition grew to an average of 91 a day. Subsequently, the aerial activity of the US and allied air power continued to grow, reaching an average of 123 sorties a day in mid-September, compared with about 90 by the IrAF. During the week starting with 4 October, the IrAF flew about 700 sorties compared with 929 by the Coalition

– and sometimes up to 50% of those flown by the Iraqis actually consisted of a stream of transport aircraft and helicopters hauling additional equipment and personnel to Kuwait.[90]

During all these months, the IrAF only periodically operated over Kuwait – sometimes using the 'buddy' in-flight refuelling capability of its Mirages. Furthermore, it temporarily moved some of its squadrons to the local air bases which were re-named for this purpose: Ali as-Salem to Adnan, and Ahmed al-Jaber to Abbas. However, both were concluded to be 'too exposed for permanent deployment', and, generally, the IrAF kept well away from this portion of 'its' airspace.

Finally, bad weather in early January 1991 reduced the IrAF's flying activity to an absolute minimum. Certainly enough, 221 sorties were registered by the Coalition on 12 January, and 142 the following day, but on 15 January only 64 transport flights were noted. By contrast, the Coalition's air forces flew 1,029 sorties during the week ending with 14 January.

DEFENSIVE STRATEGY

The mood at the HQ IrAF in Baghdad worsened during November and December 1990. The consequence was that the IrAF – following Saddam's preference for conserving it as a force in being, but also due to the realisation about enemy's qualitative and quantitative superiority – gradually adopted a defensive strategy based upon SAMs and anti-aircraft artillery. This was considered as the only realistic option to conserve pilots and aircraft. Anticipating that their interceptors would have only a limited window of opportunity to operate, after which the destruction of the Kari's infra-structure would lead to the collapse of the IrAF's ability to offer resistance, the Iraqis thus limited the role of their air force to that of surviving.[91]

Therefore, instead of trying to openly challenge a superior enemy in the air, the IrAF's interceptors were to operate against carefully selected targets: they were to scramble and fly to pre-determined control points in 'total emission control' (EMCON) – with their radars turned off, only listening for messages from their ground control, and monitoring their radar warning receivers (RWRs). Once close to the target the GCI would advise them to activate their radars, after which the pilots were to use their own initiative. The first corresponding exercise was undertaken during the night from 25 to 26 December. It promptly showed that such tactics were impossible to exercise with MiG-25s: they were much too fast. Nevertheless, other IrAF interceptors were to use it. Indeed, all those confirmed as shot down during the subsequent war were lost while not under ground control – either because their communications were jammed, or because ground radars were jammed or destroyed.[92]

Finally realizing the scope of the threat, in December 1990, Saddam sent Taha Muhie-el-Din Marouf, his Vice-President, to Tehran, to meet the Iranian leaders and struck a deal: should the US air power attack Iraqi air bases, the IrAF was to transfer its aircraft to Iran; Iran would then hold these as a deposit for the duration of the conflict. While insisting on remaining neutral, the Iranians expressed their agreement: they were not only to provide a safe haven for the Iraqi jets, but also to return them after the end of the conflict.[93]

Ultimately, Saddam's preference to conserve his air force 'won' the day and, in the long term, sealed the fate of Iraq under his rule. Determined to remain a force-in-being the IrAF parked its best aircraft inside a total of 594 hardened aircraft shelters on its various air bases, while dispersing away and hiding its fighter-bombers and older types, and flying some military and civilian transport aircraft

to Iran and Jordan even before the fighting started. Less than a handful of top Iraqi air force officers could imagine the full extent of the consequences of this decision.

PRIMARY DOCUMENTS

CIA, *Iraq's Air Force: Improving Capabilities, Ineffective Strategy; An Intelligence Assessment*, October 1987, CIA/FOIA/ERR.

DIA, *Electronic Warfare Forces Study – Iraq*, 9 August 1990, National Archives.

Iraqi Ministry of Defence, *History of the Iraqi Armed Forces, Part 17; The Establishment of the Iraqi Air Force and its Development* (in Arabic), (Baghdad: Iraqi Ministry of Defence, 1988).

Iraqi Air Force & Air Defence Command, *An Analytical Study on the Causes of Iraqi Aircraft Attrition during the Iran-Iraq War* (in Arabic), (self-published for internal use, May 1991; English transcription provided by Sadik).

Iraqi Air Force & Air Defence Command, *The Role of the Air Force and Air Defence in the Mother of All Battles: After Action Report* (in Arabic), (self-published for internal use, 5 November 1991, captured in 2003 and translated as 'A 1991 Dossier on the Role of the Iraqi Air Force in the Gulf War', by the US Department of Defence-sponsored Conflict Records Research Center (CRRC Record Number SH-AADF-D-000-396) in the course of the 'Project Harmony').

Iraqi Air Force Martyrs Website, 1931-2003, iraqiairforcememorial.com

ONI, *SPEARTIP 009-88*; *Persian Gulf Fighter Developments*, 18 April 1988 (released in response to FOIA enquiry, October 2000).

ONI, *SPEARTIP 014-90*; *Iraq Fighter-Interceptor Capabilities* (date of publishing redacted; released in response to FOIA enquiry, October 2000).

ONI, *Request for Persian Gulf Related Info*, June 1987 (released in response to FOIA enquiry, October 2000).

BIBLIOGRAPHY

Alani, Mustafa M. *Operation Vantage: British Military Intervention in Kuwait 1961* (Surbiton: LAAM Ltd, 1990).

Allen, C. E., 'Warning and Iraq's Invasion of Kuwait, a Retrospective Look', *DIA Journal, Vol.7, No.2* (1998).

Alnasrawi, A., *The Economy of Iraq: Oil, Wars, Destruction of Development and Prospects, 1950-2010* (Westport: Greenwood Press, 1994).

Anscombe, F. F., *The Ottoman Gulf: The Creation of Kuwait, Saudi Arabia, and Qatar* (New York: Columbia University Press, 1997).

Atkinson, Rick, *Crusade: the untold story of the Persian Gulf War* (Boston: Houghton Mifflin, 1993).

Ayyoubi, H. A. ar-R., *Fourty-Three Missiles on the Zionist Entity* (in Arabic), (Amman: Jordan, al-Arab al-Yawm, October 1998).

Barr, J., *A Line in the Sand: Britain, France and the Struggle that Shaped the Middle East* (London: Simon & Schuster, 2011).

Blaxland, G., *The Regiments Depart: A History of the British Army, 1945-1970* (London: William Kimber, 1971).

Cameroon, J., 'Aug 2: Day of Betrayal', *Arab Times*, 4 November 2013.

Cohen, Dr Eliot A. (Director). *Gulf War Air Power Survey* (Washington DC: US Government Printing Office, 1993) *Vol 1: Planning/Command and Control Reports; Vol 2: Operations and Effectiveness Reports*, Drs Thomas Hone (Command, Control and Organisation), Alexander S.Cochran (Strategy and Plans); *Vol 3: Logistics and Support*, Mr Barry White (Operations and Effects), Dr John Guilmartin (Weapons, and Tactics); *Vol 4: Weapons, Tactics and Training, Space Operations Reports*, Mr Richard Gunkel (Logistics and Support), *Volume 5: A Statistical Compendium and Chronology*, Dr John Guilmartin (Weapons, Tactics and Training), Mr Richard Gunkel (Space), Lt Cols Daniel T.Kuehl (Statistics), Robert C. Owen (Chronology)

Conrad, Scott W., *Moving the Force: Desert Storm and Beyond*. McNair Paper 32 (Washington DC: Institute for National Strategic Studies, National Defense University, 1994).

Cooper, T., *Hot Skies over Yemen, Volume 1: Aerial Warfare over the Southern Arabian Peninsula, 1962-1994* (Solihull: Helion & Co., 2017).

Cooper, T., *Hot Skies over Yemen, Volume 2: Aerial Warfare over the Southern Arabian Peninsula, 1994-2017* (Solihull: Helion & Co., 2018).

Cooper, T., Sadik, Général de Brigade A., Bishop, F., *La guerre Iran-Irak: Les combat aériens, Hors-Serie Avions No. 22 & No. 23* (Outreau: Éditions LELA PRESSE, 2007).

Cooper, T. & Salti, P., *Hawker Hunters at War: Iraq and Jordan, 1958-1967* (Solihull: Helion & Co., 2016).

Cooper, T., *MiG-23 Flogger in the Middle East: Mikoyan I Gurevich MiG-23 in Service in Algeria, Egypt, Iraq, Libya and Syria, 1973-2018* (Warwick: Helion & Co., 2018).

Cooper, T. & Sipos, M., *Iraqi Mirages: The Dassault Mirage Family in Service with the Iraqi Air Force, 1981-1988* (Warwick: Helion & Co., 2019).

Cordesman, A. H. & Wagner, A. R., *The Lessons of Modern War Volume IV: The Gulf War* (Boulder: Westview Press, 1996).

Crystal , J. L., 'Kuwait – Persian Gulf War', *The Persian Gulf States: A Country Study* (Library of Congress, 5 March 2011).

Davis, R. G., *On Target: Organizing and Executing the Strategic Air Campaign Against Iraq* (Honolulu: University Press of the Pacific, 2005).

Department of Defense. *Conduct of the Persian Gulf War: Final Report to Congress* (Washington DC: Government Printing Office, 1992).

Dildy, D., & Cooper, T., *F-15C Eagle vs MiG-23/25, Iraq 1991* (Oxford: Osprey Publishing, 2016).

Foss, Christopher F. *Jane's Armour and Artillery 2007-2008* (Coulsdon: Jane's Information Group, 2007).

Francona, R., *Ally to Adversary: An Eyewitness Account of Iraq's fall from Grace* (Annapolis: Naval Institute Press, 1999).

Flintham, V., *Air Wars and Aircraft: A Detailed Record of Air Combat 1945 to the Present* (London, Arms and Armour Press, 1989).

Gordon, M. R. and Trainor, General B. E., *The Generals' War: The Inside Story of the Conflict in the Gulf* (Boston: Little, Brown and Company, 1995).

Guillebon, H. de, 'base secrète en Irak, les Mirage F1 de Saddam Hussein', *Fana de l'Aviation No. 546* (2015).

Guillebon, H. de, 'Le "Bazar" de Bagdad: Les programmes secrets avec l'Irak, 1977-1984', Première partie', *Fana de l'Aviation No. 567/2017*; 'Deuxième partie', *Fana de l'Aviation No. 568/2017*; 'Troisième partie', *Fana de l'Aviation No. 569/2107*

Guillebon, H. de, 'Les "Mirage" traquent les pétroliers, Golfe persique, 1985-1988, Première partie', *Fana de l'Aviation, No. 578/2018*; 'Deuxième partie', *Fana de l'Aviation, No. 579/2018*; 'Troisième partie', *Fana de l'Aviation, No. 580/2018*; 'Quatrième partie', *Fana de l'Aviation, No. 581/2018*

Hamdani, R., *Before History Left Us* (in Arabic) (Beirut: Arab Scientific Publishers, 2006).

Hilman J., *A Storm in a Teacup: The Iraq-Kuwait Crisis of 1961* (Syracuse: Syracuse University Press, 2014).

Hiro, D., *The Longest War: The Iran-Iraq Military Conflict* (New York: Routledge, Chapman and Hall Inc., 1991).

Hooton, E. R., Cooper, T., Nadimi, F., *The Iran-Iraq War, Volume 1: The Battle for Khuzestan, September 1980-May 1982* (Solihull: Helion & Co Ltd, 2016).

Hooton, E. R., Cooper, T., Nadimi, F., *The Iran-Iraq War, Volume 2: Iran Strikes back, June 1982-December 1986* (Solihull: Helion & Co Ltd, 2016).

Hooton, E. R., Cooper, T., Nadimi, F., *The Iran-Iraq War, Volume 3: Iraq's Triumph* (Solihull: Helion & Co Ltd, 2017).

Hooton, E. R., Cooper, T., Nadimi, F., *The Iran-Iraq War, Volume 4: The Forgotten Fronts* (Solihull: Helion & Co Ltd, 2017).

Hoyt, T. D., *Military Industry and Regional Defense Policy; India, Iraq and Israel* (Oxon: Routledge, 2007).

Huertas, S. M., *Mirage: The Combat Log* (Atglen: Schiffer Publishing Ltd., 1996).

Khaled Bin Sultan, HRH General. *Desert Warrior: A Personal View of the Gulf War by the Joint Forces Commander* (London: HarperCollins Publishers, 1995).

Levins, J., *Days of Fear: The Inside Story of the Iraqi Invasion and Occupation of Kuwait* (Motivate Publishing, 1997).

Liébert, M. & Buyck, S., *Le Mirage F1 et les Mirage de seconde generation à voilure en flèche, Vol.1* (Outreau: Éditions LELA PRESSE, 2007).

Malovaney, Colonel Pesach. *Wars of Modern Babylon: A History of the Iraqi Army from 1921 to 2003* (Lexington: University Press of Kentucky, 2017).

Metz, H. C., *Iraq: A Country Study* (Washington: GPO for the Library of Congress, 1988).

MILITARY POWERS-*The League of Arab States-Irak, Jordan, Lebanon, Syria, PLO, Iran, Israel*. (Paris, Societe I3C, 1989)

Mobley Richard A. *Gauging the Iraqi Threat to Kuwait in the 1960s – UK Indications and Warning*, CIA FOIA Electronic Reading Room, April 14, 2007.

Murray, W. & Woods, K. M., *The Iran-Iraq War: A Military and Strategic History* (Cambridge: Cambridge University Press, 2014).

Navias, M. S. & Hooton, E. R., *Tanker Wars: The Assault on Merchant Shipping during the Iran-Iraq Crisis, 1980-1988* (London: Tauris & Co Ltd., 1996).

Nelson, Major R. A., 'The Battle of the Bridges: Kuwait's 35th Brigade on the 2nd of August 1990', *Armor*, September-October 1995.

Raspletin, Dr. A. A., *History PVO website* (historykpvo.narod2.ru), 2013.

Razoux, Pierre (translated Nicholas Elliott). *The Iran-Iraq War* (Cambridge: Mass, Belknap Press of Harvard University, 2015).

Sa'aydon, M. as-, *Pilot Memoir* (privately published document, 2005).

Sadik, Brig Gen A. & Cooper, T., 'Les "Mirage" de Baghdad: les Dassault "Mirage" F1 dans la force aérienne irakienne', *Fana de l'Aviation No. 434/2006*; 'Deuxième partie', *Fana de l'Aviation No. 435/2006*.

Sadik, Brig Gen A. & Cooper, T., 'Un Falcon 50 lance-missiles: Avion d'affaires contre navire de guerre', *Fana de l'Aviation No. 470* (2007).

Sadik, Brig Gen A., and Cooper, T. *Iraqi Fighters, 1953–2003: Camouflage & Markings* (Houston: Harpia Publishing, 2008).

Sadik, Brig Gen A., Cooper, T. 'The First Night: Iraqi Air Force in Combat – 17 January 1991', *International Air Power Review*, Volume 26, 2009.

Sampson, A., *Die Waffenhändler: Von Krupp bis Lockheed, Die Geschichte eines tödlichen Geschäfts* (Reinbek bei Hamburg: Rowohl Verlag GmbH, 1977).

Scales, Brig Gen Robert M. *Certain Victory: The US Army in the Gulf War* (Dulles, VA: Brassey's Five-Star Paperback, 1997).

Schwarzkopf, General H. N., with Petre, P, *The Autobiography: It Doesn't Take a Hero* (London: Bantam Press, Transworld Publishers, 1992).

Scholfield, Richard. *Kuwait and Iraq: Historical Claims and Territorial Disputes* (London: Royal Institute of International Affairs, 1994).

Schubert, F. N. and Kraus, T. L., (Editors), *The Whirlwind War; The United States Army in Operations Desert Shield and Desert Storm* (Washington DC: US Army Center of Military History, 1992).

Shaw, I., and Santana, S., *Beyond the Horizon: The History of AEW&C Aircraft* (Houston: Harpia Publishing LLC, 2014).

Slot, B. J., *Mubarak al-Sabah: Founder of Modern Kuwait, 1896-1915* (London: Arabian Publishing, 2005).

Stearns, Lieutenant Colonel LeRoy D. *The 3rd Marine Aircraft Wing in Desert Shield and Desert Storm* (Washington DC, History and Museums Division, Headquarters, U.S. Marine Corps, 1999).

Tripp, C., *A History of Iraq* (Cambridge: Cambridge University Press, 2000).

Tucker-Jones, Anthony. *The Gulf War: Operation Desert Storm 1990-1991* (Barnsley: Pen & Sword Military, 2014).

United States Navy, *The United States Navy in 'Desert shield'/'Desert Storm'*, www.history.navy.mil

Watson, Bruce W. (Editor) *Military Lessons of the Gulf War* (London, Greenhill Books, 1993).

Westermeyer, Paul W. *U.S. Marines in the Gulf War, 1990-1991-Liberating Kuwait* (Quantico: History Division, United States Marine Corps, 2014).

Woods, K. M., Murray, W., Nathan, E. A., Sabara, L., Venegas, A. M., *Saddam's Generals: Perspectives of the Iran-Iraq War* (Alexandria: Institute for Defense Analyses, 2010).

Woods, Kevin M. *The Mother of all Battles: Saddam Hussein's strategic plan for the Persian Gulf War*, (Annapolis: Naval Institute Press, 2008).

NOTES

Chapter 1

1   The first Sheikh of Kuwait thus became Sabah I Bin Jaber (1700-1762), in 1752.
2   For further historic backgrounds, see Anscombe, *The Ottoman Gulf* and Darryl Line in the Sand.
3   For Kuwait's relationship with the Ottoman Empire and its subsequent border dispute with Iraq, see the in-depth examination in Scholfield, *Kuwait and Iraq: Historical Claims and Territorial Disputes.*
4   Scholfield, p. 23.
5   Ibid & Anscombe.
6   Scholfield, pp. 65, 97 & Slot, pp. 406-409.
7   Cox drew much of the southern border on the basis of the Sykes-Picot Treaty between Britain and France (for details, see Barr, 2011). The 'official' border remained 'porous' for nearly a decade longer (see Glubb, 1948 & Glubb, 1960). Details on the Iraqi recognition of the border to Kuwait as provided by Jill Crystal, 'Kuwait – Persian Gulf War', *The Persian Gulf States: A Country Study.*

Chapter 2

1   Alani, Operation Vantage (herafter Alani), pp. 79-84; Hillman, Storm in a Teacup (hereafter Hillman), pp. 25-71.
2   Alani, pp. 11-42, 50-51.
3   Mobley, Gauging the Iraqi Threat to Kuwait in the 1960s (hereafter Mobley). According to Mobley, British intelligence – despite its traditionally good links to the Iraqi military – failed to detect the establishment of the 3rd Armoured Division, and misidentified the 4th Infantry Division as the '4th Armoured Division'.
4   Cooper et al, Arab MiGs, Vol.2, p. 71.
5   Mobley.
6   Alani, pp. 84-92, 135-154, 193-194.
7   Ibid, pp. 52-78, 157-162, 200-205, 216-231. For further details on the 'Kuwait Crisis' of 1961, see Hillman pp.73-127.
8   Alani, pp. 81, 93-118, 163-192, 206-215; Kraus & Schubert, The Whirlwind War (hereafter Whirlwind), pp.9-12 & Mobley.
9   For further details on the British build-up, see Alani, pp. 119-134, 155-157, 238-245; Cooper et al, Arab MiGs, Vol.2, pp. 70-74 & Blaxland, The Regiments Depart pp. 358-361. Hereafter Blaxland.
10 Flintham, Air Wars and Aircraft pp. 166-167 (hereafter Flintham).
11 2nd Battalion the Parachute Regiment had been scheduled to come from Cyprus, but Turkey delayed overflight permission until 3 July. 45 Commando, part of which was already in the Persian Gulf, thus had to replace this unit. The tanks were landed upon a beach selected by troops from 42 Commando. The King's Regiment relieved the Royal Marines, starting from 6 July. For related problems, see Alani, pp. 232-238; Blaxland, pp. 360-361 & Flintham, pp. 166-167.
12 Alani, pp. 232-238, Blaxland, pp. 360-361; Cooper et all, Arab MiGs, Vol.2, p. 72-74.
13 Flintham, pp. 166-167.
14 Alani, pp. 119-134, 238-247 & Flintham.
15 Malovany, Wars of Modern Babylon (hereafter Malovany), pp. 503-504.
16 Alani, p. 109 & Mobley. In the early 1960s, and until 1991, the only Kuwaiti island with a permanent population was Faylakah.

Chapter 3

1   Although still shown on most of maps of Kuwait published in English-language speaking areas well into the 1990s, the Neutral Zone on the border between Iraq and Saudi Arabia created by the al-Uqayr Treaty was partitioned between the two countries during negotiations in December 1969. Similarly, the Saudi-Kuwaiti Neutral Zone was re-organized as the 'Divided Zone' in 1966. It was during related negotiations that Kuwait City and Riyadh agreed to share all oil and gas from onshore and offshore fields equally. Similar agreements were subsequently reached between Kuwait and other nations in the Persian Gulf – both in regards of borders and offshore territories.
2   Sampson, *Die Waffenhändler*, pp. 156-157.
3   Ironically, the decision to abandon all military activity east of Suez was taken by a government of the Labour Party – the same that, in 2003, then decided to participate in the US-led invasion of Iraq.
4   Scholfield, p. 126.
5   Ironically, less than 10 years later, Kuwait was to play a crucial role in establishment of exactly such an alliance – though without Iraq – also known as the Gulf Cooperation Council.
6   Notably, the royal family was, and remains, divided into two opposing clans: the as-Salim and al-Jaber. The former had the support of the conservative segments of society – especially the wealthy merchant class – while the latter enjoyed increasing support of the professional and technical classes, and youngsters (especially students). While sharing political and economic power, the two clans had very little in common.
7   Cooper et all, *Iraqi Mirages*, pp. 23-25.

8   J. H., retired missile warfare analyst of the DIA, interview, 10/2002; D. L., retired aviator of the US Marine Corps, interview, 01/2001.
9   For details on Iranian attacks on the shipping bound for Kuwait in 1984-1986 period, see Navias & Hooton, *The Tanker War* (hereafter Navias), pp. 77-85, 98-102, 108-115 and 118-124.
10 Hooton et al, *Iran-Iraq War Vol.2*, pp. 55-77; Scholfield, p. 126. For multiple examples of the IrAF making extensive use of Kuwaiti airspace, see Miroslav Lazanski, 'Zasto Fao jos nije pao', *Start*, September 1987 & Cooper et al, *Iraqi Mirages*.
11 Miroslav Lazanski, Zatso Fao jos nije pao, Start, September 1987 & Sadik, interview, 03/2005.
12 *Whirlwind*, p. 18.
13 Sadik, interview, 03/2005.
14 Navias, pp. 132-147 & 152-154.
15 Hooton et al, *Iran-Iraq War, Vol.3*, pp. 44-55.
16 The new Majlis of Kuwait had barely begun work before the Iraqi invasion of August 1990. During a conference of Kuwaiti exiles in Jeddah, in Saudi Arabia, in October 1990, Crown Prince Sheikh Sa'ad al-abdullah as-Sabbah had to promise full restoration of the Constitution of 1962.
17 Cordesman & Wagner, *The Lessons of Modern War, Vol.1,* p. 33-36.; Malovany, pp. 504-505; *Whirlwind*, p. 22.
18 Woods, *Mother of All Battles* (hereafter Woods), p. 52 & 'Kuwait Marks 10 Years since passing on of "Amir of Hearts"', *Arab Times*, 22 April 2016. A barrel of oil is 42 US-gallons or 785 litres. According to Woods (p. 52), every US$1 drop in the oil price per barrel cost Iraq US$1 billion a year.
19 In June 1981, the Israeli Defence Force/Air Force (IDF/AF) bombed and destroyed the construction site of two French-made nuclear reactors in Tuwaitha, in the southern outskirts of Baghdad. Israel subsequently declared this strike was launched to 'prevent Iraq from developing nuclear weapons'. However, publications by top Iraqi nuclear scientists released in Arabic since the US-led invasion of Iraq in 2003, have shown that in 1981 Iraq had no nuclear weapons development programme because it had only 200 qualified nuclear scientists at the time. Ironically, it was this Israeli strike which prompted Saddam to launch a super-secret project for developing nuclear weapons. Gulf Air Survey, Vol 2 Part 2 (hereafter Survey with Volumes), p.487 & Green, pp. 135-152.
20 Malovany, pp. 497-498 & Sadik, interview, 10/2007.
21 Khaled, Desert Warrior (hereafter Khaled), pp. 136-137. Notably, the ACC collapsed dysfunctional within weeks of the Iraqi invasion of Kuwait.
22 Woods, p. 47.
23 Malovany, p. 500.
24 Ibid, p. 500.
25 Woods pp.53-57 & Khaled, p. 174.
26 Woods et al, *Saddam's Generals*, pp. 19-22.
27 Watson et al, Military Lessons of the Gulf War (hereafter Watson), p. 18 f/n 3.
28 Woods et al, *Saddam's Generals*, pp. 11.
29 Woods p.152.
30 Ibid, pp. 12-13, 52.
31 Woods et al, *Saddam's Generals*, p. 14.
32 Khaled, pp. 174-176.
33 Woods, p. 53.
34 Khaled, pp. 174-178.
35 Malovany, p. 508.

Chapter 4

1   For examples on the flawed and patronising analyses of the Iraqi military at war with Iran, see *Lessons*, and Pollack, *Arabs at War*.
2   Hooton et al, *Iran-Iraq War,* Vol.3, pp. 35-39 & US Department of Defence (US DoD), 'Final Report to the Congress: Conduct of the Persian Gulf War' (hereafter Congress), pp. 48-50.
3   Malovany, pp. 493-494; IISS, *The Military Balance, 1989-1990/1990-1991*, pp. 101-106 (hereafter IISS); CIA, *National Intelligence Estimate, Iraq: Foreign Policy of Major Regional Power*, date unclear, CIA/FOIA/ERR.
4   Sadik, interview, 03/2007; Sadik et all, 'First Night'; Malovany, pp. 494, 693. According to Sadik, Hassan was also the first IrAF commander in 30 years without training in Great Britain and without flying experience on the Hawker Hunter. Indeed, Sadik described Hassan as a 'Soviet-style trainee'.
5   Ibid, pp. 494, 754.
6   Hooton et al, *Iran-Iraq War, Vol.2*, pp. 52-53.
7   Malovany, p. 497 & Woods, p. 60.
8   Malovany, p. 497.
9   Sadik, interviews, 03/2005, 03/2007 & 10/2007.
10 For full understanding of Sha'ban's and Basu's influence, and repercussions of Saddam's decision from early 1989, see Cooper et all, *Iraqi Mirages*.
11 Woods, pp. 79, 89 f/n 27.
12 Unless stated otherwise, this sub-chapter is based on Sadik, interviews 03/2005, 03/2006, 03/2007 & 10/2007; Cooper et all, *Iraqi Mirages*; Sadik

et all, *Iraqi Fighters*; Sadik et all, 'The First Night' & Cooper et all, *La guerre Iran-Irak*.

13 According to Sammari (Shattering the Eastern Gates, p. 250), the IrAF had 620 combat aircraft, 26 Ilyushin Il-76 and An-24 transports and 243 training aircraft. US intelligence reports usually put the figure at about 700, while Iraqi documentation captured in 2003 is listing a total of 997, including 620 fighters (Woods, p. 272).

14 Sadik, interview, 03/2005.

15 SPEARTIP 014-90; Sadik, interviews, 03/2005, 03/2006 & 03/2007 & Sadik et all, 'The First Night'. According to Sadik, the reason for Iraq ordering 137, but taking delivery of only 33 MiG-29s before stopping their further acquisition was that in 1989 the decision was taken to purchase Sukhoi Su-27 interceptors instead.

16 Ibid.

17 Ibid & Cooper, *MiG-23 in the Middle East*. Iraq originally acquired at least 55 MiG-23MLs, however, 10 were sent for overhauls to Yugoslavia and at least two to the USSR, in 1988-1989. Due to an arms embargo imposed by the UN in reaction to the Iraqi invasion of Kuwait, not one of these was ever returned to Iraq.

18 For details on operational history of the Mirage F.1EQ in Iraq in period 1980-1988, see Cooper et all, *Iraqi Mirages*. Iraq is known to have received at least 60, perhaps as many as 80, Baz-AR ARMs from France, but most were expended for testing and training purposes, or during the war with Iran. Their last known combat use took place in 1987. By comparison, the IrAF acquired 115 Kh-28s and expended 104 of these against Iran. This is one of reasons why the service then decided to deploy lighter but shorter-ranged Kh-25MPs during operations against Kuwait (data based on J. H., interview, 10/2002 & Sadik, interview, 03/2006). Other details from Woods, pp. 70, 89 f/n 24, 26, 27 & *Congress*, pp. 51-52.

19 Sadik, interviews, 03/2005, 03/2006 & 03/2007 & Sadik et all, 'The First Night'.

20 Ibid & Sadik, *Iraqi Fighters*. While Iraq stunned Western observers by modifying one Mirage F.1EQ-5 for deployment of Soviet-made Kh-29 laser-guided missiles, in 1989 – which were much cheaper than French-made AS.30Ls – such an 'upgrade' never saw a fleet-wide application.

21 SPEARTIP 014-90; Cooper, *MiG-23 in the Middle East* & Cooper et all, *Iraqi Mirages*.

22 For technical details, see Lessons, pp. 436-438. Another 500 fire-control radars were supporting the work of SAM and anti-aircraft artillery batteries.

23 For Kari, see Gordon/Trainor, pp. 106-110; *Lessons*, pp. 408-409; 'Iraq's Air Defence Command' in *Jane's Intelligence Review*; *Survey*, Vol.2, Part 2, pp. 187-204-208, 210, 222-226 and Vol.4, Part 1, pp. 18-22.

24 Raspletin; Survey, Vol.2, p. 209; Woods, p. 148; Lessons, p. 134 & Military Powers, p. 200. The latter put the number of heavy flak (80-130mm) at 200, while Lessons quoted a total of 2,404 fixed and 6,100 mobile anti-aircraft artillery pieces.

25 US Department of Defence (USDoD), *The Conduct of the Persian Gulf War: Final Report*, p. 241.

26 Based on Sadik et all, *Iraqi Fighters*.

27 While every major IrAF air base was protected by one Missile Brigade, only those for which the designations of are known are mentioned.

28 Malovany, pp. 498-499, 819.

29 Ibid, pp. 499-500 & 820.

30 Unless stated otherwise, this section is based on IISS, pp. 104-105, 108-109; Cordesman & Wagner, *The Lessons of Modern War Vol 4* (hereafter *Lessons*) pp.201-203, and *Military Powers: The League of Arab States, Gulf Co-operation Council, Yemen Arab Republic, People's Democratic Republic of Yemen* (hereafter *Military Powers*), pp. 40-43.

31 There are many erroneous reports that the KLF operated Indian-made Vijayata tanks, which were licence-built versions of the Vickers MBT Mk.1: actually, Kuwait used only British-made vehicles.

32 *Lessons*, p. 201.

33 *Whirlwind*, p. 24.

34 The Matra R.550 Magic short-range air-to-air missile usually associated with the Mirage entered service only in 1979-1980. With the orders from France and Iraq having priority, KAF Mirage F.1CKs were initially equipped only with US-made AIM-9J Sidewinder air-to-air missiles. R.550 Magic Mk.Is were acquired in the mid-1980s, and by August 1990 a batch of 50 Magic Mk.IIs was also delivered. For further details on the KAF and its Mirages, see Liébert et all, p. 237; *Lessons*, pp. 203-204 & *Military Powers*, pp. 43-48.

35 Most sources, including all those from Kuwait, place this battalion on Faylaka Island. However, this SAM-site was meant to counter threats from the east and only 'leakers' from the north, while the SAM-sites on the Bubiyan and at the Mutlaa Ridge were deployed specifically to counter threats from the north.

36 Unless stated otherwise, this section is based on Scales, *Certain Victory* (hereafter Scales), p. 94; IISS, pp. 111-112, 115-116; *Lessons*, pp. 176-180; Khaled, p. 235; Westermeyer, *Liberating Kuwait* (hereafter Westermeyer),

37 For related details, see sister-publications *Hawker Hunters at War* and *Hot Skies over Yemen, Vol.1*.

38 *Whirlwind*, pp. 82-85.

39 Both types were merely export variants of the US Army's OH-58D Kiowa and UH-60A Black Hawk helicopters, respectively.

40 *Whirlwind*, p. 21.

41 *Lessons*, pp. 187-188; Lieutenant-Colonel Martin N Stanton, 'The Saudi Arabian National Guard Motorised Brigades', *Armour*, March-April 1996, pp. 6-11. Notably, RSLF also acquired 521 Commandos for internal security, while the 10th IMNSB was in the northwest of the country.

42 'Saudi Arabian Air Defence System', *AirEnthusiast*, April 1966; *Lessons*, pp. 188-193 & *Military Survey*, pp. 132-144.

43 James K Gordon, 'Debate Expected over Plan to sell Missiles to Saudi Arabia', *Aviation Week & Space Technology* (henceforth AW&ST) 2 May 1988 & Michale Mecham, 'US Support for Saudi AWACS Called Crucial to Future Sales', AW/ST, 16 May 1988.

44 As of August 1990, the RSAF had no wing-structure, relying instead upon local base-commands. This order of battle is arranged geographically, from north towards south and from west towards east.

45 Khaled p. 249.

46 *Lessons*, pp. 194-195 & *Gulf War Air Power Survey,* Vol.5, Chronology of Desert Shield (hereafter *Air Survey* with Volume number).

Chapter 5

1 Scales, pp. 42-43 & *Whirlwind*, pp. 17-18, 48-49.

2 Schwarzkopf, *It Doesn't Take a Hero* (hereafter Schwarzkopf), p. 283.

3 Scales, pp. 43-44; Gordon et all, *The Generals War* (hereafter Generals), pp. 18-19; Hallion, p. 142; *Air Survey*, Vol.5, Chronology, p. 116-117; Schwarzkopf, pp. 289, 291; *Whirlwind*, pp. 48-49, 51. By pure accident, the US Naval War College's annual Global War Game run between 9 and 27 July, also included an exercise scenario involving an Iraqi attack and occupation of Kuwait and Saudi Arabia.

4 Scales, p. 44; *The United States Navy in Desert Shield/Desert Storm* (hereafter USN History), pp. 27-33 & Westermeyer pp. 36-37.

5 *Whirlwind*, p. 42. Cheney would also continue cutting defence budgets well after Desert Storm.

6 *Air Survey*, Vol.5, Table 1.

7 *Whirlwind*, pp. 26-46; Scales, pp. 6-38; Hallion, *Storm over Iraq*, (hereafter Hallion), pp. 83-120.

8 Hallion, Table 4.1.

9 Scales, pp. 16-18, 23-25; *Whirlwind*, pp. 34-37, 71, 83-85, 90-93.

10 Scales, pp. 10-15, 20-23; *Whirlwind*, pp. 38-42.

11 *FM 100-5: Operations*, 1976 (Obsolete Manuals from Ike Skelton Combined Arms Research Digital Library, cgsc.contentdm.oclc.org).

12 Scoot-and scoot involves the gun firing a number of rounds before rapidly moving to avoid enemy counter-battery fire.

13 Scales, pp. 9-10, 12-15, 25-27; *Whirlwind*, pp. 27-29.

14 Scales, pp. 15-16.

15 Ibid, pp. 7-10 & 15-16 & Hallion, Table 4.1.

16 Hallion, pp. 74-82, 109-113, 115-120.

17 Scales, p. 10; *Whirlwind*, p. 27.

18 *Whirlwind*, pp. 29-33; Foss, *Armour and Artillery*, pp. 168-171, 446-447, 1026-1027 & 1029-1030. The 120mm gun was installed in a gyro-stabilised turret (for improved accuracy whilst moving) that was planned for future US Army tanks even before Chrysler designed the Abrams. The Bradley was delivered in two variants: M2, as an infantry fighting vehicle, and M3 Cavalry Fighting Vehicle, as a reconnaissance vehicle which carried an increased load of BGM-71 TOW missiles and a two-man scout team in place of an infantry squad.

19 For Operation Desert Storm 104 of these new rockets were delivered to Saudi Arabia.

20 Hallion, pp. 39-46, Appendices A, B and D, and relevant issues of *Jane's All the World's Aircraft*. Notably, the F-15E Strike Eagle entered service only in 1990. Most of the crews flying B-52s during the Operation Desert Storm were younger than their aircraft.

Chapter 6

1 Arabic for 'Day of the Call': codeword for the Iraqi invasion of Kuwait, with the implication of Saddam calling the Kuwaitis to 'rejoin' Iraq.

2 Ayyubi, 'Fourty-Three Missiles on the Zionist Entity', p. 12; Malovany, pp. 497, 506-501; Woods et al, *Saddam's Generals*, p. 18 & *Woods*, pp. 60, 62-71, 88; Sadi, interview, 03/2005. Ibrahim's Chief-of-Staff was Saddam's half-brother.

3 Malovany, p. 508.

4 Sadik, interview, 03/2005; Sadik et all, *Iraqi Fighters* & Sadik et all, 'The First Night'; Malovany, p. 525; Woods, pp. 71, 89-90, 101-105 & Woods, *Saddam's Generals*, p. 16. According to Sadik, the MiG-25RBs photographed most of strategic facilities in north-eastern Saudi Arabia and Bahrain.

pp. 50-51. Hereafter Westermeyer & *Military Powers,* pp. 127-132, 154-155.

5   Woods, pp. 66-67.
6   Malovany, p. 507.
7   Sadik, interview, 03/2005; Hamdani, pp. 134-135; Woods, p. 64. There have been suggestions that the Iraqis followed a plan originally developed by the British, although why London would wish to invade Kuwait from Iraq is unclear. Despite the decision not to make use of massed artillery, the RGFC's divisions deployed more than 500 self-propelled and towed guns in Kuwait.
8   Malovany, p. 506; Woods, p. 62-63.
9   Malovany, pp. 507, p. 514; Woods, p. 63 & Charles E. Allen, 'Warning and Iraq's Invasion of Kuwait, a Retrospective Look', DIA Journal, Vol.7, No.2 (1998), pp. 33-44.
10   Woods, p. 95 & Hamdani, pp. 134-137.
11   Woods, pp. 65-66.
12   Malovany, p. 500. These figures are based upon the divisions being at their normal peacetime establishment of about 80%.
13   Sadik, interview, 10/2007 & Woods, pp. 71-72.
14   Lessons, p. 205. Pending possible publication of any kind of official documentation from the period 1989-1990, it is impossible to clearly say if the KLF really had any kind of a clear defence plan. Diverse sources (see Bibliography) do indicate that the force was to hold up any kind of a land incursion at the Mutlaa Ridge with support of the KAF, and then to secure the Kuwait City pending the intervention of the international community.
15   Malovany, p. 509 & Woods, p. 89.
16   Woods, pp. 78-80.
17   Sadik, interview, 03/2005.
18   Ibid & Cameron, 'Aug 2, Day of Betrayal'.
19   Cameron, 'Aug 2, Day of Betrayal'; Levins, Days of Fear; Sadik, interview, 03/2005 & Woods, pp. 114-116.
20   Sadik, interview, 03/2005; Malovany, p. 511 & Woods, pp. 81-82. Despite numerous interviews and a wide range of authoritative publications, it has proven impossible to determine what exactly has happened during this phase of the invasion. The KAF eventually credited its fighter pilots with 16 kills, and its HAWK SAM-sites with 4 kills (see Levins). The Iraqis – probably as much shocked as ashamed over this tragedy – either tried to downplay it (for example: Sadik insisted on the loss of 'two or three helicopters', all to ground-based air defences), or explain it with night, sand and tension wires. While none of them has ever clearly cited the exact number of helicopters lost, at least one of survivors put the number at, 'more than 40'. The commander of the 16th SF Brigade recalled that his unit suffered more than 60 casualties. Whatever the figures, it is possible that this was a bigger and costlier catastrophe than that experienced during a similar operation launched by the Egyptians during the opening evening of the October 1973 War with Israel.
21   Schwarzkopf, pp. 293-298.
22   Nelson & Hamdani, pp. 134-137. The destruction of the single T-72 from the Hammurabi Armoured Division during the clash on the Mutlaa Ridge is usually credited to an 'Indian-made Vijayata tank' of the 6th Brigade, although this was – as explained above – equipped with British-made Vickers MBT Mk.1s. Although several of the Kuwaiti MBTs reportedly opened fire at the same Iraqi tank from a relatively short range, it is more likely that the T-72 in question was knocked-out by a shot from one of the Chieftains arriving in their rear. This conclusion is apparently supported by Nelson.
23   Sadik, interview, 03/2005; Levins, Days of Fear; Iraqi Air Force Online Memorial Website & Woods, pp. 108-109. While all Iraqi sources confirm the loss of their Navy's Super Frelon, whose wreckage and its Exocet missile were eventually found, most of them remain uncertain about the fate of its crew.
24   Sadik, interview, 03/2005 & Iraqi Air Force Memorial website (iraqiairforcememorial.com). According to Sadik, the IrAF had Kh-25s in its arsenal already since mid-1980s, but never used them against Iran, and this was the first known combat firing of this weapon ever. According to Levins, the MIM-23B I-HAWK SAM-site at Faylaka was credited with the downing of four confirmed and one possible IrAF fighter-bombers within three hours starting from 0455hrs. However, as mentioned above, this site was actually positioned on Bubiyan Island.
25   Sadik, interview, 03/2005; Levins, 'Days of Fear'; Iraqi Air Force Online Memorial; Woods, pp. 108-109. The air strike on Ali as-Salem AB was witnessed by elements of the 35th Brigade KLF, greatly encouraging their departure from their base nearby. Ironically, while obviously failing to protect vulnerable helicopters, intercept any of six Mirages or two A-4 Skyhawks of the KAF scrambled early that morning, or to suppress the work of Kuwaiti MIM-23B I-HAWK SAM-sites, the IrAF subsequently declared its involvement in the invasion as a 'success'. When, three years later, Lieutenant-General Rawi – now serving as the Chief of Staff of Armed Forces – openly challenged Hassan about the failure of the IrAF to prevent the Kuwait Air Force from taking off, the latter not only ignored his own failures in regards of planning and conduct of operations, but also insisted, '...when compared to the worst

case scenario, our mission was successful...despite all the challenges caused by weather and other conditions, our pilots managed to strike the Kuwaiti airfields at 0625 (Iraqi time), 1220 and 1600... and overall, the KAF should've flown 10 times the number of sorties it flew, but it didn't... because we stopped 90% of their sorties...so, the IrAF did its job...' It remains unclear if helicopter pilots of the IrAAC were sharing his opinion, but, gauging by certain related recent publications self-congratulations remained the order of the day in the proud IrAF for long afterwards.
26   Sadik, interview, 03/2005; Nelson & Levins, Days of Fear. Due to the lack of time and general chaos, the KAF failed to deploy forward air controllers with the ground forces. Therefore, the pilots first circled over their targets attempting to identify these.
27   Woods, p. 108.
28   Levins, Days of Fear. Overall, KAF Mirage F.1-pilots were officially credited with 15 kills (some sources cite up to 17). Methods used to confirm all of these claims remain unknown.
29   Hamdani, Before History Left Us, pp. 141-142.
30   Nelson & Hamdani, p. 135-137.
31   Nelson.
32   Levins.
33   Levins & interview with a source in Kuwait, which provided information on condition of anonymity, 08/2006
34   Sadik, interview, 03/2005.
35   Woods, pp. 68-70.
36   Lessons, p. 205.
37   Malovany, p. 513, 156 f/n 30 & Woods, p. 87.
38   Malovany, pp. 513 & 516.
39   For details on Operations Tawakkalna 2, 3 and 4, see Hooton et all, Iran-Iraq War, Vol.3, pp. 66-73 and Vol.4, pp. 51-55.
40   Hamdani, pp. 138.
41   Watson, pp.50-51.
42   Congress, pp. 67-69.
43   Khaled, pp. 28-32.
44   Ibid, pp. 178-180 & 183-185.
45   Woods et al, Saddam's Generals, pp. 6-14.
46   Ibid, p. 17.
47   Congress, pp. 58-67 & Whirlwind, p. 49.
48   Congress, pp. 58-67, Air Survey Vol.5, Chronology; Schwarzkopf, pp. 309-328 & Whirlwind, pp. 49-51.
49   Schwarzkopf, p. 315; Whirlwind, p. 102 & Scales, pp. 45-46.
50   Khaled pp. 30-31 & Whirlwind, pp. 52-53.

Chapter 7

1   Schwarzkopf, pp. 345-346; Air Survey Vol.2, Part 1, pp. 481-482 & Vol.5, Table 3. The KTO consisted of Kuwait and Iraqi territory south of the Euphrates and west of the Shatt al-Arab. It was officially defined as south of Latitude 31°N, west of the Gulf, north of the Saudi border and east of Longtitude 45° East. Jamieson p. 10.
2   Khaled, p. 260.
3   Westermeyer, pp. 35-40. Schwarzkopf wanted to call the Operation 'Peninsula Shield', but the alternate name was selected by the Joint Chiefs of Staff in Washington.
4   Whirlwind, p. 56. The Sheridan was actually a tracked reconnaissance vehicle mounting a 152mm gun /missile launcher using either caseless ammunition or MGM-51 Shillelagh ATGMs.
5   Air Survey, Vol.5, Table 1 & Chronology. The KC-10As were returned to their original, 'tanker' role only during January 1991.
6   Whirlwind, p. 62; Woods et all, Saddam's Generals, pp. 60-61; Westermeyer, p. 39; Air Survey, Vol.2, pp. 43-44 & Vol.5, Chronology; Hallion, pp. 136-139. In the course of all the related operations, only one aircraft was written off: on 29 August 1990, a C-5 crashed in an accident at Ramstein AB, in (West) Germany).
7   For USAF deployment see Davis, pp. 33-56; Hallion, p. 136; Survey, Vol.2, Part 1, pp. 45-46, 45, f/n 30, 47, 104, 184 & Survey, Vol.5, Chronology. For that of the US Marine Corps, see MAW 3, p. 24.
8   Khaled, pp. 222-225, 231.
9   Hallion, pp. 138-139, 187; Survey, Vol.5, Chronology, 14 September – 20 December. The tanker figures include 13 aircraft deployed in the Pacific and 94 in the Middle East.
10   Based upon Survey, Vol.5, Table 6. The column 'Combat' is including tactical fighters, interceptors, ground attack and attack types, but no types used for electronic warfare.
11   Survey, Vol.5, Chronology; Survey, Vol.2, Part 1, pp. 125-134, 183, 185-187, Tables 46-52; Survey Vol.4, and Survey Vol.5, Tables 54-57.
12   Survey, Vol.5, Table 46.
13   The Patriot proved not only a sophisticated, but also a sensitive system: on 24 October, half the deployed batteries had to be taken off the line for repairs necessary on their AN/MPQ-53 radars.
14   Congress, pp. 486-492; Conrad, pp. 23-39 & US Navy History, Section II and Appendix K.

15 Scales, pp. 87-90 & *Whirlwind*, p. 81. Some of the ships that carried the 101st Airborne Division to Saudi Arabia, had carried the same unit already to Vietnam, about 25 years earlier.

16 *Survey, Vol.5*, Table 27.

17 Khaled pp. 299-300; Scales, pp. 55-57, 73-79 & *Whirlwind*, pp. 64-66.

18 Conrad, p. 15; Schwarzkopf, pp. 341-342; Khaled , p. 285 & *Whirlwind*, p. 57.

19 Scales, pp. 60-63, 69-73, 80-82, 97-99; Conrad, pp. 36, 46; pp. 57-60, 62, 66-67 and 78-81; Khaled, pp. 285, 290.

20 For the Saudi logistics contribution, see Scales, pp. 63-65; Conrad, p. 48; Khaled, pp. 285-305; *Whirlwind*, pp. 62-64, 67-68. Eventually, the Saudis provided the coalition with fuels worth US$1.9 billion. Notably, when – on 7 September 1990 – Yeosock informed Khaled he was expecting 15,000 troops within 48 hours, the Saudis had no problem accommodating these, for there was plentiful of unoccupied housing in the Eastern Province and the country was used to housing millions of pilgrims for the Hajj every year. Moreover, the Saudis were able to accommodate not only hundreds of thousands of foreign service personnel, but also 360,000 Kuwaiti refugees. Unsurprisingly, Sultan later expressed his disappointment at the lack of Western recognition of the Saudi contribution to the logistic effort – without which all the subsequent operations would be impossible (Khaled, pp. 287 & 303).

21 Khaled pp. 266-267, 269-273, 275-279. Chevènnement would later insist the activity of French military to be restricted to Kuwait: he resigned when Mitterand overruled him.

22 *Air Survey*, Vol.5, Chronology; Khaled, pp. 292-293. The authors would like to thank Dr. Peter Johnston, Head of Research of the National Army Museum for information on British deployment.

23 Schwarzkopf, p. 351.

24 Scales, pp. 103-106.

25 Khaled, pp. 248-250 & 253-257.

26 *Lessons*, pp. 59, 195-200; Khaled, pp. 222-225, 227-231 and 236; *Whirlwind*, pp. 132-133.

27 Khaled, pp. 224-225.

28 *US Navy History*, Appendix C.

29 Scales, pp. 49-51 & *Whirlwind*, pp. 53-54.

30 Westermeyer, pp. 37-40 & Stearns, 3rd MAW History (hereafter Streams), p. 43.

31 Woods, pp. 125, 142, 164.

32 Malovany, p. 517.

33 Woods, pp. 151-157.

34 *Air Survey, Vol.5,* Chronology.

35 Woods, pp. 124-125.

36 *Congress*, p. 109. By 23 October 1990, US intelligence identified the arrival of the 6th and 10th Armoured Divisions, 1st and 5th Mechanised Divisions, and the 2nd, 11th, 14th, 16th, 19th, 20th, 26th, 30th and 42nd Infantry Divisions in Kuwait. The Guards might have had the secondary role in sense of 'corsetting' or 'stiffening' the resolve of the Army, because the Defence Ministry and the Army were all excluded from the planning for the invasion of Kuwait, while now became responsible for holding the '19th Province'.

37 Woods, pp. 142-144, 167. Notably, Rawi's plan was war-gamed at the forward GHQ in Basra, on 23 November, with unknown results. Saddam later regretted this expansion of the RGFC, commenting that the units in question were never properly trained and some displayed dubious loyalty during the uprisings in Iraq in the aftermath of Operation *Desert Storm*.

38 Scales, pp. 67-69, 112-115, 117-118, 142-145, 160, 207-210; *Air Survey, Vol.5, Chronology*; Malovany, pp. 521-522.

39 Woods, pp. 125-126, 129-130, 132-133, 165. Notably, even Kuwaiti scrap yards were searched for anything that could make a decoy.

40 Malovany, p. 528.

41 Ibid, p. 523 & Makki, interview 01/2019.

42 The plan was 'published' on 29 November 1990. CENTCOM, Operation Desert Shield/Desert Storm, Executive Summary (hereafter CENTCOM), pp. 10-11.

43 Scales, pp. 93-94.

44 Ibid, Schwarzkopf, pp. 331-332; *Air Survey*, Vol.5, Chronology.

45 Scales, pp. 66-67, 82-87, 90-93, 96; Woods, *Saddam's Generals*, pp. 66-67; Malovany, pp. 517-518; Schwarzkopf, p. 346, 348, 350; Khaled, p. 197; Westermeyer, pp. 47-48.

46 For satellites see NSA articles United States Space Command Operations. Operations *Desert Shield* and *Desert Storm* Assessment of January 1991. Jamieson p.16.

47 For U-2 and TR-1-operations see NSA pamphlet, 'The Dragon Lady Meets the Challenge', pp. 35-44. U-2s flew 284 sorties during Desert Shield and 260 during Desert Storm. Rest of the data is based on *Survey, Vol.5, Chronology*.

48 Sadik, interivew, 10/2007.

49 Khaled, pp. 310-311.

50 Scales, pp. 160-174; Khaled, pp. 308-311; *Whirlwind*, pp. 134-138.

51 Sadik, interview, 03/2005 & Woods, p. 133.

52 Malovany, p. 533, 541 & *Air Survey*, Vol.5, Chronology.

53 Malovany, pp. 521, 539 & Woods, pp. 126-127, 129, 164.

54 Woods, p. 127-129.

55 DIA, *Electronic Warfare Forces Study – Iraq*, 1 April 1990 (henceforth DIA, *EWFS*), piii, CIA/FOIA/ERR & Sadik, interviews, 03/2006 & 03/2007. Except for units of the Technical Equipment Directorate, Iraq also had a powerful COMINT system operated by the Ministry of Transportation and Communications. This Japanese-built system was operated by military officers and proved capable of intercepting internal clandestine and international communications, and civilian command and control communications.

56 Malovany, p. 717 & Woods, pp. 130-131. Iraqi COMINT-related operations are known to have caused concerns about possible flanking movement which would encircle the troops in the KTO. This is what prompted a re-deployment of Iraqi Army troops into the Wadi Hafr al-Batin area, and further west.

57 Based on DIA, *EWFS* & Sadik, interviews, 03/2005, 03/2006, 03/2007 & 10/2007.

58 Scales, pp. 167-170. The Orchidée was actually cancelled in 1990, but the sole demonstrator was then deployed to assist the HQ of the XVIII Corps.

59 Eventually, Pioneers flew 307 sorties, and clocked 1,011 hours of flight time during Operation *Desert Storm*.

60 *Congress*, p. 159-160.

61 Survey Vol 2 Part 1 p.190.

62 For Proven Force, see *Congress*, pp. 164-165; *Survey, Vol.2, Part 1*, p. 185, 338-339, 443, 447-464; *Survey, Vol.5, Chronology*.

63 *Lessons*, pp. 59-60 & Woods, pp. 105-106.

64 Data kindly provided by Albert Grandolini, interview, 11/2018.

65 *Whirlwind*, pp. 52-54, 70-72, 74, 82-83; Scales, pp. 87-90.

66 Scales, p. 41 & Khaled, p. 290.

67 USN History, Appendix C.

68 *Whirlwind*, p. 158.

69 *Air Survey*, Vol.5, Chronology and Table 18, amended by *Congress*, p. 573. Notably, the 1st Cavalry Division included the 1st Brigade of the 2nd Armoured Division.

70 *Air Survey*, Vol.5, Table 9. It is worth noting that the figures shown here are for combat-ready formations only. For instance, the statistics for British forces include only 7th Armoured Brigade; a further British brigade (4th Armoured) and considerable divisional assets (to form 1st Armoured Division) where also in-theatre and working up to operational readiness. See Nigel Pearce, *The Shield and the Sabre* (London: HMSO, 1992).

71 Scales, pp. 46, 57-60; Khaled, pp. 33-34; *Whirlwind*, p. 52. Yeosock was a quiet and self-effacing man who had been commissioned through the ROTC in 1959, after graduating from Pennsylvania State University. Having served as a project manager for modernising the SANG, he knew the Saudis and the terrain. Khaled especially appreciated his 'gruff, straight-forward manner'.

72 Khaled, pp. 35, 232, 237-240, 242; Westermeyer, p. 51.

73 Khaled, pp. 33-35, 189-198, 306; *Whirlwind*, pp. 131-132; Schwarzkopf, pp. 329-330, 334-335, 339-340. Schwarzkopf and Sultan were of similar build, and both were left-handed, but the American was 56 and Sultan was 42. They met in Khaled's office at 1600 every day for 45-60 minutes, to munch some home-made biscuits from Khaled's aunt, and drink Diet Coke. Nevertheless, Khaled observed, 'He was not an easy man to deal with'. Indeed, Khaled felt that Schwarzkopf – contrary to Horner and Yeosock (both of whom often worked over-night, using cups of extra-strong cappuccino to stay awake) – did not fully comprehend the complexities of the Middle East. Finally, Khaled observed (p. 208), '… But Schwarzkopf… had a certain impatience for matters he did not understand or did not consider relevant to his immediate mission. This was to be the source of a number of misunderstandings.'

74 For USAF planning, see *Congress*, pp. 143-159; Davis, pp. 57-110; *Certain Victory*, pp. 176-181; Hallion, pp. 143-144, 150-156; Jamieson, *Lucrative Targets* (hereafter Jamieson), pp. 17-20; *Lessons*, pp. 389-395; Schwarzkopf, p. 415, Survey, Vol.2, Part 1, pp. 55-115, 134-182, 188-189, 191-195, 274; Survey, Vol.5, Chronology; Westernmeyer, pp. 69-70.

75 Nickname 'Black Hole' came into being because, like the astronomical feature, all the available intelligence was 'sucked' by the Special Planning Group, but nothing came out (Hallion, pp. 143-144).

76 Scales, p. 121 & *Whirlwind*, pp. 54, 95-96.

77 *Air Survey*, Vol.5, Chronology; Conrad, p. 16; Scales, pp. 79-80, 116. According to Conrad, at the end of Operation *Desert Storm* in March 1991, the Americans still had 226,800 tonnes of ammunition in their supply dumps in Saudi Arabia. Notably, Schwarzkopf was not happy at such massive changes in his armoured force out of concern that his men would still be transitioning to new weapons when the offensive

began. However, the high quality of troops formerly stationed in West Germany meant there were no significant problems.

78 Malovany, pp. 524, 540.
79 Malovany, p. 540 & Woods, p. 137.
80 Woods, p. 129-130.
81 Ibid, p. 139.
82 Ibid, pp. 141-142.
83 Malovany, pp. 522-523, 530, 533-535; Woods, pp. 129, 165; Hooton et al, *Iran-Iraq War*, Vol.4, pp. 40 and 47. Notably, fearing communications break-down between Baghdad and Kuwait, the GHQ then established its forward headquarters in Basrah, which also coordinated air- and land-support for the KTO.
84 Malovany, pp. 543-544.
85 Sadik, interviews, 03/2005, 03/2006 & 03/2007; Malovany, p. 536 & Woods, pp. 144-147, 167 f/n 81.
86 Woods, p. 148.

87 Ibid & Sadik, interview, 10/2007.
88 Sadik, interview, 10/2007.
89 Malovany, p. 525 & *Survey, Vol.5, Chronology.*
90 *Survey, Vol.5*, Tables 46 and 59 & *Chronology.*
91 Sadik, interviews, 03/2005, 03/2006 & 03/2007& Woods, pp. 144-147, 167 f/n 81.
92 Sadik, interviews, 03/2005 & 03/2007.
93 Sadik, interviews, 03/2007 & 10/2007; Sadik et all, 'The First Night'.

ABOUT THE AUTHORS

E R HOOTON

E.R. (Ted) Hooton is a retired defence journalist who worked for 30 years with Moench and Jane's before establishing the Spyglass newsletters. Since retirement he has focussed upon military history and has written some 15 books covering subjects as diverse as the Iran-Iraq Tanker War (co-authored with Mr Martin Navias), the Chinese Civil War, the Luftwaffe, the Balkan Wars (1912-1913), the Spanish Civil War, Air Operations over the Western Front (1916-1918) and Eastern Front (1941-1945). With Tom Cooper he has written a four-volume history of the Iran-Iraq War on the ground for Helion's *@War* series.

TOM COOPER

Tom Cooper is an Austrian aerial warfare analyst and historian. Following a career in worldwide transportation business – during which he established a network of contacts in the Middle East and Africa – he moved into narrow-focus analysis and writing on small, little-known air forces and conflicts, about which he has collected extensive archives. That resulted in specialisation in such Middle Eastern air forces as those of Egypt, Iran, Iraq and Syria, plus various African and Asian air forces. As well as authoring and co-authoring 30 other books and over 500 articles, he has co-authored an in-depth analysis of major Arab air forces at war with Israel in the period 1955–1973, resulting in the six-volume book series *Arab MiGs*.